IMAGES OF HUMAN NATURE

IMAGES OF

HUMAN NATURE

— *A Sung Portrait* —

DONALD J. MUNRO

PRINCETON UNIVERSITY PRESS

Published by Princeton University Press, 41 William Street,
Princeton, New Jersey 08540
In the United Kingdom: Princeton University Press, Guildford, Surrey

Library of Congress Cataloging-in-Publication Data

Munro, Donald J.
Images of human nature : a sung portrait / Donald J. Munro.
p.   cm.
Bibliography: p.   Includes index.
ISBN 0-691-07330-9 (alk. paper)
1. Philosophical anthropology—History. 2. Chu, Hsi, 1130-1200.
3. Neo-Confucianism. I. Title.
BD450.M863 1988   128'.092'4—dc19   88-12661

This book has been composed in Linotron Palatino

Publication of this book has been assisted by grants from
the Horace H. Rackham School of Graduate Studies,
the office of the Vice President for Research,
and the College of Literature, Science, and the Arts
at the University of Michigan

Printed in the United States of America by
Princeton University Press, Princeton, New Jersey

For Sarah, one of my two sparkling lights,
and in memory of Marvel and George Patterson.

CONTENTS

ACKNOWLEDGMENTS

When I first began this project a number of years ago, several people helped me get started tracking down examples of Chu Hsi's use of structural images: Chiu Tze-kuan, Eugene Cha, Hu Chin-yuan, and Lyu Syau-de. I am grateful to them. Mr. Lyu and I subsequently met with some regularity to discuss Chu's philosophy and the significance of various passages involving images. I learned a great deal from these meetings, and I value the friendship that developed on the basis of a shared interest in Neo-Confucian thought.

The Asia Library at the University of Michigan is headed by a unique man, Mr. Wan Wei-ying. Mr. Wan not only knows where every book is but also what is between the covers. He has helped me immeasurably not only with sources but also with the interpretation of many passages in them. Over a period of several years, two of my colleagues in the Department of Philosophy at Michigan clarified a number of issues in the use of images by Aristotle and Descartes. My thanks respectively to Nicholas White and Louis Loeb. Another philosophy friend, Frithjof Bergmann, discussed metaphors with me in a number of enjoyable and helpful conversations.

Some of the material in these chapters was first presented as the Gilbert Ryle Lectures at Trent University (Ontario) in 1983. Along with cordial hospitality during my stay in Trent, I benefited from constructive criticism of my embryonic thoughts from many individuals, including Trent students. I want to thank especially these members of the faculty: Robert E. Carter, Bernard J. Hodgson, James MacAdam, and Thomas Robinson.

I spent several months in Peking in 1983 discussing sections of the project with several scholars and following up on readings suggested by them. My good friend Zhou Liquan of the Institute of Philosophy, Chinese Academy of the Social Sciences, prepared me well for the experience by reviewing my material. I also thank the institute for its warm reception and for serving as my host. I had fruitful discussions with Meng Peiyuan of the institute and with Mao Huaixin of the Institute of History. Zhang Dainian and Lou Yulie of Peking University's philosophy department were similarly generous in responding to my questions, as was Shi Jun of People's University. I must especially single out Zhang Liwen, also of People's University, with whom I met regularly over a period of two months. Discussing both his own works, which I read with care, and my drafts, I was able to supplement and revise portions of my manuscript. There is no question that these meetings were the most continuously productive aspects of my stay in Peking.

I was fortunate to be invited to attend a meeting in Taiwan sponsored by National Tsinghua University in 1984 at which I presented a draft of Chapter Three. Many scholars present made constructive criticisms, to which I tried to respond in revisions.

During the years in which I was doing the research and writing of the book, I had fellowships to support the work from the John Simon Guggenheim Foundation and the American Council of Learned Societies, Joint Committee on Chinese Studies. This is a project nurtured by their generosity. Similarly, the staffs of the University of Michigan's Center for Chinese Studies and Department of Philosophy helped me in so many ways that I can no longer keep track of them. But I do want specifically to mention Donna Ashton, Achla Karnani, and Trudy Bulkley from the center, and Sherri Kononetz and Doreen Fussman from the department.

I am grateful to the University of Michigan Press for permission to refer to copyrighted material in my book, *The Concept of Man in Contemporary China*. And I would like to make special mention of the excellent dissertations by John W. Chaffee and Robert Hymes, from which I have learned so much. There is a little known but excellent study of metaphors from which I first became aware of their misuses. It is Donald A. Schon's *Displacement of Concepts* (London: Tavistok Publications, 1963).

In a clear case in which the last to be mentioned deserve my greatest gratitude, I want to acknowledge a number of younger scholars who read early drafts of the entire manuscript, showed me the potholes in the road I was taking, and suggested how I might fill them in. When I think of the time spent by these persons already so busy with their own careers, and of how much I learned from them, I am deeply moved. This was collegial support at its finest. So let me salute Irene Bloom, Peter Bol, Chan Sin-yee, Robert Eno, Lionel Jensen (who beat on me with history books until I properly noted the importance of historical context to a number of chapters), Lo Yuet-keung, and Hoyt Tillman. Finally, the prose in this book has been fine-tuned by the China specialist's ideal editor, Barbara Congelosi. She has a magical power to make the murky clearer and the imprecise more exact.

IMAGES OF HUMAN NATURE

ONE

BACKGROUND AND METHODOLOGY

Chu Hsi (1130–1200), the subject of this book, is historically important because his ideas became orthodoxy in China after his death and remained so until 1905. Yet the very breadth of his writings and recorded conversations, and the long and fluctuating history of his influence in China, have made it difficult to untangle the intricacies of his philosophical doctrines. Moreover, the organization of his ideas is not easy to grasp. The occasion for this study is the application of a new methodology in the attempt to clarify one core element in Chu's thought: his conception of human nature. This methodology will reveal two sets of polarized ideas at the center of his view of human nature. Because that concept lies embedded in his conversations and writings on ethics, its extraction will inevitably involve an examination of his ethical construct, too.

Previous Western studies of Chu have relied on such useful methods as term definition, historical sociology, and analysis of the nature of Neo-Confucian orthodoxy and have clarified Chu's ideas and their transformation over time.[1] Although each attempt has yielded important new insights, each has also revealed in Chu's works some unsystematic patterns of thought. These discoveries suggest that there is more work to be done to unlock the philosophical perspectives that made his ideas coherent to himself and his followers. If a key is found, it should be possible to differentiate between what was coherent for Chu and yet may still be problematic for modern analysts.

This study will seek the key in Chu's own mode of discourse. That is, I shall articulate his conception of human nature through an analysis of certain dominant structural images that Chu employed to express his ideas. While mindful of historical background, I intend to focus on doctrine. By tailoring my method to the formal structure of philosophical discourse, I can reveal cohesive arrangements of previously elusive ideas, thus making possible an analysis of Chu's views of human nature that is both clear

3

and simple. As the portrait takes form, I will also consider the issue of the distinctiveness of Chu's ideas in comparison with Western philosophical traditions and, at the end of the work, the echoes of Chu's images of human nature in the modern age.

It may seem at times that the pictorial images play too central a role in this study in comparison with the doctrine of human nature that they are meant to elucidate. I have found no way to avoid this, because the doctrine emerges clearly only from the pattern disclosed by the images.

The large philosophical question in which I am interested is: how does the mode of human thinking affect the content of thought (with special attention to the formulators of original theories)? It is in this connection that I was drawn to the use of pictorial images in the explanation of philosophical theories. I was first alerted to the matter by noting the centrality of the images of the human organism to explain nature and society and of light to explain cognition in classical Western thought, and of the machine (especially the clock) to explain nature and humans in Renaissance writings. The methodology is one that I suspect is equally valid for the study of Western and Chinese philosophy.

In sum, this work has three interlocking themes. The first is Chu's views about the nature of human beings, which turn out to involve two sets of polarities. The second is its methodology, identifying and analyzing the structural images that reveal what Chu's conception of man is. And the third is the fitting together of his disparate ethical positions, because they constitute the philosophical source material from which the images of man emerge. Before beginning to discuss these themes, however, I want first to say something briefly about Chu's school. Then I will note the historical background in which the ideas developed. This information helps in understanding some of the reasons for the significance and future course of Chu's thought. Finally, I will lay out in detail precisely what the methodology is that serves as a new key for dealing with Chu's historically monumental doctrines.

THE SCHOOL

If the earliest Confucians were famous as teachers and practitioners of rituals (ªli), their Sung descendants were noted for their theories about ᵇ*li* (principle). Among his Sung predecessors, Chu acknowledged the greatest debt to Ch'eng I (1033–1107). He claimed that a metaphysical concept (ᵇ*li*) that Ch'eng had worked into his teachings came to play a central role in his own thought. Originally standing for the grain in wood or jade, of which the carver must be mindful, ᵇ*li* refers to natural patterns in things or events. In Ch'eng's writings, it means the eternal, changeless, and non-empirical (my rendering of Chu's *hsing erh shang* or "above form") source of both ordered change and the classification of things. Each class of things, such as humans or plants, and each member of a class, has its ᵇ*li*. A knowledge of it reveals the behavior or action that is natural to a class or individual. The ᵇ*li* in the teachings of Ch'eng I and Chu Hsi caused some commentators to refer to their doctrines as the "School of Principle" (*li-hsüeh*). This designation was made in the second half of the thirteenth century.[2] Their ideas were known as "the learning of the Way" (*tao-hsüeh*) and, to underscore the importance of the innately moral mind in its teaching, as the "learning of the mind" (*hsin-hsüeh*). In this study the term "Neo-Confucianism" refers to this school.

Chu did not always agree with Ch'eng I (see Chapter Four). The present work cites Ch'eng's writings and/or those of his brother (Ch'eng Hao, 1032–1085) as additional illustrations of positions shared with Chu for which there is documentation. Chu Hsi's ideas, expressed in his commentaries on Confucian classics of the Chou period (1122 or 1027–256 B.C.), were inculcated by the curriculum studied by candidates for the civil service. To base the examinations on his works was to ensure, among an elite group of scholarly leaders, some degree of shared assumptions about humans and their values and about the societies and natural world in which they lived. This movement toward orthodoxy occurred in three stages. Although factional disputes led to the formal proscription of his doctrines in the 1190s, only a decade after his death the throne began to award him posthumous titles. In 1211 it published his collected commentaries on the *Four Books* (the *Analects*, the *Mencius*, the *Great Learning*, and the *Doctrine of the Mean*). The year 1241 marks the second watershed in the progress toward national acclaim of his philosophy, for in that year the earlier proscription was condemned.[3] Just a few years earlier Chu and his philosophical predecessors in the Northern Sung (960–1125) were elevated to the rank of "former sages."[4] The climax occurred shortly after the collapse of the Southern Sung in 1279, when the Mongol emperor decreed that the examinations would require familiarity with Chu's commentaries. The *chin-shih* ("presented scholar") examination, which was reintroduced in 1314–1315, thenceforth was based to varying degrees on these texts.

Taking note of Chu's place in Confucian orthodoxy should not be limited to mentioning only acts of the throne. Chu himself contributed to the notion that the body of truths he expounded was alone worthy of being transmitted. He suggested that these truths were known to Confucius (551–479 B.C.), his disciple Tseng Tzu, and the Confucian moral intuitionist Mencius (372?–289? B.C.). Chu said that on the death of Mencius they were lost, until several Northern Sung figures—Chou Tun-i (1017–1073), Ch'eng Hao, and especially Ch'eng I—rediscovered them.[5] According to Chu, leading figures from the Han (206 B.C.-A.D. 220) through the T'ang (618–906), when the tao (moral path) was lost, were unworthy of emulation by those who seek it.[6] This idea of a "transmission of the tao" owes something to the Buddhist practice of master-to-disciple transmission of sometimes secret or esoteric teachings.

Chu further claimed that there is a set of core truths, and that up to his own time only a limited number of persons had had access to them. One truth is that the mind is innately capable of discriminating between hierarchical differences and proper relationships, and this capability corresponds to the objective order in nature as a whole. Such a view of mind differs from that of the Buddhists, for whom the ideal state of consciousness is devoid of such categories. Second, although the individual's mind is one, it can be bifurcated in terms of the object on which it focuses. This leads to a separation into a higher and a lower self, between which there will be conflict until the former conquers the latter. All persons possess the higher self, and so there is an assumption of perfectibility. People should regard single-mindedness in the nurturance of the higher self as a cardinal value, along with maintaining the mean. And, finally, these truths are capable of being passed on, as they were from the earliest sages to Confucius.

During Chu's own lifetime, and long before his doctrines became state orthodoxy, he helped nurture society's acceptance of his doctrines by both revitalizing scholarly teaching academies and contributing personally to their curriculum materials. Chu earnestly hoped that more and more people would understand these truths. But the claim by Chu and his like-minded colleagues that there is a "learning of the Way" (*tao-hsüeh*) to which they had access was perceived by many others as a belief in exclusivity. I will return to this point again.

Scholars traditionally divide the Confucian philosophies that emerged in the Sung and continued to flourish through the Ming (1368–1643) into two schools. That which stands juxtaposed to the Ch'eng-Chu teachings has been called the School of Mind (*hsin-hsüeh*). But we may accurately ascribe that term to either Chu's school or that of his most famous critic, Wang Yang-ming (1472–1529).[7] Conflicts between the schools dwell on the relation between mind and principle (are they one or two?) and on the relative importance in self-improvement, respectively, of either scholarly textual study or spontaneous intuition and service activity. This second topic, in fact, reveals much about the personality differences between the chief proponents of the two schools. Chu Hsi was a bookish intellectual, most at home in the solitude of his study. Wang Yang-ming, on the other hand, was an idealistic monist who identified mind and principle and was probably happiest when actively engaged in the solution of civil or military problems. He often risked his life in the process. But it is time to turn to the polarities revealed in Chu's images of human nature and to the historical facts of the age in which he lived that helped shape them.

Two Polarities and Their Historical Context

Somewhat before Chu's time, political factors in the Northern Sung had already begun to play a decisive role in a turn toward early (meaning Chou) Confucian fundamentalism. As George Hatch has argued, the gentry from south-central China, a region benefiting from increasing commercial wealth and urbanization, lacked the great landed wealth and hereditary titles of the T'ang

(618–906) aristocracy based largely in the north. To compensate, they demanded political and social status by virtue of a claim to the principles of early Confucianism.[8] By the 1060s these principles were dominant, advocating restoration of early doctrines, including the ritual rules (*ali*), as guides to political and social practice. In addition to these changes, there were the immediate threats from non-Chinese tribes such as the Khitans and Tanguts in the north and northwest. Fan Chung-yen (989–1052) was a restorationist reformer who advocated evaluations of bureaucratic performance. He rose to prominence on the battlefield fighting the Tanguts, and he remained acutely sensitive to the need to reform the society thoroughly in order to save it.[9] The practices of the early sages were there as the appropriate model.

Looking back on the early classical Confucian teachings that carry the wisdom of the sages, it is possible to identify two specific issues that became significant in Chu's own philosophy. The following passage in the *Analects* contains one of them:

> The "Duke" of She addressed Master K'ung saying, "In my country there was a man called Upright Kung. His father appropriated a sheep, and Kung bore witness against him." Master K'ung said, "In my country the upright men are of quite another sort. A father will screen his son, and a son his father—which incidentally does involve a sort of uprightness."[10]

The passage indicates clearly Confucius' priority in a conflict between duty to one's own family and the claims of either the family that lost the sheep or the laws and customs of the state in which the event took place. At the same time, the *Analects* prizes humaneness (*jen*), which includes loving people in general.[11] Although rooted in kinship affection, love can and should be extended to persons outside the family. Chu Hsi accepted both the family preference and the obligation for altruism beyond the family. The first issue, therefore, is the potential incompatibility between family duty and duty to those outside the family.

Mo Tzu (ca. 479–ca. 381 B.C.) criticized the Confucian preferential love for family members as both inefficient and often ignored even by its advocates (leaving for a distant mission, they entrust their families to practitioners of universal, not partial, love). It is also contrary to heaven's universal-mindedness. Mo Tzu thus found an impossible conflict between the value of family partiality and that of altruism and advocated abandoning the former in favor of love equally distributed to all. Mohist universal love also differs from Confucian humaneness in the following respects: the former is an obligation, but the latter is a natural disposition; universal love is more like fair treatment of others than an emotional response, like Confucius' humaneness or compassion; and Mo Tzu often justifies universal love on utilitarian grounds, whereas for Confucius humaneness is to be practiced because it is natural and therefore intrinsically right. The Mohist critique of Confucianism constitutes an early identification of an incompatibility seen later by others between Confucianism's family love and the altruistic Confucian ideal of loving those outside the family. Chu Hsi frequently criticizes the Mohist position because it denigrates natural family sentiments and would eliminate natural gradation of worth.[12]

The second issue is the relative weight to assign to self-discovery of morally relevant truths and to obedience to those objective rules of conduct (ritual rules, [a]*li*) formulated by others. Mencius emphasized the centrality in man's universally shared innate endowment of the moral sense ([a]*i*) and the ability to discriminate between right and wrong (*shih-fei chih hsin*). Another prominent Warring States Period (403–221 B.C.) Confucian, Hsün Tzu (ca. 298–ca. 238 B.C.), also made a place for the moral sense.[13] But, consistent with the practice of many Confucians, he believed that the brutish qualities also present in man's innate endowment require the individual to undergo an exhaustive inculcation of the ritual rules. The early classical Confucian works contain no definitive position on the optimal balance between these two sources of formative standards for the individual.

Chu Hsi himself did not directly focus on these issues. Among other things, he was interested in constructing a metaphysics that could answer those questions which had already received sophisticated treatment in Buddhist philosophy, such as the content of human nature (*hsing*) and mind (empty of innate moral truths, according to the Buddhists), and the existence of a unifying entity

9

immanent in the many disparate things. And he was interested in the classics as educational materials. Yet as he grappled with these more immediate matters, including constructing a theory of human nature as an alternative to that found in Buddhism, the conflicts in these classical polarities emerged to color his answers. And they are relevant to any attempt to evaluate his doctrines as a system.

The present work is an examination of these two older sets of polarities that keep cropping up in Chu's theory of human nature. The book ends with a consideration of the implications for modern Chinese thought of Chu's treatment of each set. In the first set, the juxtaposition of family love and altruistic love of people beyond the family, the seeds of both poles are innate to human nature. Altruism grows out of the same innate trait as does family feeling. The second set, self-discovery of truth as contrasted with reliance on objective authorities, also emerges from Chu's theory of human nature. The important principles that inform people about all things in nature are innate. Yet the actual cloudiness of the mind, inevitably caused by one's physical constitution, requires momentary reliance on the guidance of external authorities as a supplement to self-effort in grasping these principles.

Part of my examination of these polarities in the theory of human nature concerns weaknesses in Chu's doctrines. These weaknesses help account for the form of the inheritance of Chu's thought in the late imperial and modern periods. Briefly, in Chinese society, family-oriented priorities dominated among the gentry. Unlike many of his Confucian contemporaries and successors, Chu tried in his ethics to accommodate both the value of preference for family and that of public-spirited altruism. The ethics seem addressed to all people. I will try to show that he was unable to harmonize the two values successfully, in part because of the social categories in terms of which he thought and wrote about the altruist and "the people." His concepts of love and of people often assumed differences in the economic status of altruist and recipient. In addition, his doctrines lack detail about how to act altruistically. Chu's doctrines eventually became state orthodoxy and were studied by the elite, who had a wider impact on the society. Since Chu was unable to give a clear account of how the individual could accommodate both family role fulfillment and public duty, the result was that many of those who studied his doctrines found weak practical guidance with which to overcome the actual family priorities that were prevalent in their social group. In the long run, the weaknesses undermined the panhuman or humanitarian intentions of his ethics, robbing it of potential validity in the eyes of questioning readers as late as the twilight of the imperial era and China's entry into the modern age.

With respect to the other polarity, I will try to show the simultaneous existence in Chu's thought of claims for both self-discovery of moral truths and reliance on various types of external authority. There is no clear guidance as to which takes precedence. One long-term consequence was to justify as within the hallowed Chu Hsi tradition scholars and rulers who wished to tilt toward one or the other of these authorities. Textual sanction existed for both, and for a moral stature for advocates of either authority.

Role Fulfillment and Equal Worth

The Sung (960–1279) bureaucratic scholars may have been Confucians. But Buddhism retained the allegiance of other Chinese up and down the social ladder. Chu himself criticized the emperor for saying that the "three teachings" (Buddhism, Confucianism, and Taoism) were essentially the same. Local elites were actively involved with Buddhist priests and temple life.[14] At the popular level, Buddhism provided a structure for socializing that cut across class, professional, and gender lines in much the same way that involvement in church fellowships or auxiliaries does in American society. The following passages, dating from the Sung, reveal the nature of the Buddhist societies with which so many people were involved:

> Every birthday of the titular deity, the shop owners of various guilds form groups. There are different ways in which they greet the deity and make offerings. . . . Jewelry shops offer "the seven toys" in organizing a society. There are also the . . . Rich and Poor Gambling Society, . . . the Girls' Pure Voice Society, . . . a society of the fruit shops that offers seasonal fruits, a society of people from eastern and western Ma

11

Ch'eng which offers wondrous things like unusual pine and juniper trees, the fish guild which offers unusual turtles and fish.[15]

There are also virtuous females—wives and women from the mansions of the provincial and local officers. They formed a . . . group in which they chant the *Sutra of Perfect Enlightenment*. All wear precious jewels and head ornaments when they attend meetings. People call it a "high fashion competition."[16]

Although these passages reveal Buddhism adapting itself to the routine of ordinary Chinese life, Confucians like Ch'eng I and Chu Hsi singled out for criticism those Buddhist teachings and practices which undercut standard (especially family) social role duties. They had in mind the retreat of monks and nuns to remote monasteries, which removed them from family obligations. Family duties and expectations were at the center of Chu's ethics. Other condemned practices were the exemption of monks from taxation and public labor service.

It is ironical that much altruistic philanthropy during Chu's time (medical treatment, hospitality for the traveling stranger) was carried on by monks in their temples or by members of the Buddhist societies. The latter did everything from forming "Tea and Soup Groups" that distributed free food to the people, to paving the streets: "The Brightness Group of the Upper India Temple consists of members all of whom are wealthy. They pave the big streets with large stones and bestow huge candles and incense on the temple."[17]

These few references to Sung Buddhist societies point to an issue related to altruism, namely, the assumption that people have equal worth and an equal possibility for improvement. There was a society for everyone, rich and poor, male and female. Popular Buddhist doctrines as well as philosophically sophisticated teachings had an egalitarian message. The Pure Land school, for example, preached that sincere invocation of the name of the Buddha Amitābha is sufficient for anyone to gain release from this world's sufferings. The practice spread to other sects as well. It was not necessary to be literate and read sacred scriptures or understand doctrines to attain the common goal of all persons in that age, namely, to enter a paradise called Sukhāvatī. On the more sophisticated level, the Ch'an, or Meditation, school taught that, because the Buddha nature is present in all sentient beings, a person can become enlightened about it in the course of routine daily activities, such as chopping wood. No scriptural training is required. This position carries the message that persons are equally worthy of compassion (*karunā*).

There is ambivalence in Chu's philosophy about these Buddhist ideas. In part he was repelled by them, because they are incompatible with the Confucian doctrine of a hierarchical concern for others as found in the ritual rules (ᵃ*li*). This is the spirit behind his powerful criticisms of Mohist universal love and may constitute the direct historical motive for his vehemence. And yet, he was also a partisan of the expression of selfless love beyond the family to all other people and creatures, an altruism that resonates with Buddhist compassion. It is plausible, then, that he was mindful that there is an incompatibility between family love and altruism, even if it was not an incompatibility that he consciously accepted and purposively tried to overcome; indeed, his straightforward thesis doubtless eliminates the incompatibility for him.

When I speak of Chu Hsi as inheriting some aspects of Buddhist egalitarianism with implications for the altruism in his ethics, I am referring to the idea that all principles are equally present in each person, giving equal worth to all. As in many Confucian writings, there is vagueness in Chu's work about the set of humans that he actually would include in the group of equally worthy persons, all deserving of concern. He says that everyone deserves relief from poverty. And sometimes Chu speaks as though education is for everyone, which implies the equal perfectibility of all humans. At most other times he directs his teachings at potentially superior men (*chün-tzu*). In such cases, his concern is with a Chinese group of literate males, and this excludes barbarians and members of pariah classes. When future references are made to "equal worth" or "equal perfectibility," these qualifications of the reference group should be remembered.

An altruist selflessly cares for the welfare of a broad range of people. There are traditional Confucian categories that identify persons within the family who should be objects of concern, such as husband and wife, father and son, and older brother and younger brother. It is more difficult to determine how Chu identified people outside the family to whom the altruist has obligations, and what the relation of the altruist to them should be—in short, how he envisioned what is today called society and the Confucian's relation to it. Some detailed observations on these issues are presented in subsequent chapters, especially Chapter Four. But at this point it is appropriate to take preliminary note of historical facts concerning the political organization of Chinese society as Chu understood it and to mention their relevance. These facts emerge from Chu's memorials to the throne and from his letters. They reveal that he thought of "the people" in terms of the standard administrative categories into which China was divided in his time.

> Therefore, a family has its own principles and a nation has a nation's principles. So communities [hsiang] are governed by the county [ahsien], the counties by the prefecture [chou], prefectures by the different circuits, circuits by the central government departments, the departments by the premiership, and the premiership coordinates and makes decisions with the emperor, which result in policy and promulgations. These are the world's principles.[18]

Early in the twelfth century there were 254 prefectures and 1,234 counties. According to the census of 1102–1106, the population of one such prefecture, to which Chu would one day be appointed prefect, was 112,343. Within it there were three counties.[19] A community might be just one village, and there were many villages in a county.

The unit of primary welfare concern to a sometime Confucian official such as Chu was the ahsien, or county. Repeatedly he speaks in his memorials and letters of the need to attend to the poor at the county level by reducing their taxes.[20] He wanted to lessen the gap between poor and rich counties.[21] Of course, he also addressed other official welfare obligations, such as providing education, attending to proper sacrifices, reducing the scale of army recruitment, and appointing good officials. Chu referred to

14

the masses inhabiting the counties as the "sons and daughters of the [ᵃhsien] magistrate." Even a prefect's concerns were formulated in terms of the individual counties that fell within his prefecture. Occasionally Chu also referred to the official's need for concern with the welfare of communities (hsiang). He advised the emperor to issue an edict to encourage officials to establish community granaries as he himself had done, to lend grain to poor peasants at low interest rates. Noting that government-run charitable granaries may not have extended their charity beyond the prefectural city, Robert Hymes has discussed the evidence that in one Southern Sung circuit (overlapping with the modern Kiangsi Province), social welfare was supposed to be the concern of local men of wealth and name, which was the rationale for the institution of the community granary. Chu Hsi modified a plan for such granaries developed and implemented by a friend and proposed it for the empire in 1181.[22] I will refer again to this institution in Chapter Four. Chu bemoaned the fact that the central government had an inadequate idea of local conditions, and he therefore placed special obligations on county magistrates to look after the communities in their areas.[23]

References to Confucian literati who perceived society in these terms are to people whom Chu speaks of as ju (Confucians). They form a subdivision of scholars (hsüeh-che, shih-ta-fu), some of whom are "bad eggs."[24] Among the Confucians, some are true Confucians (chen ju),[25] and some are even superior men (chün-tzu) whom the emperor has actually invited to serve in government.[26] But there are also vulgar Confucians, people of shallow learning, and false Confucians.[27] Chu claims that since the Ch'in and Han dynasties, such false Confucians have focused on the memorization of texts and have dabbled in Taoism and Buddhism.[28] From the language that Chu uses, the reader infers that he considers ordinary people intellectually inferior to true Confucians, who aspire to help people through public service, and that their relation to true Confucians is that of children to parents. On impeaching an official, Chu writes that a Confucian should be "hardworking, rectifying himself, and leading those beneath him, so as to spread forth the proper transformation and nurturance of the masses" (lit., "mean people" [hsiao-min]).[29] Chu's own compassion cuts across

15

occupational lines, encompassing peasants, soldiers, and merchants.[30]

Chu's writings thus indicate that in addition to the standard occupational divisions such as officials, peasants, soldiers, and merchants, and the basic social role sets (prince and minister, husband and wife, father and son, and so forth), society consists of the emperor, good and bad literati, some of whom have official posts, and the people who are hierarchically subordinate to the good Confucians. He viewed the latter group as uneducated occupants of administrative zones for whom some official should have a parental type of responsibility. For purposes of this study, the significance of all of this is that it contributes to an understanding of the audience for whom Chu wrote and the nature of the recipients of altruism. The audience consisted of potentially superior men and the recipients were the ignorant, childlike masses. This status difference and the relationship it involves color Chu's discussions of "loving people," or selfless altruism outside the family. The idea of such selfless love is for him inextricably bound up with the notion of official duty, if one is a Confucian.

The value of altruism has roots in both the early Confucian conception of humaneness and in egalitarian Buddhist doctrines about the equal presence of the Buddha nature in all persons. The latter was a popular Ch'an teaching about the mind that Chu Hsi praised, along with certain other aspects of the Ch'an views on the mind.[31] One was the relation between reducing desires and heightening the mind's clarity. But the intensity with which he also maintained his commitment to the value of hierarchical role fulfillment, starting in the family, reveals that at the same time he was a guardian of the early Confucian cultural heritage that was being challenged by egalitarian Buddhist ideas and the societies in which they were exercised. In this connection, in his last years, especially after preaching in 1189 the idea of an orthodox transmission of the tao, he strengthened his emphasis on ritual training. Ritual concerns proper behavior between people of different hierarchical positions. Practice in the rites can be regarded as a way of making the value of role fulfillment concrete. Through ritual training, the early traditions are rediscovered and preserved in the face of Buddhist social leveling.[32] To the end, Chu both absorbed aspects of Buddhist egalitarianism and reacted against its threat to social hierarchy based in rites. It is necessary now to sort out these strands within a philosophy that tries to make a place for both.

Confucians never forgot that Buddhism was a foreign import. The Sung government experienced severe threats, not only from the Khitans and Tanguts, but also from the Tungusic Jurchen people who originally came from Manchuria. In 1125–1127 the court abandoned North China to them entirely, and the Southern Sung (1127–1279) house had to face protracted attempts at annexation of the south by the Jurchen. These tensions fertilized the xenophobic root of Confucian attacks on Buddhism.

Self-Discovery and Objective Authority

In the eyes of Chu Hsi, the presumed Buddhist advocacy of withdrawal from social duty contrasted with the Confucian value of "serving man." Though he was bookish by preference, Chu also believed in the social service ideal. His nine years of government service seem proof of that. The figure "nine" may seem few to those spending an adult lifetime in such service, but for those preferring the solitude of the study, it is a substantial contribution. Chu was an activist administrator, advocating tax cuts for the poor, building granaries to protect the people from famine when there was a bad harvest, and rebuilding schools. Through these acts, he concretized his personal response to the idea of monastic withdrawal. It should be noted, however, that the methods he chose aimed at solving individual local problems hindering people from securing a livelihood and education. He was not a social reformer on a grand scale, the way the Northern Sung Confucian Wang An-shih (1021–1086) had been.

Wang was leader of a faction that drew its support from officials in Kiangsi and Fukien provinces. These south-centralists were the arrivistes of their day, deriving their wealth from rich agricultural lands. Members of their families had only recently become successful examination candidates. Wang's conservative northern opponents, on the other hand, often came from families with a long tradition of official rank.

Wang was an advocate of a powerful central government that

17

would reform the country through edict. He initiated sweeping programs that included state control of commerce and state loans to farmers and proposed the division of all land into equal units in order to bring about a fairer land tax. If, years later, anything could drive someone with a bookish bent back into the study, it was the example of the failure of these large-scale reform efforts. In the short run most were abandoned. In the long run, the Jurchen successfully conquered North China. And Chu's own spiritual mentor, Ch'eng I, and some like-minded scholars had opposed Wang An-shih. In Luoyang, out of favor, they had turned away from a desire for official positions toward the goal of becoming virtuous individuals through teaching, scholarship, and self-cultivation. These practices contrasted with the reformist attempt by Wang to use state power to change China's institutions by decree.[33]

If the memory of this unsuccessful reform effort provided background, Chu Hsi and many other Southern Sung Confucians found a more compelling argument for focusing on individual self-cultivation (rather than on social reform) in the number of scholars who failed the civil service examinations. According to John Chaffee, in the Sung one out of every thirty adult males took the prefectural examinations every three years.[34] Because of the low success rate, many spent years studying only to face repeatedly dashed hopes (increasingly, competitive advantage in examinations and careers went to kin of high officials). The type of academy sponsored by Chu was critical of the very goal of studying in order to pass the examinations and become an official. Its competing goals—inquiry into ethically relevant aspects of nature and man and self-cultivation—intersected nicely with the prevailing cynicism about the tests caused by the disillusionment of so many failed candidates.[35] Chu prized moments of solitude as part of the self-cultivation process. The utility of such a practice had to do with self-development, not examination success. Certain historical factors, then, reinforced Chu's advocacy of practices that involve introspective self-discovery. These were not without their Buddhist tinges.

This orientation of some opponents of Wang An-shih in the Northern Sung, and of students cynical about examination prospects in the Southern Sung, seems to emphasize the individual and his own moral intuitions. Chu agreed: self-cultivation is the goal, not official success. There were other concrete historical aspects of Chu's era, however, that drew him to advocate the value of uniformity, or conformity, as opposed to individual judgment, and the importance of objective authorities. One was the harsh reality of factional life in Chu's China. Its roots lay in the Northern Sung split between the Wang An-shih reformers and their opponents, led by the conservative northerner Ssu-ma Kuang (1019–1086) but also including Ch'eng I and, in the west, Su Shih (1037–1101).

Southern Sung factionalism pitted those who wanted to negotiate a peaceful resolution to the Jurchen problem against the war party. Politically, Chu was a hawk, especially in his youth. Although his criticisms of the war party during his later years caused some to paint him as a traitor, he remained committed to the liberation of the north.[36] Philosophically, his claim that he and selected others had access to the correct transmission of the tao was, as a matter of historical fact, conducive to fragmentation of the scholarly world. John Haeger has drawn attention to the following sentiment about the perceived elitist pretensions of the advocates of the "learning of the Way":

> As for this so-called *tao-hsüeh* phrase, both benefit and harm are involved with it, and it does not belong to Chu Hsi alone. From early times, petty men have caused harm to loyal and good men, and there has regularly been the designation [of divergent positions] with names. Some because they like the name, some because they stand at odds with the mainstream and some to found a clique—recently [men] have gathered under the rubric of *tao-hsüeh*.[37]

In sum, the use of the term *tao-hsüeh* makes a partisan issue out of the tao and implies that those who use it to describe their field of learning have a monopoly on understanding it. Yet Chu saw himself as someone working to reconcile or eliminate factions.

In desiring a uniformity of values in a community of scholars and officials having "one mind,"[38] he was, in fact, no different from that other symbolic factional head, Wang An-shih. Like Chu, Wang sought to achieve uniformity through education. Wang's

19

method was to require that examination candidates study only the commentaries on the classics by himself or by his son. Their writings would constitute the objective authorities to promote a society with one mind. As he was rising to power, Wang sent the following memorial to the throne:

> At the present talented men are scarce; moreover, scholarly skills are dissimilar. Each man has an interpretation [of the classics] and for ten men there are ten interpretations. When the court wants something done, the various arguments are confusing and no one is willing to obey instructions. This, in general, is why the court is unable to achieve a single morality. To achieve it, we must therefore reform our schools, and if we wish to reform our schools we must change the examination regulations.[39]

Even earlier (1057), Ou-yang Hsiu (1007–1072) had made changes in the examination system that also had the effect of promoting uniformity in ethical and political thinking. Candidates had to master a classical curriculum and be able to answer questions about its relevance to contemporary problems. In addition, they had to use a new prose style, the *ku-wen*.[40] The Sung trend toward uniformity is manifest in the eventual elimination of all specialized examinations at the capital and the retention, at the highest degree level, of only the *chin-shih* examination.[41]

This interest in the examinations is part of the general growth of education during the Sung, which Chu Hsi helped to promote. There were many watersheds in this movement as well as efforts that were soon aborted, such as the 1044 edict requiring the establishment of state-sponsored schools in each prefecture. This act, initiated by the reformer Fan Chung-yen, was important in setting a precedent and style of state education that was realized toward the end of the Northern Sung.[42] Although the Southern Sung government was often not actively involved in the management of government schools during that period, the schools remained vibrant.

This growth of education is directly relevant to an aspect of Chu's thought sympathetic to the role of objective authorities in providing direction in people's lives. Schools need texts and a cur-

riculum for both young and old students. Ch
tered on what later became known as the *Four*
the *Six Classics*[43] and the dynastic histories. The
prised the *Analects* of Confucius, the *Mencius*, the
and the *Doctrine of the Mean*. The last two were origina
in a late Chou or early Han work, the *Book of Rites (Li-*
extracted, edited, and elevated them to prominence. He de
how and in what sequence these various classics should be
ied, and he wrote commentaries on them. A common, ob
curriculum of the kind that he provided was useful to the
class, which could then defend its privileges on the basis of
of access to its truths.

Of course, the elements intrinsic to Chu's philosophical move-ment as a whole that also contributed to the idea of an authorita-tive teaching include his claim that the early sages had grasped the tao, which carried the injunction to copy the minds of those sages. Academies were places where sages could be properly wor-shiped,[44] and Chu is famous for having reestablished the White Deer Grotto Academy during the years 1179–1183. Many acade-mies had their own block-printing facilities, which permitted them to publish interpretative and curricular materials reflecting the viewpoints of the scholars in attendance. This both enhanced academies' significance as instruments of national education and made them a potential threat to court figures intent on palace con-trol of thought.

In advocating the need for objective authorities, Chu was also thinking of training the young in the ritual rules of conduct de-scribed in books and taught by rote in the schools. One function of such training was to help the individual develop habits that would reduce his desire for material goods. In short, it promoted the value of frugality (a matter discussed in Chapter Five and Chapter Six). This is an appropriate place to caution the reader about another historical reality. Chu's ideas were not always con-sistent with either the beliefs or the practices of other members of his scholar-official class. If those others stressed frugality, it was sometimes only to ensure the survival of the family as a property-owning unit, not, as Chu would have it, because indulging desires

...g in itself. Pursuing wealth to increase the family's
m... was a value absent from Chu's ethics.

...lyst should be mindful that he is dealing with a unique
...eing whose environment had its own intrusive character-
...Chu was a student of classical texts, content with the soli-
...that both scholar and monk found so appealing. Yet, simul-
...eously, he prized "serving man" above monastic retreat.
...though his academies taught self-cultivation, this was not equiv-
...to teaching an iconoclastic sort of self-absorption in which
...person is the measure of truth. An advocate of uniformity of
...ues among the scholar class, Chu did his best to realize it
...rough curricular innovations that others after him sought to uni-
versalize. And at the same time that his political positions and philosophy were perceived as highly partial, he sought to reconcile
factional disputes in order that all participants might be of "one
mind."

METHODOLOGY: STRUCTURAL IMAGES

That humans think exclusively in images used to be all but assumed by many Western philosophical writers.[46] A moment's reflection reveals the implausibility of such a proposition. Human
thought processes make regular use of terms for which no likely
graphic images can be suggested. Yet, it is also true that people
rely heavily on graphic imagery in thinking. Some people think
predominantly pictorially. This is true even in such fields as mathematics and physics, where one might not expect it. The mathematician S. M. Ulam wrote in his memoirs, "It is said that seventy-
five percent of us have a dominant visual memory, twenty-five
percent an auditory one. As for me, mine is quite visual. When I
think about mathematical ideas, I see the abstract notions in symbolic pictures."[47] British-born physicist Freeman Dyson has revealed his own gradual ability to mesh two modes of thought:

Dick [Feynman] just wrote down the solutions out of his head
without ever writing down the equations. He had a physical
picture of the way things happen, and the picture gave him
the solution directly, with a minimum of calculation. It was

no wonder that people who had spent their lives solving equations were baffled by him. Their minds were analytical; his mind was pictorial. My own training, since the far off days when I struggled with H. Y. H. Piaggio's differential equations, had been analytical. But as I listened to Dick and stared at the strange diagrams that he drew on the blackboard I gradually absorbed some of his pictorial imagination and began to feel at home in his version of the universe.[48]

Most people probably shift constantly from the verbal (if they are not solving equations) to the pictorial and back.

I am not concerned in this study with the occasional images everyone uses to illustrate a point ("My daughter is like a tiger"). Nor am I concerned with the everyday images that may structure ways of conceiving routine experiences; for example, a recent study identified the metaphor of war as structuring the view of argument ("Your claims are indefensible"; "He attacked every weak point in my argument").[49] Instead, the focus here will be on those images which help to define abstract theories, like the image of the ladder that informs theories of evolution and progress (the ladder indicating upward movement as well as stages within the process of change). Images serve special functions for theories. And, because each image is generally associated exclusively with a particular theory (or set of theories), the appearance of multiple images within one systematic philosophy can reveal much about the mix of theories it contains.

Study of the pictorial images used by Chu Hsi to explain his theories reveals that they perform two functions, structural and emotive.[50] An image structures the relations between disparate facts to which a theory applies, calling attention to certain aspects of the relationship. And, because of its familiarity within the culture, it also elicits an emotional response to those facts, thereby uncovering a value that Chu Hsi wishes to affirm. These are functions that the analyst can identify today, not ones of which Chu Hsi was necessarily aware.

Philosophers, like scientists, deal with facts about man, society, and nature, and they formulate theories about those facts. Theories purport to explain the relations between facts. In the case of

Chu Hsi, structural images enter the scene as a third factor, after facts and theories, to serve the facts in ways that theories cannot. They are explanatory devices that clarify the integration among facts by giving an example of a familiar structure in which the parts are clearly related. The choice of the term "explanatory" is purposive, to indicate that Chu's structural images go beyond mere illustrative examples. They demonstrate something about the world, namely, that all physical phenomena are interrelated in a variety of ways. Examples include how members of a family, with their respective duties and expectations, are related within the family group, and how roots, seed, trunk, and leaves are related in a plant. Chu Hsi's theories are so abstract that they do not adequately explain the integration in the case of any specific set of facts, and so he was forced to rely on structural images. At the same time, as I have argued elsewhere and will argue again below, Confucians tend to merge accounts of facts and values. It is not surprising that the images Chu employs also reveal values that he is trying to persuade the reader to accept.

I have purposely chosen not to use the words "metaphor" and "analogy" systematically in this work because of the academic debates attending these terms.[51] Using them would necessarily bring these arguments into the discussion, which is already complex enough. The structural and emotive uses examined here emerge directly from the material, and the word "image" conveys simply and directly the device Chu Hsi uses in explanations. The use of images may be thought of as analogical in the ordinary sense of the word, but I do not want to make a technical issue of that term. Images can be deployed in analogical ways, but people also use them to persuade. And images have properties that analogies do not. They link themselves together or pattern themselves on a separate level from that of the objects to which they refer. For example, in Chu's case, water and silt link together on the same level, that of things having visible form, while [b]li (principle) and [a]$ch'i$ (material force), to which they are respectively compared, link on the two separate levels of things without visible form and things with such form.

Pictorial images are especially significant for the analyst because they reveal what is likely to be original in a philosopher's works, if, indeed, a philosopher is creative and has new ideas that need explanation. Such images are common elements in the works of Chu Hsi, appearing often when concepts new and unfamiliar to his readers or listeners are introduced. This is one reason the *Classified Conversations* (with disciples and others) is the most suitable place to search for the images, which were frequently prompted by Chu's encounters with inquisitive students. Altogether there are twenty thousand conversations with ninety-seven disciples. Most date from the time when Chu was about forty-five until shortly before his death; many are from his last decade, so the present work is not an intellectual biography. It deals with the doctrines and images of Chu's mature years. The polarities discovered are manifest in the organization of his ethics. They are not revealed by episodes of personal anguish over his developing life.

Some of the images he selects may, of course, have been invoked by other writers in other periods. What is unprecedented is their use in conjunction with what Chu regards as his new ideas: a theory of human nature that incorporates both profound discontent about the present form of that nature and energizing optimism about its possibilities; a Buddhist-inspired vision of the potentially equal worth of all people, based on belief in universal traits of mind (to which Confucians also contributed); a theory of knowledge that preserves the distinction between self and things while proposing a way to unite them psychologically; a view of nature as having objective worth (seen in the processes of life and growth); and, finally, an admonition to single-mindedness of purpose without extreme asceticism. These are not necessarily the ideas that outside analysts will find significant in his work.

The study of structural images is a good way to unravel the various theories that are intermingled in Chu Hsi's writing. Chu does not make much attempt to differentiate among theories; the terminology developed in one is freely used in another: for example, ᵃ*li* (propriety) is ᵇ*li* (principle), and the latter is *jen* (humaneness, present in living things as their principle of life).[52] Part of this equationist approach has to do with the desire to harmonize doctrines, a goal that can be achieved by claiming that X is really Y, if one takes the proper perspective. In contrast, it is not so easy to say that a stream is a tree, or that any concrete object is really some other object. Using images as a point of entry, the analyst can pick apart and differentiate among the theories that Chu Hsi rather haphazardly weaves together.

Another argument in favor of the image approach is that Chu Hsi's philosophy is not well revealed simply through an analysis of abstract terms. His key terms commonly serve a variety of functions, with respect to somewhat discrete areas of theoretical concern. Because the same terms crop up regularly in different areas (*jen* plays a role in ethics and metaphysics; [b]*li* cuts across ethics, psychology, metaphysics, and the theory of knowledge), it is often difficult to detect the organization of the facts to which Chu's discussions of ethics or psychology or some other area pertain. Terms that should form solid pillars of a theoretical structure behave unpredictably because they are called upon simultaneously to perform different functions in other areas. But the structural images so often employed by Chu are generally coterminous in structure with a particular area of theoretical concern.

Those of Chu Hsi's theories that require structural images often pertain to phenomena for which no sensory explanation is available. Chu mentions unobservable entities of a kind that positivistic thinkers call "explanatory fictions," meaning that they are purported to be the sources of all sorts of observable regularities, from seasonal change to predictable human behavior. In fact, according to the positivists, since all that can ever be known of these fictions is the regularities they ostensibly explain, introducing them adds nothing to human knowledge. Examples of such "fictions" would be [b]*li* (principle), *tao* (the Way), *t'ien* (heaven), *t'ai chi* (the Great Ultimate), and *hsing* (human nature). Each can be invoked to explain the cause of any regularity in nature. "Fiction," of course, is a pejorative term. It may be preferable to use a term that does not assume the correctness of positivism, such as "explanatory device." In any event, in Chu Hsi's writings these unobservable entities cry out for something familiar to explain them. And the graphic images of commonplace objects serve that purpose.

Inasmuch as the *Classified Conversations* contains an enormous number of images, the obvious next question concerns the criteria by which those studied here were selected. The answer is that a rather limited number of them appear repeatedly in the attempts of Chu or his disciples to explain his theories, whereas the others occur only once or a handful of times.[53] Frequency of use and use in philosophically significant contexts therefore became two associated criteria for selection. The first thirteen *chüan* of the work alone contain more than thirty uses of the water image in explaining philosophically important terms; over twenty of light and related images (mirror, sun); at least ten of the human body or of the literal image of embodying something; at least eighteen of the ingestion of food, an indirect way of explaining how knowledge or experiences are embodied; and at least seventeen of the plant and related notions (seeds, trees, growth cycles). Needless to say, not every philosophically important image occurs in every *chüan*. The family image, for example, is well represented in some *chüan*, yet found not at all in others.

A third criterion involved in the selection process is that a given image is basic because it spins off related, subsidiary images. These, in turn, meet the first two criteria. For example, the basic image of body or embodiment is associated with several subsidiary ones—I have just mentioned eating. But it also is related to the picture of taking medicine (correcting defects in the body) and of a fan (for example, abstract virtues require a person to embody them, just as paper becomes useful for our comfort only when it has a skeletal framework to adhere to). The basic image of water shifts to the subordinate image of blood when the discussion turns from the principle accounting for cosmic movement to its concrete substantiation in the vitality of the human body. The basic image of light source (mirror, sun) or light spins off the related image of the pearl. The translucence of the pearl is apparent only when light is permitted to touch its surface. The act of ruling also constitutes an image, which in turn spawns such secondary images as fighting battles (as between motives guided by moral principles and those guided by selfish desires), conquering, and shooting arrows (aiming at a single target).

Using these three criteria, then, this book identifies six images that seem to play a major role in Chu Hsi's explanations of his theories about man. These include the family network and the stream of water, both of which are applied to all things. The family and its structure—reciprocal duties and expectations linking a hierarchy of social positions—provide an example of integration that Chu believes is characteristic of all natural phenomena in the cosmos. For its part, the stream of water links an original spring of pure water to an infinity of channels that constitute the water's natural path and that always contain, in the form of sand and rock, the potential for pollution or obstruction of the natural flow. The stream image suggests the relatedness of all things, in the sense of coming from a single source and of being penetrated by a single pure entity. The juxtaposition of these two images, family and stream, seems to place the individual in the paradoxical position of having to conform to hierarchically distinct natural role relations at the same time he is given reason to believe in the equality of human worth.

The third and fourth primary images are the light source and the body. The mirror (or lamp) provides a structure for understanding the dynamics of light, the incorporation of the light itself, things that obscure or stop light, and the light's effect. Chu uses this image in his theory of knowledge, treating the mind as similar to a light source in its capacity to clarify the inner principles of things. The body provides a way of understanding empathy, by treating things distinct from the self as if they were parts of one's own body.

The plant, the fifth image, introduces the idea of stages of change and suggests the relation of nurturance to growth. It enters the discussion to teach the individual how to develop both his own mind and the minds of others, emphasizing especially the nurturance of innate traits, universally shared.

Finally, the picture of ruling explains the relationships among aspects of mind. Even though there are universally shared human traits (a mind able to intuit principles innate to it), it cannot be assumed that everyone's mind will be equally cognizant of them; thus, some ruling is required by certain aspects of the mind with respect to other aspects, and by the minds of ancestors, emperors, or teachers over the minds of others. Ruling is needed because everyone needs a master to ensure that he lives by the principles revealed in the mind. The inner ruler is often obscured, and only clean minds can know these principles; therefore, external rulers should supplement what limited inner resources are available.

Not every theory requires a structure of the kind provided by a pictorial image. Numerical classification theories constitute a good example of those that do not. It is often difficult to identify any common structural attributes among the objects classified together, and so it is difficult to make the case that imagistic thinking is being employed. In his work *Symbolic Classification*, Rodney Needham remarks,

> In other cases—probably the majority—the ethnographic evidence provides no reason to think that the members of a symbolic class are connected by features that are common to all. The Javanese scheme of correspondence [involving the number five] is very explicit to the point that of one member of a class it can be said that it is one or another member; but beyond this statement the source offers no ground to infer that there is any common feature that unites, e.g., east, reserved, food, verandah, and propitious.[54]

The same could be said of many of the objects classified together in a set by the Chinese five-element scheme, including noses and metal, mouths and water. No common structure links them.

This book will examine the concept of man in the thought of Chu Hsi and related values in his ethics. Theories about the one are linked to conclusions already formulated about the other. The method used to clarify that concept of man is the study of the structural images that are philosophically significant to the theories. Although important in explaining what a person is, the images are absolutely crucial to persuading Chu's audience what to do about it.

Values

In addition to informing his theories, Chu's images often have a special function—that of indicating the appropriate emotional response to a given set of circumstances, a response appropriate to nature, society, or humankind (the three factual realms). The desired response is significant, because from it the individual can infer values. In other words, when Chu Hsi summons up a structural image to explain a theory, his choice of image also discloses a value.

The term "value" refers to anything Chu Hsi considers to be morally good or desirable, where "good" is defined in terms of either accord with nature (*t'ien-tao*) or consistency with the constant principles and rules of conduct (ª*ching* or ª*li*) found in classical texts. The good may be intrinsically desirable, or desirable as a means to things good in themselves. A value can include fulfillment of a duty or an obligation, and/or it can refer to an enduring condition of a person or society. Thus, a reference to the emotional response suggested by an image is also a reference to the duty inspired by the emotion involved; fulfillment of the duty actualizes the value with which it is associated. One can generally infer from such duties and from other evidence the values associated with the person or system that are considered desirable.

It is not surprising that Chu Hsi's abstract theories about nature, society, and persons have some built-in biases. Confucians regarded the mind that knows and the objective regularities that it knows (the subject matter of theories) as, each in its own way, linking together factual and evaluative matters. In Chu Hsi's case, the regularities are the predictable behaviors of all things belonging to a particular category. His usual example is the behavior of occupants of specific social roles (the classes of sons, daughters, mothers, princes, peasants, and so forth).

As will be discussed in Chapter Three, Chu Hsi believes that certain moral principles are innate to the mind. The mind can and should link any individual piece of knowledge to one of its innate moral principles, thereby pairing a factual matter with an evaluative tool. For example, knowledge of breeding patterns in animals, linked with the moral imperative to sustain and protect life's natural cycles, results in the conviction that certain animals breed at X time *and* should not be hunted at X time.[55] Knowledge is considered deep or thoroughgoing only when this kind of association occurs. In this portrait of what might be called integrated knowledge is one of Chu Hsi's major contributions to the Confucian fusion of facts and values.

Moreover, Chu Hsi has no conception of a cognitive faculty that operates independently of the emotions. Pure cognition is a Western idea, associated with the separation of immaterial mind from material body. Chu Hsi believes instead that every mind possesses universal emotional predispositions along with cognitive powers. Moral sentiments may be aroused by and directed toward the same object that an individual is engaged in cognitively investigating; that is, one may simultaneously know and approve of or feel compassion toward something. Feelings carry value judgments. The point is that the mind knows and evaluates at the same time. This clustering of facts and values has its roots in the Chou period, when Confucians used the phrase *shih-fei chih hsin* to refer to a sensibility that discriminates between "correctness" and "incorrectness," a cognitive function. Yet the same phrase suggests some sort of evaluation: to ª*shih* something is to approve it, to ª*fei* is to disapprove. These are matters of feeling. In Chu Hsi's philosophy, then, the mind concurrently makes cognitive distinctions and affective evaluations.[56]

Chou Confucians believed that the external objects of knowledge also exhibit both descriptive and prescriptive information. One such example is the Chinese equivalents for natural law. Hsün Tzu turned the term "propriety," or "rules of conduct" (ª*li*), into a cosmic principle. In human society it stood for the ritual rules governing the relations among occupants of hierarchically arranged social roles. As a cosmic principle, it imputed to plants, rivers, and other natural objects regular movement, a moral duty to behave in a certain manner, and rank. As Hsün Tzu notes,

> [ª*Li* is] that whereby heaven and earth unite, whereby the sun and moon are bright, whereby the four seasons are ordered, whereby the stars move in their courses, whereby rivers flow, whereby all things prosper, whereby love and hatred are tempered, whereby joy and anger keep their proper places. It causes the lower orders to obey, and the upper orders to be illustrious; through a myriad of changes it prevents going astray. But if one departs from it, he will be destroyed. Is not ª*li* the greatest of all things?[57]

To know the courses of the stars is to know both how the stars predictably will move and how they should (in a moral sense) move; that is, there is a principle for every class of things that both describes the patterns of movement, or actions, of things in the class and prescribes how things in the class should act.

31

This tendency for facts to be linked with values should be borne in mind during an examination of Chu Hsi's theories and their associated structural images. The image, because of its temporal and cultural associations, is a key to the value embedded in a theory about nature and facts about human behavior. Whenever an image appears in Chu's philosophical discourse, it not only provides information about the structural relations between objects (a factual matter); it also conveys suggestions as to how one should feel about and react to them (an evaluative matter). The image is employed to provide information about something that cannot be seen. In this case, it points to the values that are supposedly immanent in the objective world. The experience of enlightenment described in Chapter Three includes understanding how all things and events fit together to form an orderly whole.[58] This being the case, it is evident why the very idea of the coherence or integration of some facts (demonstrating these is the first function of structural images) itself carries emotionally persuasive overtones. It is an instance of universal interconnectedness. When Chu presents a theory that explains how some things in nature are integrated, the particular structural image that he uses not only helps to persuade the audience to accept the theory about the interrelations between those facts, but also emotionally promotes complete integration as a value. It encourages the value of understanding and facilitating a holistic approach in the individual's own behavior. Study and empathy are the means of attaining that approach, which can be encouraged by several very different images. The family and the plant both explain integrated structures and induce an acceptance of the value of completeness, or being part of a whole.

Some examples of other values promoted by images are in order. Like Hsün Tzu, Chu Hsi accepted the theory that the rules of propriety (ª*li*) exist in nature, meaning that hierarchy and duty have objective status. Like his Confucian predecessors of long before, Chu Hsi used the image of the family network to explain the interrelationships among all natural phenomena. Once read into nature, reciprocal obligations such as those existing between fathers, mothers, and children are seen to integrate planets, mountains, rivers, and so forth. The image gives support to the value of role fulfillment, and its content of reciprocal duties and expectations, for that is what makes good family members, whether the members are human beings or cosmic bodies (the pole star "rules" and other stars obey). It reinforces the primacy of family in any listing of natural structures, because all other organizational structures are derived from it. As long as that primacy is recognized, the image can be called on to encourage in the reader a sense of familial affection for things dead (human or not) and things yet to be born, as well as for all that is part of the here and now.

Other structural images do the same thing. Water suggests the possibility of purity and, therefore, worth. By extension, it suggests the duty of purification. Projecting light suggests the value of empathic expansiveness (of feeling), of reaching out beyond the self to other things. The plant suggests the value of growth and the duty of nurturance. The image of a ruler or a general commanding soldiers implies the value of conquest and the duty of submission. Subsequent chapters will flesh out these statements and show how these images and their values are related to Chu Hsi's concept of man.

In most cases, the values associated with the images had existed in Chinese culture long before Chu's time. Han cosmologies reveal the value of role fulfillment in association with the family image, applied to explain nature. Chou-Han Taoist descriptions of the sage's mind provide examples of the value of purity in association with the images of water and the mirror. Buddhist texts introduce the value of clarity and avoiding obscurity through depicting the enlightened mind as a light source. The *Mencius* alerts the reader to the value of nurturance by explaining the mind's innate traits as akin to barley seeds. And the Chou Confucian works give the value of willful commitment (*chih*) to a moral standard. They do so by describing facets of the mind through the analogy of the ruler-ruled division in society.[59] In the case of the committed person, all desires spontaneously submit to the commands of the moral mind.

Focusing on a philosopher's structural images and their psychological impact is a way of understanding theories that has applications far beyond Chu Hsi. For example, Western studies of social contract theory have become bogged down when they have followed the usual Western route of appealing to logic to verify statements about the derivation of state authority from a citizen's contractual agreement. There is no way to verify such claims. The debate becomes interminable and boring when one attempts to take the claims as stating that societies began when people met and made a contractual agreement to band together as social units. There is no way to test such claims. As Margaret MacDonald has shown, the real importance of such statements lies in the psychological impact of the contract image.[60] The statements encourage the attitudes that social institutions are man-made and can be changed, that citizens should be critical rather than reverential toward rules, and that rulers are responsible to the governed. I would add that the psychological effect of such statements is the strengthening of the political values of independence and flexibility.

Of the structural images used by Chu Hsi, some are static, such as the family and still water, but many more are process images. "Static" simply means that movement or change, especially between poles, is not among the most significant aspects in descriptions of the image or in any account of the facts to which it applies. Alternatively, in the case of process images, movement or change is an important feature. For example, while Chu recognizes that people's roles within the family are bound to change as they mature, the important idea for him is the unchanging nature of the image—the family as a fixed network of hierarchical roles. When still water is used to explain the original mind or the sage's mind, it is assumed that sages, too, continue to develop. But in this context the image is meant to convey the static tranquility, nonprejudicial equilibrium, and clarity of the sage's mind. In contrast, the very essence of the stream image is movement from the pure-spring source through silted channels to the sea; and in the case of the plant, the focus is on change, represented by the seedling's progress through all the stages of growth to decay.

The preponderance of process images in itself suggests a value that is revealed in various ways by many different images in Chu's theories—that of harmonizing conflicting beliefs or explanations. The notion of a process in Chinese philosophical writings suggests accommodating superficially polarized or contradictory entities:

the process of breathing, for example, includes expansion and contraction; yin and yang alternation applied to seasonal change explains both heat and cold; and the process of change itself accommodates tranquility and movement. Chu Hsi seems to have focused particularly on process images because of their utility in harmonizing conflicting beliefs. Process images can accommodate different and even seemingly conflicting positions by assigning them to different points in the process (the conflicting beliefs mentioned in passing here will be discussed in subsequent chapters.) One could argue that, in addition to providing support for the value of conflict avoidance or resolution, a writer like Chu Hsi had another reason for being partial to process images; their vagueness permits those encountering the image to read into it a wide range of reactions from personal experience, thereby providing the opportunity for some individualized use of the teachings.

In any case, the value of conflict avoidance is often a background theme, not the central value flagged by each of the process images. For example, in Confucian literature, the stream is a symbol of timelessness, eliciting feelings of awe at its ceaseless flow and admiration for its original clarity.[61] In Chu Hsi's writings the process image of the stream, flowing from a pristine spring and passing through all living things, harmonizes conflicting ideas about human nature. In addition, it instills both reverence for its presence and an obligation to feel unity with all of the things through which it flows. At the same time it suggests a duty to purify: "Washing away dirt."[62] In sum, this image communicates the values of the potentially equal worth of all living things, of empathy, and of maintaining the purity of the "source" as it exists within each thing. The plant image suggesting the growth process may harmonize conflicting values by identifying them with different stages of growth. But, as Chapter Four will show, it also promotes other values.

Uses and Misuses of Structural Images

In studying structural images, I am not taking a reductionist approach. Information derived from the methodology used in this volume can serve neither to bolster nor to undercut the adequacy, utility, or truth of any theory in question, and, indeed, this is not the intent. Instead, my aim is to unravel theories that overlap, identify what is original about them, and clarify their content. In addition (and more problematic for the analyst), I seek to assess how persuasive some of the images were in establishing belief in Chu Hsi's values in subsequent generations of Confucians.

Pictorial images perform a number of functions for the theoretician. One of these is simply to clarify for his audience the structural relations among facts to which his theories apply; without the image, the reader might fail to note that the facts in question are related at all. In the process of providing this clarification, the image can highlight or call attention to certain features of the relationships that are deemed especially important. For example, the image of the family network applied to all natural objects suggests to the reader that natural morality is built on reciprocal duties and expectations (such as exist in a family). The water image applied to all people or living things highlights the fact that they have a source, just as water has a spring as its source, and that they can be purified or muddied by their physical surroundings. The plant discloses that change occurs in stages, as in a plant's growth from seed to bud to blossom.

Another service rendered by images lies in their emotive effect. They may evoke in the reader a response sympathetic to the theory, prompting him to think about its content in a new way. The image of light projecting from the mind (see Chapter Three) is unlikely to be accepted by the reader as literally accurate, but it may dispose him to think about the mind's expansive characteristics or its ability to project the individual beyond his immediate physical self.

The images' worth as explanatory tools is most compellingly indicated by their continued vibrancy and endurance as later Confucians passed on Chu's teachings. This much has long been obvious. What is less obvious are the misuses to which the images are subject. The primary reason for misuse is the writer's lack of limitations on their use. The most commonly encountered shortcoming is the application of an image's dominant features, without qualification, to the world as a whole or to social organizations, thereby tempting the philosopher or his audience to infer that some aspect of its structure must have a direct counterpart in the real world. In fact, the inference may have no more support than the mere presence in the commonplace object used as an explanatory image of some actual or imagined attribute.

The point is that the most familiar attribute associated with a structural image may not be the only one worthy of attention in the entity to which the image is applied. Most Confucians apply the family image to all complex structures, whether social, terrestrial, or celestial (see Chapter Two). Providing stability for nurturance and reproduction is a familiar, plausible core function of actual families. Stability is achieved by each person's performance of what custom determines to be his basic social roles; parents nurture, children obey so as to learn and grow "naturally." But should ensuring stability be viewed as the major function of a military unit, a weaving mill, or a dam-building team? Obviously not, yet this would be the appropriate inference to be drawn from the use of the family image to explain the organization of these phenomena.[63] It is important to avoid analogizing from concrete families to ersatz ones and assuming without question that the claimed core function of the one should be central to the other.

Chu Hsi uses the image of a spring and its derivative stream to explain the relation between principle and things. He occasionally even uses terms such as "source" and "fountain" to describe "natural principle" (*tao-li*), the life principle *jen*, and the Great Ultimate (*t'ai chi*). [b]*Li*, he says, is the source from which things emerge.[64] Many of Chu's readers have assumed that the attributes of a spring of water can be transferred almost in toto to the [b]*li*, especially the state of being temporally prior to and the producer of things (as springs are to streams and rivers). So the Great Ultimate or the [b]*li* are taken for the original generator of the universe. But such an interpretation is consistent neither with the fact that Chu rarely says "[b]*li* produces the yin and yang [a]*ch'i*," nor with his general position that principle and matter are inseparable, and the one has never existed without the other.[65] The idea of a water source has obscured the boundary between "origin of" and "explanation of." The [b]*li* are "prior" (or "source") in the latter sense, that is, what account for something, but not in the former. They are eternal patterns that explain why things belong to certain classes or categories, why things in given classes both have certain qualities (e.g., fire is hot) and should have them (filiality in sons), and why their behavior or movement has predictable patterns or expressions. An explanation differs from an origin in that the former does not assume a point in time before which there was a source but no universe. It addresses itself to traits, not existence. The stream image is a source of ambiguity in Chu Hsi's own thinking and hence, not unexpectedly, in the thinking of his interpreters.

Another picture, a corollary to the stream image studied in Chapter Two, involves the capacity of flowing water to absorb silt from the streambed. Chu Hsi would have his audience infer that, plausibly, principle can absorb from its material container something that is capable of polluting it. This is no explanation of the origin of evil, simply an unsupported inference from the stream image to Chu Hsi's claims about the real world.

Misunderstandings about the nature of the image easily transform themselves into erroneous claims about the real world. Those who use the light image often automatically assume that light always clarifies. Yet everyone has personal experience of light's capacity to distort as well as clarify (the light of the sun obscures the stars, making the sky appear blue), and so one must acknowledge that visual evidence is not necessarily an accurate reflection of reality. A mental assessment of the world can be erroneous in the same way, even when everything seems logically clear.

In addition to fostering fallacious inferences, a structural image can increase the likelihood of a theorist's failure to probe characteristics of the world simply because they do not conform to those of the image. This is a phenomenon that recalls Thomas Kuhn's insights into the way some scientific paradigms can inhibit the acquisition of new knowledge. This misuse can be illustrated with examples drawn from a number of Chu Hsi's key images. The popular Chinese wisdom about flowing water is that it moves in a single direction (down). Locked into thinking of morally positive emotional responses (^{a}ch'ing) such as compassion as manifestations of the pure stream that interpenetrates all living things, Chu Hsi draws a connection between this quality of flowing water (its "singularity" of direction) and the nature of morally good human motives. The image reinforces the Confucian stress on "either/or" motivation as a picture of how people are or should be (e.g., either study or seek profit). Chu is thus primed to offer simplistic explanations of human behavior. This is not the only image that reinforces such explanations. Chu assumes that people can be directed toward a single goal (see Chapter Two and Chapter Five) and describes the sagelike person as having a single motive, unlike lesser beings whose motives are varied (*tsa*). In reality, of course, people's motives are always mixed; some are self-serving, perhaps, and some are altruistic. The point is that the choice of the image may inhibit one from noting this fact. To use Chu Hsi's terms, the choice may prevent one from understanding the variety of ways in which the *ªch'i* of the self affects the *ᵇli* in the mind. The temptation is to rest content with statements on the order of "All affairs have only one of two fonts: the right one is the impartiality of heavenly principle, and the wrong one is selfish desires."[66] More likely, all affairs have about ten fonts.

Similarly, in discussing choice, I introduce Chu Hsi's balance-scale image, intended to explain how the mind selects alternatives. The scale image in fact oversimplifies any actual decision-making process. As Chu Hsi explains it, the individual weighs one choice at a time against the dictates of the moral sense (*ªi*) to see if it balances. In actuality, decision making involves the comparison of many alternatives that are undergoing constant revision. At best, images can only explain aspects of given sets of facts, yet they may lull one into thinking that they are explaining everything about these facts.

Chu's employment of the image of plant growth to explain change (see Chapter Four) primes one to watch for cycles similar to seasonal stages of growth. Since cycles imply repetition of what has happened before, new developments, which may be entirely different qualitatively from anything observed previously, are in danger of underestimation—or of being overlooked completely. What is not observed is then unlikely to alter traditional theories of change.

Chapter Five deals with decision making, and particularly with choices between means, between conflicting rules, and between competing goals. The most important choice is the last, and the image used to explain it is ruling. Some goals (e.g., realizing "heavenly" moral principles) constitute the ruler, while others (fulfilling the desires, ª*yü*, or human desires, *jen-yü*) make up the ruled. Chu Hsi is so concerned with the image of acquiring and maintaining dominance that he all but ignores clarifying the ruler and ruled. The reader is never totally sure whether "heavenly principles" refers only to the social role duties and rights, or whether it encompasses the patterns of behavior of all natural classes of things and affairs as well.

Chu Hsi never clarifies what the term "desires" covers: physical desires, antisocial activity, activity contrary to natural laws? Sometimes he says they are selfish, which is true of the second and third definitions but not necessarily the first. Sometimes it seems that he claims there is a difference between "desires" (ª*yü*) and "human desires" (*jen-yü*), the former denoting life-sustaining needs (food, drink) that are morally appropriate and the latter, hedonistic gratification, which is always selfish.[67] In this view, the human desires are all bad and should be conquered and destroyed. Yet elsewhere, Chu contradicts this idea. What is finally left is a muddle that tilts in the direction of claiming that the ideal man is a truncated man. That part of him which contains ordinary human experience that lies beyond the satisfaction of survival needs has been declared immoral and dispensable. The core issue of which parts to dispose of and why is never clearly addressed. The reason is preoccupation with the process of self-mastery, or ruling, and the consequent trivialization of interest in the nature of what is ruled.

Mindful of the potential dangers of the influence of structural images on the thought process, an analyst can at least be on guard in evaluating Chu Hsi's arguments and in using such images himself. This is one virtue of studying them.

In the last chapter of this book I will make the case that Chinese theoreticians will probably continue in the future to employ "explanatory fictions" and the structural images that support them. Awareness of their shortcomings does not cancel out their positive functions. Chinese philosophers will not become positivists, content with statistical guidebooks that reveal regularities in nature. This is because the images serve a variety of nonscientific ends that no statistical guidebook can further. One of the most important of these ends, and one that plays a central role in this book, is the elicitation of emotional responses from the reader or listener. The images are capable of extracting fear, zeal, anger, or almost any other powerful sentiment. The emotions generate responses that can be interpreted as duties, and these duties are associated with specific values or goods. The ability to engender an emotional response allows the structural image to explain some facet of reality and simultaneously to justify a particular moral duty associated with that facet. Confucians found the images to be a persuasive teaching device because of their emotive meaning and the utility of that meaning in fostering compliance with duties.

CONCLUSION

Clarifying Chu's ideas by a study of his structural images is the first step toward explaining his concept of human nature. The methodology reveals Chu's attempts to harmonize ideas that appear polarized to modern readers, though they did not appear contradictory to the Confucians. In other words, it is worth remembering that as one uncovers Chu's concept of man and the values with which it is entwined, two polarities at the heart of the philosophical issues are revealed. One is the dichotomy between family love and love for people outside the basic role relationships. The other juxtaposes self-discovery of nature's principles and reliance on objective authority. Analysis of this particular concept of man in the context of early modern China thus simultaneously enables one to note and evaluate the place of these culturally important polarities in this period. I will judge the adequacy of Chu's efforts at making a place for each value in each set of the sets that I consider polarized.

In putting together Chu's portrait of what a human is, an analyst can learn something about how *he* thinks. The very act of unraveling Chu's positions on the mind and related ethical issues reveals assumptions in one's own views that may hitherto not have been adequately questioned. Among others, these include the assumption that there are no alternatives to distinguishing in the self between the subjective or the psychological realm that is private (in the sense of accessible only to the individual) and the objective realm of publicly observable behavior. In short, there may be other

41

ways of analytically splitting the person. Another common assumption is that free choice is a crucial aspect of being human and is central to the virtuous life. Chu's doctrines can stimulate a questioning of whether the idea of free choice has only a European history or is a universally understood notion. One can wonder when and why it became so central in the Western view of man and whether it is possible to think of the moral life without assuming it. Rather than serving as convincing replacements for Western doctrines, those of Chu can force a reexamination of presuppositions and place them on a firmer foundation. From time to time in this study I will introduce pertinent examples from the Western philosophical tradition in order to facilitate learning a bit about the way Westerners think.

The analyst also begins to sort out features of Chu's doctrine that can have dangerous implications for political problem solving. His portrait of a mind that fuses matters of fact and value means that the primary considerations in investigating the facts in any social situation will be the moral standards of either the investigator or any human participant in it. When the former are correct, the factual judgments are assumed to be accurate, and when the latter are proper, the situation will be propitious. Needless to say, this perspective on problems limits the dimensions of a real life situation that one deems pertinent to understanding it. The approach may ignore economic and organizational variables.

TWO

THE FAMILY AND THE STREAM:
TRANQUIL HIERARCHY AND
EQUAL WORTH

Chu Hsi uses a great many pictorial images in his explanations. Of the banquet of options before him, he settles on a very few that then change their functional nature. Instead of being simply heuristic descriptive devices, they become conceptual frameworks used to structure the relations between increasingly complex sets of facts. These sets of facts may pertain to anything, from parts of an individual person to nature as a whole. Chu Hsi's repertoire of dominant structural images includes the family, the stream of water, and the plant. The first two of these will be examined in this chapter. The three as a group constitute the images adopted by Chu Hsi to explain his most comprehensive theories of nature.

Each of these images implies one or more values. Explaining nature in terms of the family image provides a cosmic justification for social role fulfillment, a value that, once realized, points to a more generalized realm of value. If practiced universally, this value results in the realization of the societal value of a tranquil, orderly, hierarchical system.

Explaining nature in terms of the stream of water indicates the duty to purify oneself and others. Purification is a value, and pursuing it points the individual toward knowledge of people's potential equal worth; that is, purification reveals the original nature with which all human beings are equally endowed. This claim of equal worth has two rather different bases. One is the present condition of all people now, namely, their possession of an "original nature" in the form of the principle of life and of life's moral rules. This nature is revealed in actual life and in a moral sense that intuits these moral rules. Chu says that all men "possess the principles of humaneness, righteousness, respectfulness, and knowledge that emerge as compassion, shame, reverence, and the ability to distinguish right and wrong. All men have these."[1] People possess this nature by virtue of a common source of being, suggested in the image of a pure source or spring for a stream of water. The other basis of equal worth is the assumption that human beings are perfectible, which makes this a matter of potentially equal worth. Chu Hsi does, however, identify limits to the perfectibility of some people: "Confucius said that some people definitely do not change. They do not do so because of their physical nature. How can we say that they can change? They are called the most stupid, and the reason why they have become most stupid is because of their physical nature. Confucius' theory is perfect."[2] The important point about these bases is that they do not hinge on social roles. They are universal. The first basis of equal worth, that associated with the stream source, implies a direct and similar affinity among all humans on the grounds of a common origin. The family image, in contrast, implies ranked personal relationships, with preference being shown to those in one's actual family, toward whom one has standard, role-associated responsibilities.

Philosophically, there is no necessary incompatibility between the ideals associated with the two images, the family and the stream. Their contrasting emphases, however, provide a substantial ground for tension unless Chu adequately deals with how the individual accommodates both. In both theory and practice, the family image serves to highlight the values associated with an individual's position in a hierarchical society. These include loyalty, respect, filiality, and preferential affection for kin. In contrast, the stream emphasizes that which is common to all human beings instead of that which differentiates them.

The notion of equal worth therefore coexists with the values of role fulfillment and hierarchy. This is one of the central themes of this book. I will examine the potential incompatibility that exists between these values, its long-term implications for Chinese society, and how Chu Hsi's position purports to harmonize the values. It is important here to point out that Chu Hsi does not himself explicitly treat the family as a dangerously restrictive entity that narrows people's concerns to those with whom they have genealogical ties. It is analysts who identify it as such, much as the Mohists did when disciples of Confucius were treating filiality as the primary virtue, the root of all altruistic love. And in Chapters Three and Four it is as an analyst that I sort out Chu Hsi's thesis, based on the light source and the plant images, that in his philosophy serves the function of dissolving all conflict between the values associated with the family and stream images.

THE FAMILY

I begin with abstract theory. As Ch'eng I says, "[W]e can see from the superiority of heaven and the humble status of earth that $^a li$ [rules of propriety] are already established. From the arrangement of things according to types and their divisions into classes we can see that the $^a li$ are already in operation."[3] "Nothing stands alone"[4] in this cosmos; all things are viewed as existing in complementary, and usually hierarchical, pairs. The idea that proper relationships exist between all things is manifest when Chu speaks of the "rules of propriety" that underlie their orderly divisions.

Theoretical statements about an orderly, hierarchical universe do not answer the obvious question: what holds the whole thing together? The theory requires information about the reason for the integration of the myriad parts and the nature of the relationships among them. There is another way of putting the matter. Chu and his disciples accepted the existence of patterns ($^b li$) in the universe in the sense of something that accounts for classes of things, for predictable courses of change that members of each class undergo, and for the fact that the patterns and things all are somehow related. But the belief in pattern does not provide enough detail to explain the nature of integration, which is an additional issue.

The image of the family network works well in this context because a family is a unit that bears a clear explanation for the integration of its parts: reciprocal obligations based on what each member provides the others. Parents provide food for children, and children constitute old-age insurance for parents; ancestors watch over the family's good fortune, and family members give food and other sacrifices to ancestors. Each provision binds the recipient. The whole is held together by a network of psychological expectations and reciprocal, specialized duties. The structural image of the family serves a key function in Neo-Confucian ethics

45

by providing a natural justification for the values of role fulfillment and tranquility within a hierarchical system. Before introducing the details of the structural image, however, I will note its roots.

Origins of the Image

To consider the government an extension of family relationships was a policy of Chou feudalism; early Chou rulers addressed feudal princes by familial names. It is not surprising, then, that the family or clan has been used metaphorically to explain society since the Spring and Autumn period (722–481 B.C.). In discussing government, the *Book of Odes* refers to the feudal lord as the "father and mother of the people" (*min chih fu-mu*),[5] and down through the Ch'ing dynasty, magistrates were characterized as "parental officials" (*fu-mu kuan*). Like good rulers, good officials "treat the people as kin" (*ch'in-min*).[6] In the Sung period Ch'eng I said that "heaven is the ancestor of the myriad things, and the king is the ancestor of the myriad states."[7] And as Chou Tun-i remarked, "There is a model for the government of the world. It is the family."[8]

Turning to a unit smaller than society or the state, one finds that the Confucian classical texts treat the master-disciple relation as akin to that between father and son.[9] As a modern Chinese commentator has noted,

> Regarding social life, the Chinese people essentially expanded or extended family life into a larger area. . . . While the Chinese respect for the tutor was an extension of filial piety, the respect of friendship was, as an expansion of tutorship, also an extension of filial piety. The closely knit patterns of relatives, clansmen, fellow countrymen, and tutors, together with friends, were all interwoven around the filial axis in the Chinese community.[10]

Explaining society in terms of the family is not unknown in the West, though the image is less pervasive. Aristotle was perhaps its most famous classical proponent, and he made only sparing use of it.[11] It is significant that one must root around among far lesser figures to find modern advocates, such as Locke's target, Sir Robert Filmer (d. 1653), in *Patriarcha*.[12]

By the Former Han period (202 B.C.-A.D. 9), the image of the family had also come to be employed in the service of cosmological theories claiming that nature is composed of objects integrally related to each other in a hierarchical manner. The *Classic of Filial Piety*, which gained popularity at this time, states: "Tseng Tzu said, 'How great is filiality!' The master replied, 'Filiality is the constant principle of heaven, the moral rule of earth, and the standard for conduct of the people.' "[13] At the bottom of this reading into nature of family duties and relations is the early Chou claim that the social distinctions, among which those of the family are basic, derive from heaven.[14] Hierarchical position, a characteristic of all things from planets to people, is the key to the rules of proper behavior that apply to everything. Planets that behave in accordance with the rules are "obedient"; those that do not are "contrary."[15]

The *Classic of Filial Piety* also explains proper social organization as an extension of family relations. "The superior man is filial in serving his parents. Therefore such loyalty can be transferred to his ruler. In serving his elder brothers he is deferential. Therefore, such obedience can be transferred toward those senior to him."[16]

The Sung Confucians, then, cannot be credited with introducing the family image into Chinese philosophical thought. It was a legacy of the past that became part of their own doctrines. The most prominent form in which the image was passed down to them is found in the *Book of Changes*. The first two trigrams, *ch'ien* and *k'un*, were respectively regarded as father and mother (the qualities of *k'un* were described as those of a "mare"). Through their intercourse, the universe was created. The other six trigrams are their three "sons" and three "daughters."[17] As trigrams, *ch'ien* and *k'un* describe nature as a whole and heaven and earth more specifically. As viewed from the perspective of their early analysts, however, *ch'ien* and *k'un* introduce to nature the idea of complementary familial obligation. *Ch'ien* symbolizes the obligation to beget children, to be creative, to nourish. *K'un* stands for the obligation to bear the children or to bring things to fruition. Together they constitute a "family," bound by the complementarity of their duties. Such a model would offer any holistic cosmological theory a plausible basis for explaining the interconnectedness of things. It also introduces the value that will be considered in Chapter Four in connection with the plant image, namely, nurturance of life.

Ch'eng, Chu, and the Family Image

Within Sung cosmologies, then, there is an early Confucian strand. And it is in the early cosmological ideas that the Sung figures inherited that nature is first described in terms of the core attributes of clan society. These societal characteristics together are described in the subordinate image of a net that has one central and numerous secondary cords (though it may be more helpful to think in terms of several nets, not just one). The family and society thus are viewed as having a spatial dimension, that is, as a picture of positions (social positions) in a net. Since the Han period, the three basic sets of social relations ("Three Bonds," *san kang*) have been identified as those between ruler and minister, father and son, and husband and wife. As Chu Hsi describes the term "bond" (*kang*), "*Kang* refers to the principal cord in a net. In the three bonds, the ruler is principal cord for the minister, the father for the son, and the husband for the wife."[18] Chinese writers down to the present have continued to refer to the explicit image of the net when describing these *kang*.[19] And Chu Hsi refers to an artery through which a vital force flows from a central base, connecting all kin, including ancestral spirits: "As long as [each kinship group] has its own central base, when descendants' bodies are here, then the ancestor's vital force will be here. There is an artery that links them."[20]

The most important societal attribute contained in the family image comprises social roles, which are conceived spatially. Early Confucians had no monopoly on this idea. The *Han Fei-tzu* states that "things have their proper place, talents their proper use. When all are in their proper place, then superior and inferior may be free from action."[21] But the idea is central to Confucianism. All of the terms used by Confucians to refer to social roles have spatial connotations and literally mean "position": *so, fen* (allocated portion), and *wei*. Most frequently, they stand for both routine social roles and the duties associated with those roles. (It is interesting to recall F. M. Cornford's conclusion that the earliest meaning of the Greek term *moira* [fate] was "part" or "allotted portion," something spatial rather than temporal.)[22]

The classic statement of roles and their associated duties appears in the "Li yün" (The conveyance of rites) section of the *Li-chi*:

> What are "the things which men consider right?" Kindness on the part of the father, and filial duty on that of the son; gentleness on the part of the elder brother, and obedience on that of the younger; righteousness on the part of the husband, and submission on that of the wife; kindness on the part of elders, and deference on that of juniors; with benevolence on the part of the ruler, and loyalty on that of the minister;—these ten are the things men consider to be right.[23]

The *Mencius* had referred to a set of "Five Relations" and the duties central to each: "[B]etween father and son, there should be affection; between sovereign and minister, righteousness; between husband and wife, attention to their separate functions; between old and young, a proper order; and between friends, fidelity."[24] Against the background of these classical descriptions, the formulaic sets became the "Three Bonds" and the "Five Relations." Chu Hsi cited the Five Relations in the first part of the "Rules of Study" for the White Deer Grotto Academy, which he began to restore in 1179.[25] When the literati are considered as a group, it is necessary to note that there are additional reciprocal obligations beyond the family. For example, there is the set composed of superior persons (*chün-tzu*) and lesser people (*hsiao-min*). As an individual and as an official the true Confucian has duties to nurture the people in his community or county, and the people have the duty to be responsive to the nurturance. Sung Confucians customarily explained this relation paternalistically with the family image. The true Confucian was the father of the people, a concept that will be dealt with further in Chapter Four.

In the Han period, Tung Chung-shu (179?–104? B.C.) had used the phrase "Three Bonds," encompassing three of Mencius' Five Relations. For Tung, the idea of proper family-based role relations had become central in Confucian ethics. When Chu Hsi pressed for a return to strictness in observing the hierarchical element in early Confucianism, he was pressing for a return to an aspect of the ethics that had had its flowering in the Han.[26]

Each individual role is a *fen*. In their day, the Ch'engs always claimed these were inadequately or improperly filled.[27] In order to convey the idea that the role duties reflect immutable values, they were called "heavenly allotments" (*t'ien-fen*). When actually practiced by people, the duties become known as the "human allotments" (*jen-fen*).

A second societal attribute in the family image is the existence of boundaries that separate one social position from another. Boundaries suggest the impropriety of the occupant of one position engaging in the activities appropriate to another position. Not unexpectedly, most of the early words for "wrong" mean basically to overstep or transgress a boundary (e.g., *kuo*, [b]*yü*, and *p'an*). In the philosophical record, the roots of this attribute and the one previously discussed go back to the Chou-period principle of the rectification of names (*cheng-ming*).[28] Rectification requires action appropriate to the name of one's social role. The prince must remain a prince, the minister a minister, the father a father, and the son a son. In the Ch'eng-Chu works, the idea of bounded positions is conveyed in the saying that, under the rule of sages, "each person will occupy [or attain] his appropriate social role" (*ke tang ch'i fen* or *ke te ch'i fen*).[29] Moreover, each will be and should be (the two senses are fused) tranquil (that is, at ease, content) in his position (*ke an ch'i fen*), without a desire to seek the activities or privileges of some other role.

The third attribute in the family image is relational. The basic social roles come in sets of two, and each set functions in a hierarchical manner. One role carries the duty of exercising authority; the other, the duty of obedience.

The fourth and final attribute, also relational, is composed of the emotions that tie the various related roles together to form a unified social organization. The principle that ties everything together is humaneness (*jen*). When roles are occupied by actual people, the emotions that link the positions together are love, respect, and loyalty. Love ties parents to children and children to parents. In all other sets, love proceeds from the superior to the inferior, while respect proceeds from the younger to the elder, or the inferior to the superior, and loyalty proceeds from the subjects to the emperor. Influenced by the family image from the Chou period, Ch'eng I traced all love to family sentiments: "Benevolence focuses itself in love. No love is greater than love for family. Therefore, Confucius said, 'Filial piety and fraternal love are the beginning of practicing humaneness.' "[30]

Long ago some Western sociologists began to regard this kind of stratified role differentiation as best explained by the functionalist theory of society:

> As a functioning mechanism, a society must somehow distribute its members in social positions and induce them to perform the duties of these positions. It must thus concern itself with motivation at two different levels: to instill in the proper individuals the desire to fill certain positions, and, once in these positions, the desire to perform duties attached to them.[31]

In Chu's doctrine, to claim that there is a natural basis to the roles within a natural structure similar to that of the familiar family is to assist people's motivation to perform social duties. The Western sociologists explain the motivation in terms of societal rewards.

The Family Image in Nature

Each of the four societal attributes identified above can be applied to nature. First, not only persons but all objects in nature have allotted positions within whose "space" (or with whose duties) they must abide. "Position" includes the idea of function. One of the Ch'engs said, "The sage has an impartial mind. He exhausts the principles of heaven, earth, and all things so that each may gain its proper place [fen],"[32] and "Each of all things and affairs has its place [so]. When a thing obtains its place there is tranquility; when it loses it there is disorder."[33] Chu remarked, "The heavenly order [t'ien-hsü] is natural sequence. It makes the prince rest in the position [wei] of prince."[34]

Second, boundaries between positions are present throughout nature, not just in society. This is conveyed in the quotation, paraphrase, and echo of passages from the ken hexagram in the Book of Changes. Ken means "keeping still." Most frequently quoted is the commentary, "Keeping [one's] stopping still means stopping in [one's] place."[35] In mentioning this, the *Erh Ch'eng ch'üan-shu* says, "*Ken* means stopping in one's place [*so*]. When all things stop in their places, there is no indeterminate position [*fen*]."[36] Stopping in one's place means doing what is appropriate for that place and not transgressing its boundaries. The texts speak of things (*wu*), not merely of people: "Whenever there is a thing, there is a rule for it. Each thing should stop in its place."[37] A planet has a proper position and should not encroach on the orbit of another heavenly body. The superior man who wishes to pattern himself on nature's order looks to the *ken* hexagram for guidance: "The superior man observes the *ken* hexagram and thinks of what his stopping place is and of not going beyond his position [*wei*]."[38] Ch'eng I makes the following comment on this hexagram:

> When anything exists, there must be a pattern for it. For a father, this consists of paternal affection; for a son, filial piety; for a ruler, benevolent love; for a subject, respectfulness. There is no single thing or affair that does not have its own place. Gaining this place, there is peace; losing it, there is disorder. The sage's ability to give orderly coordination to all things does not derive from an ability to create the patterns for these things. It lies simply in the fact that to each he gives its proper place.[39]

Extending the family image to nature also introduces the attribute of hierarchical relationships, which involve authority and obedience. The hexagrams *ch'ien* and *k'un* designate principles that apply throughout nature. Analogizing from family to universe, Chu Hsi says that just as a person's father and mother are his parents, so are *ch'ien* and *k'un* the parents of the world.[40] Just as *ch'ien* is in the leading position with regard to *k'un*, so is the husband with regard to the wife, and the natural principles with regard to all things in the universe.[41] In human society, the rules of propriety ([a]*li*) specify the proper duties and expectations of persons related in hierarchical sets. Similarly, the rules of propriety describe such relationships in nature at large: "From the arrangement of things according to types and their divisions into categories, we can see that the [a]*li* [rules of propriety] are already in operation."[42]

Social roles come in hierarchical sets. Such sets are found in nature as well, where the images of ruler and family dominate. Chu Hsi regularly describes the source of the natural pattern that is at the core of his entire doctrine (bli, principle) as the ruler (tsai, chu-tsai). Ch'eng I says, "That which causes material force to be able to move or be still is bli, which acts as ruler."[43] And he says that when a reference is made to bli from the standpoint of the many phenomena in which it is manifest, one must remember the differences in rank that it institutes among things, "just like in the human family."[44]

It should be noted that there are passages about things coming in sets of two that contain no reference to the image of family or society. In other words, the tendency to employ dualisms extends beyond hierarchical structural images. For example, "Among all things in the universe, there is none that does not have its complementary counterpart. Where there is yin, there is yang; where there is humaneness, there is righteousness; where there is good, there is evil; where there is speech, there is silence; and where there is action, there is tranquility."[45] The idea of authority-obedience is muted in this statement of relationships, and the idea of complementarity is emphasized, as evidenced by the juxtaposition of humaneness (jen) and righteousness (ai), and action and tranquility. The principle of complementary pairs is presented as the way in which the production and reproduction of things in the world occurs: "All principles necessarily have opposites; this is the origin of production and reproduction."[46] In the beginning there was only the one material force. It became the two material forces, yin and yang, which produced all things in the universe. And so all things have their opposites. Where there is birth, there is death, and so forth.[47] The existence of such a classification scheme independent of the family reinforces the assignment of persons to social roles that come in sets of two.

Within the family or society, cohesion among the various roles is supplied by attitudes and emotions. In the case of the family, the emotion is love, counterpart of the life force that parents give their children. As the cosmic principle of life, this love is humaneness (jen). Almost every social virtue is defined as some form of jen, the cosmic principle of growth or creativity (discussed at

53

length in Chapter Four).[48] This is true of respect ([b]*ching*),[49] reciprocity (*shu*),[50] loyalty (*chung*),[51] and impartiality (*kung*).[52]

Values: Hierarchical Role Fulfillment

As a persuasive device, the image of the family writ large in nature is intended to have an emotional impact on those who accept it. They should react with family-derived sentiments (love, respect, obedience) to the heavens and the earth, the animals, and the trees in nature. They should have these feelings about things that have died and things that will exist as well as about the currently living. Everything—whether part of the past, present, or future— is part of one integrated, extended family. The feelings themselves will depend on the objects' respective positions in the hierarchical order. Establishing contact with any living thing, and certainly with strangers, is therefore the occasion for classifying the new relationship in terms of the gamut of prescribed family relationships.

Despite the implications of this statement, it must be noted that the appeal to love people or things beyond the immediate family is more developed in passages influenced by the water analogy. In the context of the family analogy, it remains only a pious message. The vital missing element is a prescription for *how* to extend one's range of concern beyond one's own family. A key point in this connection (a focus of Chapter Four) is that the altruist, or the man of broad compassion, never abandons his basic social roles; for example, he benefits those outside his real family in his role as imaginary father of the people, or as a caretaker of his "cosmic brothers." In other words, there is no role-neutral philanthropy. This will be a key issue in my criticism of Chu's attempt to make a place for the values of both family love and altruism.

At the same time, and more central to my argument, the family image suggests to all individuals the duty of social role fulfillment, because one becomes a good "family" member by obeying its rules. Claims about the hierarchical positions occupied by all things and linked by reciprocal duties and expectations served as a powerful argument in persuading people to believe in the naturalness of human social roles. The assertion is that positions (*fen* or *wei*), whether cosmic or social, are natural. They are in accordance with the "heavenly arrangements" (*t'ien-hsü*),[53] and the heavenly arrangements are a natural order, meaning that they are assigned by heaven. Appeals to such authority provided a useful psychological tool for generating a willingness to adopt both duties and the feelings that should accompany them.

One of the most frequently encountered sets of value terminology in Chu Hsi's writings is that of *kung*, meaning unselfish impartiality, and its opposite, *ssu*, meaning selfishness. As a set, these terms have two rather different specific meanings when used in the context of the family, on the one hand, and the plant and light images on the other. In the former case, *kung* refers to the value of role fulfillment, and *ssu* to failure to fulfill one's role obligations. Because all of nature is explained by the family image, all of the roles in question are valued as "natural" ones. The roles and duties are specified in the Chou-period rules of propriety (ᵃ*li*) (and in the "heavenly principles" [*t'ien-li*], when those were thought to be synonymous with the rules of propriety), as well as in the heavenly allotments (*t'ien-fen*) and in human relationships (*jen-lun*). These passages typify this sense of unselfish impartiality:

Content in attaining one's heavenly position, without a selfish mind. . . .[54]

When one can conquer the self and get rid of the selfish mind, one naturally can return to the rules of propriety.[55]

In looking, hearing, speaking, and acting, when one does nothing contrary to principle [ᵇ*li*], this is acting according to the rules of propriety [ᵃ*li*]. The rules of propriety are principle. Whatever is not in accord with heavenly principle is selfish desire.[56]

Being basically without selfish intention is nothing but obeying heavenly principle.[57]

The third citation establishes the connection of ᵇ*li* (principle) and ᵃ*li* (rules of propriety) in the context of *Analects* 12.1 on the conquest of self. Rather than show discipline or obedience by conforming to natural duty, the selfish person satisfies his private desires. In this manner, the Ch'eng-Chu writers equated the distinction between unselfish impartiality (*kung*) and selfishness (*ssu* or *ssu-yü*) with the early Confucian contrast between doing what is right (*ai*), that is, what is called for by the rules of propriety, and doing what brings personal gain (*cli*).[58]

This understanding of impartiality explains many of the Ch'eng-Chu criticisms of Buddhism. The Buddhists fail to abide by the duties of the natural social roles into which humans must fit. This failure to regard themselves in terms of such relationships constitutes selfishness. Chu says that the reason these Buddhists want to destroy heavenly principles and get rid of human relations is that they are selfish.[59] In addition, they fail to note the other natural rules to which they are subject, such as the rule of complementary pairs, the generalized dualistic notion that, as has been shown, strongly reinforces the family image as an explanatory device. Where there is joy, there is suffering; where there is life, there is death. Buddhists are bound as well as other human beings to obey these rules. Yet they try to avoid suffering and even death—truly, the height of selfishness.[60] The contrast between the Confucian sage and the Buddhist on all of these issues is apparent in these words: "The sage develops to the utmost his selfless mind and exhausts the principles of heaven, earth, and all things so that each thing can occupy its proper place. However, the Buddhists do everything for their personal selfishness."[61]

Discipline—submergence of personal desires that do not conform to role duties in the selfless impartiality required by the family image—ensures order. No wonder those in positions of power continued to bless it and to link it with order.

When all persons fulfill their roles, they realize the value of selfless impartiality. This means that duty on behalf of the whole takes precedence over any transitory personal desire. Tranquility comes through observing proper relations with a *limited* set of people, especially those making up the Three Bonds and the Five Relations. The societal value of a tranquil hierarchy is thereby attained. In addition, each individual thing is content ("tranquil") in its position (*ke an ch'i fen*) within the integrated cosmic whole. Although a person may change roles, the idea of inviolable boundaries makes the hierarchy static. Foremost are those with whom one has direct family ties. Although Chu accounted for and justified a static hierarchy, he also envisioned extensive institutional reforms in the areas of taxation, education, food supplies, and local initiative. I return to this matter in Chapter Four.

THE STREAM OF WATER

The clear water represents the goodness of the nature. Flowing to the sea without being polluted indicates that the material endowment is clear and has been good since childhood. The sage follows his nature and retains the heavenly nature in its entirety. That stream that is already polluted after flowing just a short way indicates a person in whom the physical endowment is distorted and variegated and has been evil since childhood. . . . However, although a person is muddied by his material endowment and so flows into doing evil, it is never the case that his nature is not there within him. . . . Therefore, because of this, "men should not fail to exert the effort to purify themselves." Only if a person is able through study to overcome the material endowment will he know that the nature is vast and never decayed, and is the "original water."[62]

When this citation is placed beside others given below, the portrait is of principle as the pure water from a spring source that flows through and interpenetrates all things. The quality of its presence is a function of the material endowment that principle encounters.

If the structural image of the family provides a natural justification for the values of role fulfillment and tranquility, the stream of water offers a sharp contrast. It simultaneously explains the structural relations among and the potential equal worth of all living things by claiming a common source. This is accomplished through the image of water's penetrative power, referring to something originally pure that "flows through" all living things, linking them. By virtue of their participation in that which is pure, all things are provided with something of similar worth. The image generates both reverence for the original pure source and feelings of unity with all that is linked by the flow. The picture of water sullied by dirt is intended also to motivate action to purify that which is sullied. Whereas the stream as a structural image underlies the value of purification (which is the key to realizing equal worth among all things), as a process image (the stream proceeds from source to outlet) it also explains how two seemingly inconsistent descriptions of human nature can coexist, claiming that they refer to different aspects of the process. In one theory human nature is visualized as pure, in the other as dirtied. As both, it reinforces the value of doctrinal harmony, or making apparently contradictory doctrines compatible.

Chu Hsi uses the water image to explain his theory of the relation between a unifying principle in nature and the many concrete individual things that can regard that principle as their common source. This is the theory on which the value of equal worth rests. It should be noted, however, that water played a role in cosmology and physiology prior to Chu Hsi and is found elsewhere in Chu's own philosophy. In other words, when his whole and part theory needed explanatory support, he turned to a preexisting image to provide the structure and the emotive associations.

The importance of water as an explanatory device dates back to early texts. There is a collection of works from at least as early as the second century B.C. that is attributed to Kuan Chung (d. 645 B.C.), a powerful statesman in the state of Ch'i. The present version of that collection, edited sometime between the years 37 and 32 B.C., contains a section on the cosmic place of water that helps in understanding the origins of the stream as a structural image.

> The earth is the origin of all things, the root of all life, that from which beauty and ugliness, value and valuelessness, eminence and insignificance come into being. Water is the lifeblood of the earth, flowing through its muscles and veins. . . . Water is all-pervasive and omnipresent. It occurs in the heavens and in the earth. . . . Man is largely water.[63]

It is not surprising that at least as early as the time this work was edited, thinkers had described the motion of yang and yin as wavelike; thus, the importance of water as an explanatory device was established long before it became part of Chu Hsi's theorizing.

Chu Hsi maintained that the earth is at the center of all that exists and is surrounded by water. The physical substance of the earth is formed from sediments in the water. Chu inherited from

58

the Chou and Han periods a vision of cosmic motion derived from a cosmology based on the water image. Building on this foundation, he explained the motion by reference to the principles (^b*li* or *tao*) that determine its pattern of movement.

At the cosmic level, the "substance of the *tao* is great and inexhaustible,"[64] and so the "heavenly *tao* flows forth,"[65] or the principle of mind flows through everything, like blood through the veins and arteries[66] (blood being a subsidiary image to the stream, with which it shares characteristics). The heavenly *tao* does not involve more. It simply provides, through the ^b*li*, the patterns for the movement of material force (^a*ch'i*).[67] These passages thus refer to the cosmic movements using images derived from water's flow.

In addition to its role in explaining cosmic patterns of change, the water image is used by Chu Hsi to explain human nature in its potential and actual forms. Two attributes of water, its natural and directional movement (down) and its capacity for illumination (degree of clarity), become significant descriptive aspects of human nature. By showing how the same principles apply to both nature and man, Chu Hsi had a cosmic sanction for whatever value was suggested by the image.

Chu includes the supporting image of blood, which circulates in the individual living creature and is the flowing life force at work. ^b*Li*, as the principle of life that makes the blood flow, is called humaneness (*jen*). It operates by guiding the flow of blood. One of the Ch'engs once remarked on feeling someone's pulse that in this manner one gains access to humaneness.[68]

In addition to this biological aspect of the life force, there is a psychological aspect. Chu Hsi speaks of human nature (*hsing*) as water from which actual movement has been abstracted, and he says that "feeling is the flow of water."[69] In other words, conscious human action follows patterns of movement in the same way that water and blood do. It is appropriate to call such movement righteous (^a*i*) when the flow is in the proper direction; thus, humaneness flows forth as love of parent for child and the filiality of child toward parent. "Flowing forth" (*liu-hsing*) thus describes both physiological life processes, or movements, and psychological ones (the latter, of course, are also basically physical functions for a philosopher who has no mind-body dualism). To some degree, then, humans and their natures link up with patterned cosmic movement, a streamlike flow that permeates nature and the individual.[70]

Although it has become clear that humans and all natural things are subject to the same flowing movements, there remains the question of how disparate humans are linked to the cosmic source of such motion and to each other. Coexisting in Chu Hsi's metaphysics with the cosmological doctrine about natural movements caused by principle in nature and man is a very abstract theory about the relationship between a whole and its parts. The explanatory image of water becomes especially important at this juncture.

Chu's theory is that the cosmic heavenly principle is a "whole," and its presence in each thing constitutes its parts. This theory owes much to Chinese Buddhist thought, especially the idea that the Buddha is One Mind, present in all things. According to Chanjan (711–782), ninth patriarch of the T'ien-t'ai school, "even inanimate things possess the Buddha-nature."[71] In the Ch'an school, Huang Po said, "All the Buddhas and Bodhisattvas, together with all wriggling things possessed of life, share in this great nirvanic nature. This nature is Mind."[72] There is a formulaic expression that sums up the relationship of one to many: "Principle is one but its manifestations are many" (*li i fen shu*). It first appears in the Buddhist writings of Tao-sheng (d. 434).[73] Both Hua-yen and T'ien-t'ai masters affirm that each phenomenal object is a manifestation of the One Mind in its entirety, so between the One Mind and things there exists a macrocosm-microcosm relation.

Chu Hsi made substantial use of this legacy and the formula that expresses it. He redefined [b]*li* so that the "One," or whole, is no longer One Mind but the single ordering principle by which things are divided into interrelated classes. Each individual thing in a class participates in principle and possesses it as its original nature. For Chu Hsi the formula can mean that there is one Great Ultimate, the aggregation of all principles. The Great Ultimate comprises the principles of everything that exists. Each thing is a microcosm, possessing the Great Ultimate within itself. Alternatively, the formula permits discussion about the one ordering principle or pattern of the universe and about its presence in individual things as their particular nature, partially a function of their material endowment (*ch'i-chih chih hsing*). That endowment also works to divide things into classes, like animals and birds, each with its own ᵇ*li*.

The idea of a unity that remains a whole despite its simultaneous presence in apparently discrete individual things is difficult for most people to grasp. Plato noted this fact long ago in criticizing his own doctrine of the Forms:

> How are we to conceive that each of them [i.e., each Form] being always one and the same and subject neither to generation nor destruction, nevertheless is, to begin with, most assuredly this single unity and yet subsequently comes to be in the infinite number of things that come into being—an identical unity being thus found simultaneously in unity and in plurality. Is it torn in pieces, or does the whole of it, and this would seem the extreme impossibility, get apart from itself?[74]

It is understandable why the Neo-Confucians depended on several graphic images to explain this concept. The abstract theory of one principle in many things does not of itself suggest any plausible account of how something can be both one and many. Chu Hsi turned to the image of the stream of water that is easily comprehended by all, already in use in his metaphysics, to explain it.

The Water Image in the One and the Many

Chu needed a plausible account of the structural relations between individual things and also between things and the unitary principle. On occasion, he tried the moon—one moon, reflected in its entirety in many different rivers. But there was a limitation on its usefulness, namely, the static nature of the image. Although, perhaps, it could convey something of the idea of the presence of the one Great Ultimate in its totality in each individual thing,[75] a static moon could convey nothing of the dynamic nature of principle—its ability to provide patterns for the ceaseless production and reproduction of life. For this purpose Chu Hsi needed a process image, and the stream of water met his requirements.

The moon image, nonetheless, served as a useful subordinate image, and its value and limitations are therefore worth noting:

[Someone asked:] "Then there is the reality of the single ᵇ*li* [principle], and all things manifest it as their essence. Therefore, among all things, each possesses the single Great Ultimate. But in this case, is the Great Ultimate cut up into parts?" Chu Hsi answered, "Originally there is only the single Great Ultimate, and all things receive it respectively and have the entire Great Ultimate in themselves. It is like the moon in the heavens. There is only one moon, and yet it spreads out over all the rivers and we see it [reflected] from place to place. We cannot say it is divided up into parts."[76]

Although Chu Hsi did not use this image frequently, the passage just cited is quite famous, probably because it purports to clarify, by means of a picture, the complex relationship of one and many. The structural image itself derives from Buddhism. The Indian sutras, translated into Chinese, employ it chiefly to convey the idea of illusion or of the dependent nature of things. Reflected moons are unreal, just as the objects perceived by human consciousness or contemplated by conceptual thought are unreal.[77] The important idea is the reflection, not the moon. The *Laṅkâvatāra-sūtra* makes the following point: "The skandhas [components of personality], with consciousness as the fifth, are similar to reflections of trees in water; they should be seen as a mock show, and a dream."[78] In Chinese works favored by the distinctively Chinese Buddhist schools, however, the moon image is used to explain the one-many, macrocosm-microcosm relationship. The seventh-century Ch'an monk Chen-chüeh, said:

The one Buddha nature perfectly penetrates all natures. One dharma everywhere comprises all dharmas. One moon everywhere is manifest in all bodies of water. All the moons reflected in the water are gathered together in the one moon that they reflect. The dharma-body of all Buddhas penetrates selfhood. Selfhood at the same time is one with the Tathagata. One stage in the path is equivalent to all stages.[79]

Chu Hsi had good reasons for not making more use of the moon image. For this Confucian, the chief problem in the one-many theory was not reality-illusion but *how* the one-many relationship can take place—precisely the same problem that plagued Plato. The moon image supplies no compelling answer to this problem. But the water image, also found in Buddhist texts, does.[80] This familiar image provides the second holistic theory with an explanation of how disparate things are integrated to form a whole: interpenetration by a substance present in everything.

Water has a known process of flow, moving from one source into many interconnected channels. It gives the philosopher's audience a familiar, and therefore plausible, picture of interpenetration by one flowing substance as the means whereby all things are linked to form a single whole. At the transcendental level, Chu Hsi says that all things are penetrated by the flow of principle (^{b}li), or by "integrity" (^{a}ch'eng), which describes principle as patterns of growth and reproduction.[81] Unlike the carpenter, who remains distinct from the house that he makes, this "originator" remains integrally tied to things through which it flows:

> "Great is the ch'ien beginning. Everything begins by means of it." It is the source of integrity. This is to refer comprehensively to one single flowing source. The ch'ien changes and each thing gains its proper nature. Integrity flows forth and each thing has its own settling place. When it is a person, it is also this integrity. When it is a thing, it is this integrity. Therefore we say, "Integrity is thus established. It is like water. Its emergence involves just one source. After it flows forth and branches into myriad outlets there is still only this [single] water."[82]

The water image helps to resolve the question of how principle (^{b}li) can be localized, so that one can look for the ^{b}li of a thing or a man. There is nothing in the conception of ^{b}li by itself that clearly indicates where or how ^{b}li is located in things. Water, however, is localized by means of a vessel or container (^{b}ch'i)—a bowl, a ditch, a riverbed; thus, the container of ^{b}li, some physical substance that can surround it, must be found. "Without physical substance, there would not be any place for the nature endowed by heaven to be; like a spoonful of water, without the thing to hold it the water would have no place to settle."[83] The thing that holds the "nature endowed by heaven," its "container" (^{b}ch'i), is mind.

There are difficulties intrinsic to building a metaphysics and an ethics on a "nonempirical" (my rendering of Chu's *hsing erh shang*, or "above form") claim. In basing his philosophy on the concept of cosmic "principle" ([b]*li*), Chu had a potentially weak foundation whose existence others could challenge. The water image helps in understanding principle. At the same time, it strengthens the case for the existence of something nonempirical by providing an example of a known case in which one can infer from something perceived to something not perceived. People commonly infer from a flowing stream that is before their eyes to the existence of the unperceived clear spring that is its source.[84] They are certain that such a source exists even though it is not seen. We infer three things. First, something is unperceived (neither the stream source nor the [b]*li* are perceived, yet exist); second, [b]*li* has something of the nature of a source or origin; and third, a thing's source can be clear (like a mountain spring) even though the thing itself (the stream observed flowing through the plain) is dirty. The heavenly tao or the heavenly principles are the source, just as the clear flowing stream is a source. "Great is the *ch'ien* beginning. Everything begins by means of it. This is to discuss a single flowing source."[85] Source does not refer to a point of origin in either a spatial or temporal sense; it is not to be seen as a creator or womb. It is instead that which is responsible for the ceaseless repetition of action into certain "channels" (*ch'ü*) that may be blocked or free. [b]*Li* as humaneness works in this way.[86] The heavenly principles are the source of the directed flow of action in all that lives. They are present in all movements as the reason why they exist.

Away from the transcendental level, material force ([a]*ch'i*) connects all things by flowing streamlike through them, as water flows through the gills of a fish; the nonempirical principle ([b]*li*) in its flow determines the pattern of the actual movement in matter.[87] What is happening is that principle ([b]*li*) now explains something in addition to source: it also explains the direction of movement or "current" in all minds. The relationships among apparently disparate concrete things, and those among apparently disparate principles, are described in terms of interpenetration by that which flows through both the nonempirical and the physical realms. These considerations reveal that, among its other uses, the water image serves to bridge what can be called the mind-body dichotomy, by causing the reader or listener to think of the two as actually contiguous.

These conclusions about the role of the water image in providing a structural account of the relations among many people, many things, and one cosmic principle can be summarized by these words of Chu Hsi: "Heaven and man are one thing, the inner [mind] and outer [things] are unified as a single principle that flows through and interpenetrates all, originally with no obstructing barrier."[88]

Values: Potential Equal Worth

The *Analects* describes Confucius observing a flowing stream and saying, "It passes on just like this, not ceasing day or night."[89] With this citation as the authority, flowing water has continued to be a symbol of ceaselessness, generating a response of awe and reverence among later observers. In addition, water eventually became a symbol of purity. By using the image of "original water," claiming it is "good," and pointing to its penetration of all things, Chu Hsi helped to engender in his audience feelings of reverence for the original nature that is present equally in all persons (though obscured, or sullied, in most). Each person's original nature is equally worthy and constitutes the basis for improvement. One of the Ch'engs had stated it explicitly like this: "Every person has something prizeworthy; it is that by which all persons can become a Yao or a Shun."[90] The potential for equal worth is actualized in individuals as they achieve sagehood.

Prizing this nature in all persons is a value rooted in Mencius' doctrine that everyone is born with a good nature. But there are grounds for inferring that the Ch'engs and Chu Hsi inherited the idea most immediately from the Chinese Buddhist thesis that the One Mind is present in all things; therefore, every person should be regarded as a potential Buddha. The plausibility of the inference rests partially on two points already discussed: the Buddhist use of the idea that "principle is one but its manifestations are many," and the Hua-yen and T'ien-t'ai Buddhist assertion that each phenomenal object is a manifestation of the One Mind in its entirety. In speaking of a net made with various treasures, a Hua-yen text says that in the qualities of one pearl are revealed the qualities of all pearls.[91] But there is the additional point that the Hua-yen writers foreshadowed Chu Hsi in using the structural image of water to convey the idea of the equal interpenetration of the many by the One Mind.

> It is like water and waves. What goes up and down and is moving and churning is the waves. What is wet by nature and the same throughout is the water. When you talk about waves there is no such thing as waves different from the waves of water. So the waves serve to illustrate the water. When you talk of water, it is no different from the water of the waves. So the water serves to illustrate the waves. The mind is like the water's waves. The fact that the waves and the water are one does not preclude their difference.[92]

Chu Hsi has a preference for the single stream and the many channels into which it continues to flow rather than one water, many waves. There is a convergence of Chu's evaluative description of the original nature as "good" or clear and that of several Chinese Buddhist schools, which describe it as "pure," as in "human nature is originally pure" (*jen-hsing pen ching*).[93]

In this context, the stream image suggests the need to care not only for oneself but for all persons. The characterization of the original nature as a stream of water, clear, light, and pure at its spring source but becoming increasingly dirty (like an actual stream) the farther its distance from the source, elicits the impulse to cleanse it. The capacity of water to reflect light depends on its clarity. This suggests the need for self-purification in order to maximize the capacity of the mind to be illuminated. With illumination comes an understanding of two things. One is that built into human nature are sentiments and obligations to care for a wide range of people. The other is that these people are deserving objects because they possess the original nature and are perfectible.

Chu refers to the person who is ruled by humaneness (*jen*) as seeing no difference between other people and himself or between other things or creatures and himself.[94] He says that humaneness is the principle of love, and it is expressed in loving people and living things.[95] In the spirit of Mencius, he often says that humaneness is being bonded to parents, loving the people, and being kind to living creatures and things.[96] The point here is the obligation to expand concern beyond the family. Once again, the idealized form of the value of altruism should probably be qualified by noting that in Chu's philosophical discussions, his message often was directed at male, educated aspirants to the life of the superior man (*chün-tzu*). In his personal capacity as an official, however, according to recent research, he tried to educate all the people under his jurisdiction to observe the basic Confucian norms (especially filiality) and the rites, and to aid family members in time of poverty and help neighbors in time of marriage and death.

The idea of purification, then, along with the idea of the equal worth of other persons, impels involvement with persons and things external to the family networks. The theme of the next chapter, achieving purification or mental illumination through the study of those external objects, is intimately related to the issue of equality discussed here.

The Problem of Impurities

Other aspects of the Ch'eng-Chu theory of the human endowment raise questions about the idea of potential equal worth, and these must be dealt with. Unlike the original nature, physical endowments are not equal. According to Chu Hsi, the physical nature of some people so obstructs or beclouds the [b]*li* that they can never thoroughly "purify" themselves.[97] Differences of intelligence and strength among people, a function of the material endowment, must be taken into account. Ordinary people must study hard to become aware of things that sages are born knowing.

Fixed at birth as a function of climate and dominated by one of the five elements, the physical endowment can be changed to some degree, but not without considerable effort. Physical endowment is cited also as the basis for traits not normally associated with character, namely, degree of wealth and length of the life-span. Chu Hsi probably brings these in because in the *Analects* Confucius is reported to have said that they are part of man's endowment (*ming*). Ever since, Confucian writers have included them and attempted to explain the influence of physical heredity on them. Physical endowment also explains personality. Chu's conception of personality relies on an a priori standard governing what should be included or excluded from consideration. The character types from which Chu Hsi draws the traits he felt worthy of consideration are exemplary moral models, public servants, and literati.[98] In contrast, modern cultures that have been influenced by the ethic of individualism draw many of the traits they prize from the artist and inventor—for example, the ability to work independently, creativity, and imagination.

From Chu's perspective, the refinement or density of the individual's physical endowment provides a basis for differences of worth. In part innate, worth changes over the course of a life as a function of efforts to purify the physical self. Hierarchy is therefore required by the patterns of heaven and earth and justified directly by the existence of social roles invented by the sages to realize hierarchy (and hence order) in human society. The legitimacy of any individual's place in it derives from the purity of his material constitution.

Whatever the influences of the physical endowment, individuals still have the obligation to purify their minds. There is an optimistic tone about the ability to be successful in this endeavor if the correct mix of study, self-examination, and discipline is observed. Humans are perfectible—the roots of this concept are Mencian.

Mencius was not the only philosophical ancestor of the Ch'eng-Chu Neo-Confucians, however. Hsün Tzu's observations about human brutishness would seem to invalidate the Mencian optimism about human nature. But the stream resolves any apparent contradiction between these two positions in Chu's doctrine and thereby upholds the value of doctrinal harmony.

In their writings on human nature, the Chou Confucians left a contradictory legacy for their descendants. On the one hand, there is the empirical argument, identified by Mencius, that people are capable of spontaneous moral sentiments and acts of compassion. Mencius assumed that anyone seeing a child about to fall into a well would instinctively respond compassionately and attempt to prevent harm to the child. This led him to conclude that human nature is originally good. There are powerful psychological reasons for accepting this conclusion. It is optimistic about man's moral capacities and can inspire ordinary persons to strive for self-improvement. It provides a justification for Confucians to assume the role of teachers in society and make good their claim to be able to nurture these perfectible humans. And it allows everyone to hope that the ideal humane society can be constructed if one king somewhere recovers his good nature and serves as a model for his morally rectifiable subjects.

On the other side of the debate, Hsün Tzu pointed out some of mankind's less admirable qualities: man is envious and full of hate and lust, and he craves praise. Hsün Tzu maintained that all people possess some brutish qualities from birth and that these are a part of their nature (hsing).[99] This is not the same as the commonplace observation that there are brutish people in society; indeed, an important departure of Ch'eng-Chu Neo-Confucianism from Mencius and Hsün Tzu lies in the fact that the Neo-Confucians spoke of the descriptive inequality of men's innate endowments (a function of the mix of original nature and physical constitution). Mencius and Hsün Tzu, however, although differing on the content of the innate endowment, agreed in stressing its similarity in all people. Chu Hsi held that that inborn inequality produces at birth a range of people with differing capacities for sagehood. Mencius, in contrast, explained human deficiencies in terms of defects in the social environment. People's inborn natures are the same. According to Hsün Tzu, people at birth equally share brutish tendencies and a moral sense.

The immediate problem is that Hsün Tzu's thesis about man's original nature may have pessimistic implications. This is because people can use it to undermine the notion of perfectibility or, at least, the value of self-cultivation in man's quest for improvement. Indeed, Legalist philosophers of the late Chou had assumptions about man's brutish nature in some ways similar to those of Hsün Tzu, and they scorned a ruler who relied on people's self-cultivation as akin to an arrow maker who relies on self-straightening bamboo.

A Confucian legacy from the Chou was therefore the problem of reconciling Mencius' theory, based largely on a positive outlook, with the thesis of Hsün Tzu and its possibly negative implications. The solution to the problem was, first, to make a distinction between the original nature and the physical constitution of the person in which it resides. Second, a distinction was made between the original nature considered in the abstract (not embodied, something possible only in thought, not in fact) and that same nature in embodied form. Chu Hsi gave credit to Chang Tsai and the Ch'eng brothers for introducing the idea of the physical constitution, which made the breakthrough possible.[100] As a result, Chu Hsi could say that the nature of which Mencius spoke is the original nature, abstracted from its physical setting and perfectly good, whereas the nature of which Hsün Tzu spoke, that of imperfect and evil man, is the embodiment of the original nature in the physical person. The theoretical formulation of the solution goes like this: "Man's [original] nature is uniformly good. Yet some when born are good and some when born are evil. This is because of differences in their physical endowment."[101] One might well ask how there can be a human nature before embodiment, since embodiment is presumably what makes it human.

Chu Hsi claimed that previous theories could not account for all the facts. The virtue of the new theory was that it could. He expressly recognized this in the following passage:

> If we only say that humaneness, righteousness, propriety, and knowledge are the nature, then how is it that in the world some are born immoral? It is merely due to their physical constitution that they are like this. If you do not discuss this physical aspect, then your explanatory principles are not comprehensive and therefore are not complete. If you only discuss the physical endowment, treating this one as good and that one as evil, and do not discuss the single source [the original nature], your explanatory principles will be unclear. Since the time of Confucius, Tseng Tzu, Tzu Ssu, and Mencius, who understood this, no one put this principle into words.[102]

The idea for the solution originated with Chang Tsai and the two Ch'eng brothers, according to Chu Hsi, and he himself worked it through by employing the water image. As one of his students remarked,

> A while back, as a result of this issue, you [Chu] used the analogy of water to explain the nature and therefore you said

that the heavenly Way is purely a unitary principle like water which is originally clear. When the yang and yin and five elements mix together and produce turbidness, it is that water has been muddied. The reason why the darkness and muddiness can be returned to clarity is only because its maternal source is clear.[103]

Chu Hsi affirmed the accuracy of this explanation. The qualities of water that make all the difference are its source and flow and its capacity for light. Reconciling pious Mencian hope with brutish reality required that one think of original nature as pure, and physical constitution as sediment of varying density that pollutes or muddies the flowing water. Combining the original nature and physical constitution is possible in the same way that combining pure water and sediment is possible, and to similar effect. This solution neatly explains both the cause of evil and the Mencian faith in the perfectibility of humans.

Just as water is subject to pollution from its surroundings, including its container, the ditch or riverbed, so the purity of ^{b}*li* will be subject to contamination from its container, the physical endowment. And just as the clarity of water varies as a function of "the differing colors of the bowls" or "the cleanliness" of the bowls or channels in which it is located, so, too, will people's actual natures differ as a function of the pure ^{b}*li* mingling with the various physical endowments.[104]

There is some disjunction between the actual existence of human evil, attributed to contamination by physical "sediment" (causing selfishness), and Chu Hsi's claims about the possible triumph of order (^{b}*li*). His abstract theory of ^{b}*li* offers no clear basis for such confidence. But water does. It offers an example of relationship between a ceaseless source (the spring) and temporary murkiness or obstacles to the flow of water therefrom.

Of course, like all structural images, while providing solutions to some problems by clarifying structural relationships, the stream image may confuse its user with regard to other relationships. Not all attributes of the physical objects involved in the image can be readily applied to phenomena to which the theory pertains. For example, it is easy to say that the dirt on a bowl can interact with the clean water it contains (both are material), but how can a person's formless, transcendental nature interact with his physical self? Although contiguous, they are entirely different kinds of things. How bowls get dirty is evident, but why is the physical nature of some people corrupt while that of others is pure? Where does evil come from? Finally, can qualities observed in the physical world apply meaningfully to the transcendental? One can speak of greater or lesser amounts of water, but what can it mean to speak of greater or lesser quantities of principle in a thing, as Chu Hsi sometimes does?[105]

The other trait of water to which Chu Hsi often refers is directional movement; however, he is vague on how humans can participate concretely in any directional movement (other than in terms of their blood flow). This trait seems to allude to his assertions that morally appropriate feelings occur repeatedly in certain patterns. The plant analogy, discussed in Chapter Four, will provide more answers.

Conclusion

The family and water images have helped to uncover a number of aspects of the self as conceptualized by Chu Hsi. One is a person's naturally determined set of social roles. An individual can at once be, for example, father, son, and farmer, all defined relationally in terms of duties to or legitimate expectations from other social roles. A second aspect is the individual's share of the interpenetrating principle that links all living things and reveals itself (as described in Chapter Four) as vitality, growth, and the sentiment of love for things that live. The third is the individual's capacity to envision or understand the principle and act upon it (corresponding with water's capacity for light). Varying from person to person as a function of differing physical endowment, this capacity manifests itself in actions arising from compassion, shame, modesty, or evaluation (from the idea of man's "four fonts" in Mencius). The fourth aspect is that a person's innate physical endowment is directly responsible for other traits as well. As with the cognitive capacity, there are limitations to the changeability of any traits influenced by this endowment. But there is an optimistic tone about the consequences of purifying the mind if proper procedures are followed.

As all four of these aspects of the self come to light, so, too, are the ethical values associated with this concept of a person simultaneously revealed: hierarchy, role fulfillment, caring for those of potentially equal worth, and purification or knowledge. Concepts of man and human values thus implicate one another.

To summarize, then, the images applied to cosmic theories, the family and the stream, structure the relations between sets of facts, small and large. Units as small as a few people and as large as all of nature have similar structures. Considered as parts of a whole, the constituent elements of a social group or of nature either fall into established slots (*fen*) having previously defined relations with one another, or they are all interpenetrated by the same nonempirical principle. There is a single structure that ties together increasingly complex sets of things. These explanatory structures simultaneously justify values.

At least one problem is left, however. This is how to reconcile the boundaries of role fulfillment, justified by the family analogy, with the egalitarian panhumanism of the stream. The family image gives cosmic justification for ranked personal relationships. Family relations dominate the "Five Relations." The water image, in contrast, implies a direct kinship among all humans by virtue of shared "paternity." The shared principle, often envisioned as a stream's source, thus contributes to an outlook on one's fellow humans that is akin to the "Brotherhood of Man as children of God" in Christian theology. To external analysts, the attempt to reconcile responsibility to kin and to those outside the family is the core dilemma of Confucianism. Although Chu Hsi's philosophy has built into it a position that purports to accommodate the two values, there are many reasons to think that the tension between them was never successfully resolved and that the consequences of this failure have been inestimably negative for Chinese society, especially in the modern period. These issues are addressed in Chapter Four and Chapter Six.

Water's capacity to conduct light is significant in understanding Chu Hsi's use of the water image. This capacity reveals his confidence that principle is intelligible. Accordingly, the principles in the mind are self-bright, as will be discussed in Chapter Three. The self-brightness of these principles enables a person to know them if he makes an effort. Water can be purified by removal of sediment, and light gradually reappears as water reverts to its sourcelike purity—hence the belief in human perfectibility. It is time now to consider the impetus to become involved with other people and things that Chu Hsi maintains comes from illumination and from recognition of the potential equal worth of all people.

THREE

THE MIRROR AND THE BODY:
INTERNAL KNOWLEDGE AND
EXTERNAL EMBODIMENT

The theme of psychological separation is a remarkably pervasive background concern in the thought of Sung Neo-Confucian writers and also in that of medieval and early modern Western philosophers, from Augustine to Descartes. What is revealing about their concern, however, is the variety of objects from which it is claimed that man may become separated. Throughout their history, Confucians have argued for man's obligation to be an engaged participant in the social and physical world in which he lives. Its "human affairs" (*jen-shih*) are his proper concern. They have shied away from metaphysical positions that question the worth of such involvement. In the same vein, the Ch'eng-Chu school concentrated on reaffirming the possibility and duty of such engagement in the face of Buddhist doctrines perceived to cause separation from it. The Western thinkers, in contrast, worried about man's separation from God.

This is an absolutely crucial factor in understanding cultural differences between Ch'eng-Chu Confucian and Western philosophies that can be pinpointed with the contrasting terms "horizontal separation" (from the phenomenal world) and "vertical separation" (from God). An examination of separation will show that a structural image (light) that solves the separation problem in Chu Hsi's philosophy is quite capable of raising the problem anew in the work of European thinkers.

This present chapter must be read on two levels. Most directly, it deals with the epistemological theory devised by Chu Hsi to reaffirm the value of participatory engagement by providing a method to end the separation of mind and things. This is a theory concerning links between the subjective knower and what he knows. Chu had to show how significant relationships of a cognitive sort can be established between the self and objective things. Practically speaking, he also had to show why it is desirable to do so, and this raises an issue whose importance goes beyond Neo-Confucianism: whether philosophical and psychological claims about mind and cognition may not be value-neutral. In the case of Chu Hsi, his theory of the mind and cognition is intended to reflect his belief in the desirability of the individual's participatory engagement in the world. Other thinkers who have dealt with this question may believe their own accounts to be of a purely descriptive or scientific nature. But this study of Chu Hsi's theories and the comparisons I will make between them and the positions of some leading Western rationalists raise the conjecture that supposedly descriptive accounts may assume or be molded by value commitments.

On a second level, in terms of the structure of this book, the epistemological theory simultaneously serves to reconcile family and altruistic love, the matter just examined in Chapter Two. In his attempts to work out the theory, Chu relies on two structural images, the light source (mirror, lamp) and the body. These images are crucial to removing any incompatibility between the proper objects of love. This chapter concerns the nature of his method for doing so, which centers on study of the objective world. The other doctrines pertinent to this reconciliation deal with being able to avail oneself of the method. This is a different issue, to which many considerations in Chapter Four are relevant.

Like so many Confucian literati of his time, Chu believed that Buddhist teachings caused people to fear involvement with phenomenal things on the ground that such things can elicit desires and entrap people and also cause them to regard the illusory as real. More precisely, he believed that Buddhism had caused people to withdraw from, rather than minister to, first their families, and then all fellow humans and other creatures. For example, many Ch'an Buddhists claimed that man's mundane mind, the one that receives sensations, perceives the world in an illusory manner. This is because of its tendency to think dualistically and to form concepts or categories in terms of which it sees things, thus imposing something on reality that is not there. The Ch'an master claims that this mind constructs the world according to individual and human prejudices and fantasies. Confucians regarded the belief that the world and human relations are illusory constructs (*huan-wang*) as responsible for Buddhists' advocating withdrawal to remote Buddhist communities, away from families and other people.[1] In fact, however, many T'ien-t'ai and Ch'an Buddhists often said that one can be a good Buddhist at home or even doing official service. Confucians, nevertheless, besides condemning Buddhists' failure to pay taxes and do military service, especially condemned Buddhist monks for the retreat to monasticism. Chu condemned their "withdrawal as they abandon prince and parents and reject wife and children to enter the mountain forest, sacrificing their lives in pursuit of some so-called place of emptiness and extinction to retreat to."[2] Chu was echoing a sentiment expressed earlier by Ch'eng I:

> Someone asked how it is that one could hate external matters. Ch'eng I replied, "It is because they do not understand. How can one hate things? Buddhist learning is like this. Buddhists want to reject affairs without asking whether the affairs have evil in them or not. If they are evil [i.e., if evil is an objective fact of their existence], how can you screen it out? If they are not intrinsically evil, then naturally there is not any evil there in the first place, and so what is there to be rejected? The Buddhists passively go along with things and actively try to achieve inactivity. And they retreat far away to the mountain forests. They do not understand principles."[3]

Ch'eng I and Chu Hsi agreed that Buddhists taught men to dislike the things that inhabit the objective world and to advocate man's separation from human affairs. The charge is not simply abdication of ethical responsibilities, because that phrase is not rich enough to convey the explicit idea in their terminology. They frequently use the term *t'ao* (lit., to escape, to withdraw, to retire from) to describe the Buddhist course of action with respect to worldly affairs or social bonds. They also say the Buddhists wish to transcend the world.[4] They use phrases like "transcend the ways of the world" (*ch'ao-ch'u shih-ku*) and "withdraw from family or from society" (*ch'u chia, ch'u shih*). And they say the Buddhists wish to avoid life and death. Abdicating responsibility and separation from affairs go together.

If Chu's strongly felt positions included a critique of Buddhist withdrawal, they also included the need for the individual to end the separation between the self and objective things. To say that the former position helps to explain the passion of his advocacy of the latter is a conjecture that fits the formulation of the two positions and the historical facts of his age. Even if one were to dispute the cause-effect connection, his advocacy of ending the separation remains a fact, and this chapter is chiefly concerned with that issue. I will begin, however, by assuming the linkage of the charge against Buddhism with his appeal for the reunion of self and human affairs or things.

Setting aside the accuracy of the charge against the Buddhists, it is clear that Chu Hsi's response was to affirm the complementarity of the individual and things. According to Chu, the crucial variable responsible for Buddhist withdrawal from worldly affairs is the Buddhist conception of the mind. They treat it as empty, rather than as innately predisposed to identify and enter into relationships with people and things. Such relationships are counterparts of those in nature as a whole (as shown in Chapter Two). In place of Buddhist separation from human affairs, Chu idealized the situation in which "heaven and man are one thing; the inner [mind] and outer [things] are unified as a single principle that flows through and interpenetrates all, with no obstructing barrier."[5] The external things tend to be affairs and activities but may also be concrete things. He referred to the mind or self (*wo*) and external things (*wu*) as host and guest, suggesting the complementarity of perceiver and objective thing.[6] He asked two questions about them: (1) What is their relation to one another? and (2) Can people be led to experience external things in such a way that they not only perceive affinities between themselves as subjects and the objective things, but also embrace, rather than reject, the world of objects and affairs?

Chu's answer to the first question is that each individual's mind innately possesses the principles of all of the objective things, principles also individually present in the externals. The principles form part of an integrated whole, in which all things are linked by a variety of hierarchical, interpenetrating, and organic connections. Subjective and objective principles, though different, resemble each other. Mind and things are therefore related through the sharing of principles. The function of these principles within the mind is illustrated with the image of light. Principles are light, standing in relation to the mind as light does to its source (the mind as mirror or lamp). Within the mind, they are self-bright and capable of illuminating their objective counterparts. Chu Hsi's motivation in raising the second question was the need for a compelling alternative to what he regarded as Buddhist advocacy of separation from the phenomenal world, especially from the realm of human affairs. Positively stated, his answer served as an argument to literati for feeling responsible for the world around them. Nature is so constructed as to permit responsible engagement to be successful.

Chu's alternative approach conceded the difference between and separateness of the self and objective things. The individual would not have to reach out to things (ke wu, chi wu) unless they were separate. Wang Yang-ming criticized him, saying that the way he put it "has inevitably opened the way to the defect among scholars of regarding the mind and principles as two separate things."[7] Chu insisted, however, that this fact is not incompatible with affirming their simultaneous tight interrelationship. Distinctness need not lead to psychic separation. The antidote for separation is knowledge and affection. Knowledge reveals that the principles of objective things have content and are linked to corresponding principles within the self. Affection solidifies the links. In focusing on knowledge and affection as an antidote to separation, Chu resembles some Western rationalists—among them, Descartes—for whom the contrasting separation is between self and God. I will turn to that matter further on.

To be fair to the Buddhists, it must be noted that Chu Hsi was neither clear nor accurate about the nature of the Buddhist self that is estranged from worldly matters. Nor was he completely accurate about their "fleeing from human affairs." If the analyst juxtaposes self and things and thinks of self in terms of mind, there are "two minds" to cope with, because human beings have the capacity not only to think, but also to reflect on their thinking. When the Chinese Mahāyāna schools encouraged the individual to "become enlightened about his mind and his nature" (*ming hsin chien hsing*), they were often focusing on the self-reflective capacity of the mind, in order to claim the existence of an original pure mind (*jen-hsing pen ching*) that is good and pure in some special sense that is different from ordinary purity and goodness.[8] Attention to worldly things confuses attempts to perceive this mind. The mind that conceptualizes, in contrast, belongs to the realm of dharmas in the mundane sense, that is, to the realm of illusory phenomena. Such a mind is itself a worldly thing and therefore illusory.

In his own theory of the mind Chu Hsi differentiated between the Buddhists' "original, pure," self-reflective mind that supposedly can see itself and the mind that can perceive principles in things. He rejected the existence of the former.[9] In his interpretation of the Buddhist position, however, he unfairly charged the Buddhists with abandoning entirely the latter mind in favor of the self-reflective one. In fact, although Ch'an Buddhists approved of attempts to discover the original pure nature (which might typically involve some meditative activity), they did not advocate permanent termination of ordinary cognitive activity. Many actually encouraged involvement in mundane affairs, claiming that the Buddha nature can be found functioning within the ordinary mind as it participates in this world. Chu Hsi ignores this approach to Buddhism, preferring to dwell instead on the doctrine's apparent disdain for the realm of things, expressed by the Buddhists' reclusiveness and monasticism.

Chu Hsi took up the challenge of countering Buddhist aversion to things while simultaneously affirming the difference between self and things. He claims that direct links (akin to touch) are established between the mind and external things through the related psychological acts of knowing and empathizing.[10] Ultimately, the reason for any such epistemological claim is to strengthen the ethical position that involvement in mundane affairs is morally preferable to separation from them. In saying that the humane person's mind "has no division between the internal and the external,"[11] and that "what is called 'self as juxtaposed to things' is a selfish understanding of the self,"[12] Chu Hsi denies that there is anything necessary or permanent about the subject-object split. Indeed, the existence of such a split is a moral failing to be overcome. In his formulation, he mixes normative terms and concerns to fashion a "factual" description of cognition.

In any case, the theory needs the support that only structural images can provide to illustrate convincingly what such abstractions as ending "the division between the internal and external" might involve. Two pictorial images provide Chu with an easily accessible explanation of how a gap can be bridged. They also provide the psychological impetus to fulfill the social responsibilities that he wishes his audience to feel. The images simultaneously express the difference between and separability of subject and object and, by explaining their interrelationship, the sense in which they can be unified.

The images are light and embodiment, and both involve the projection of one thing onto another. In explaining cognition, Chu introduces the image of light projected from a source onto an object.[13] This light makes possible "cognitive awareness" (chih-chüeh), which is a higher functioning of the mind involving comprehension of principle, something of which children are not capable because their minds are undeveloped.[14] In explaining the affective aspect of bridging the gap, a process that coexists with cognition, he introduces the idea of embodiment (t'i), or the imaginary projection of one's self into something else. Embodiment entails both affective and cognitive processes.

The Mirror and the Duty of Knowing

Chu Hsi envisions the mind as a light source, such as a mirror or lamp. In his day mirrors were made of polished bronze. The principle(s) within the mind, or humaneness, is like the brightness of the mirror. It is self-bright. In response to a query about the Analects passage, "For three months he did not deviate from humaneness," Chu Hsi replied, "Humaneness is man's mind. The mind is like a mirror. Humaneness is the mirror's brightness. The mirror has always been self-bright. It is only because of some obstructions that it loses its brightness."[15] The light emanates from principles when they are present in the mind; it is not a feature of the mind itself. Mind and principles remain different. Contrary to the usual

81

Western way of thinking about mirrors, Chu sees the mirror as its own light source.

The mirror image appears in Chou-Han Taoist sources to explain the passive mind of the sage, which reflects all things without prejudice or desire. Buddhist literature often invokes the mirror (along with dreams and the moon in water) to illustrate the illusory character of sensible things. The unenlightened take a reflection for reality. This is true of the images in the *Laṅkâvatāra-sūtra*, which was so influential among Ch'an masters. Chu Hsi's portrait of the mirror image as light source is different. But it still includes aspects that emerged in earlier Taoist and Buddhist sources.

Earlier accounts of the mirror are a useful background to Chu's idea of the mirror (mind) as a light source. Centuries before Chu's time there was a belief, even at the popular level, that mirrors possess the interrelated capacities to project light onto objects and, thereby, to achieve some magical power over them. Many T'ang-dynasty (618–906) short stories refer to these capacities. For example, one contains the following passage, which describes the use of a mirror as light source on a dark night:

> When he was touring in Chiang-nan, he was about to cross the Yangtze River. All of a sudden, dark clouds shrouded the stretch of water. Dark storm gales whipped up the waves. The boatman turned white, afraid that the ship would capsize. Liu got on the boat with his mirror and shined it into the river a few feet, whereupon the water was brightly illuminated all the way to the bottom. The gale clouds then shrunk on all sides, and the waves then quieted down.[16]

If this episode says something about popular beliefs concerning the light-projecting power of mirrors, there is ample precedent for the association of radiating light with mirrors in the philosophical literature. The idea dates back at least to Seng Chao (374–414), who served as disciple to the Indian monk and translator Kumarajiva (343 or 344–413). Seng Chao's essay "Prajñā Has No Knowing" ("Po-jo wu-chih lun") contrasts the knowing of the sage or holy man (*sheng-jen*) with that of ordinary men. The work blends the Buddhist idea of Prajñā (wisdom) and the Taoist concept *wu chih* (no human knowledge). The sage has Buddhist and Taoist traits.

He possesses Prajñā, which is an ability to mirror or illuminate (*chao*) the transcendental Absolute Truth (*chen ti*): "There is nothing that the mirror of Prajñā does not search to the utmost. For this reason, when it meets [crucial instants], it does not miss anything; when it matches [the Absolute Truth], it does not affirm anything. Calm and in repose, it has no knowing, yet there is nothing that it does not know."[17] From the standpoint of their essences, there is no self and other distinction between Prajñā and Absolute Truth, and Chu Hsi continues the use of the term *chao*, meaning "to illuminate." The most famous T'ang-dynasty reference to the mind as a bright mirror is in the *Platform Scripture* poem: "The body is the tree of perfect wisdom. The mind is the stand of a bright mirror."[18]

Of course there were light sources other than the mirror.[19] Six Dynasties Taoist writers described the immortal as able to absorb the essences of the sun and moon and to project colored lights long distances. The term *nei-chao* refers to the inner vision that he can focus on his internal organs, themselves newly luminous.[20] T'ang Taoist writers refer to the projecting power of the inner light possessed by the individual skilled in practices of meditation: "The presence of the spirit of light in the personal body can be compared with the light in a basin lamp. . . . All distinctions made between beings and principle, all knowledge of even the finest and subtlest, does ultimately come from the spirit shining forth. Thus we speak of the light of the spirit."[21] So the adept is able to radiate light. Prajñā or insight (often *hui*, continuing the use of borrowed Buddhist terminology) is projected into the outside world.[22] Insight radiates forth to illuminate all things, because the insight aims to reach the tao, which accounts for the change of all things.

Various pre-Sung explanations of cognition as radiation include the belief that knowledge is of something nonempirical, that it is achieved through meditative practices, and that the ultimate goal is comprehensive or total understanding. Chu Hsi inherited these associations from his Taoist and Buddhist predecessors as tools to explain the mind's cognition. At the same time, he differs from some of them in important ways in his use of the image. First, unlike the Chou-Han Taoists, Chu treats the mind as a self-bright light source, not as a mere passive receptor. He shares with the

Taoists the idea that the sage's mind is without prejudice, although in Chu's case it is free of selfish interests that distract his responses from accord with his moral standard. Second, unlike some Buddhists, he does not generally use the mirror to suggest illusion. Third, the objects at which the mind's light is directed now are principles (^{b}li) inherent in concrete things. They can be penetrated incrementally, one by one, though in the end Chu believes in the possibility of total or integrated insight into all principles; that is, the mind may suddenly illuminate the unitary pattern that links all things. Obstructions in the mind can prevent the penetration and total insight.

On occasion Chu shifts to other images as explanations of cognition that also predate him, namely, the sun or the lamp,[23] but in every case the pictorial image is of a light source that "illuminates things" (chao wu). For example, a lamp in a room can project on a single book or, in the case of complete knowledge, light up the whole room.

Chu Hsi may not directly state that the inner light shines on the principles outside it; however, his use of the mirror, lamp, or sun image to explain how it illuminates the principles of things makes legitimate the inference that this is the way he understood the cognitive process.

> When the mind is unstable, then we are unable to perceive principle. Now, if you want to study, you must first stabilize your mind and cause it to be like still water or like a bright mirror. If a mirror is dark, how can it illuminate things?[24]

> The sentiments of compassion, shame, modesty, and the discrimination of right and wrong emerge from our own minds. Whichever of them is touched, then that sentiment will emerge. It has never been not bright. It is because it is covered by desire, so that its brightness is easily clouded over. It is like a mirror, which is originally bright. When it gets spotted by something external, it becomes not bright. But after you polish it, then its brilliance can illuminate things again.[25]

What is illuminated in this manner is not the sensory characteristics of the affair, activity, or physical object or situation, but its principle, as is evident from the expressions *chu li* and *ming li* (to illuminate principle).[26] Hypothetically, the light within the mind can project itself anywhere, illuminating all objects of knowledge. Chu Hsi says that "extending knowledge" involves recognizing that the original mind is like a mirror. Originally, it is illumination itself. Its original brightness fades or dims only as other elements intervene. If one then polishes the mirror, removing all obstructions, one will see that its brightness again projects everywhere.[27] Chu holds that the mind can regain its original brightness as selfish thoughts fade away. The objects of knowledge may be either concrete things, like the bamboo plant, or ideas, such as may be found in texts. Textual study, aiming at uncovering the principles recorded in books, is thus an essential part of self-cultivation, and the illumination of the wisdom in texts is a part of sagehood. At times it seems that Chu Hsi has textual study in mind more than the investigation of concrete objects; in fact, he worked out a curriculum of texts.

Chu Hsi's disciples, such as Chen Te-hsiu (1178–1235) of the Fukien school, continued to explain the workings of the mind in terms of the projection of light. Accordingly, they describe the mind as a place made bright by the original nature or principles within it; like a bright lamp, it is able to illuminate things (*chao wu*).[28] And they portray the role of the emperor as, by his example, enabling the people to illuminate their own minds. In short, this image plays a central role among the lasting elements of Chu Hsi's conception of man.

The image of the mirror permits Chu Hsi to structure in familiar terms the relation between the subjective and objective principles and the role of cognition in uniting the two. The mirror (mind) to which an object presents itself already has an image of one kind in it, namely, a subjective counterpart of the principle within the object. The same light that projects outward and illuminates the external principle in turn brightens even more the subjective image (principle). This circular movement, from illumination of the object (external) to illumination of the mind (internal), describes the nature of knowing.

It is Chu's imagery that reveals the existence of a return process. This implicit stage is manifest in the double meaning of *chao*, used by Chu to describe the relation between the knowing mind and an external thing. *Chao* simultaneously means "to illuminate" and "to reflect." So the mirror mind both illuminates the principles in the external thing and also brings about an equally bright "reflected" image of it in the mind. The reflected image is now the brighter subjective principle corresponding to the principle in the objective thing. At the same time, however, the mind must be kept empty of previous "images" in the sense of selfish prejudices. Chu Hsi intended here that feelings appropriate to a given object or situation should not be allowed to remain active, since they would then displace themselves onto new situations for which they would be inappropriate. To summarize a pertinent passage: because the mind is like a mirror, it is originally clear, and so it can reflect things. But if some previous image (i.e., feeling) remains in it after some occurrence, then when some new event occurs, the mind will respond in a prejudicial way rather than with an appropriate feeling.[29] It takes time to clear the mind.

Through knowledge the relation between the subjective and objective principles is understood, and any attitude of aversion on the part of the self toward things is dissipated. The first stage of internal and external unification is achieved as the light flows from the mind to the object, then returns, to brighten even more the corresponding principle in the mind. In response to a question about the investigation of things, Chu Hsi said, "The internal and external are never not united. If you know the ᵇ*li* of objective things are like something, and respond to things in accordance with the naturalness of their ᵇ*li*, you will be able to see the unity of the internal ᵇ*li* with the external ᵇ*li*."[30] The "external" phase of seeking to understand particular objective matters involves both knowing the ᵇ*li* of one or more objective things and responding to it (them) properly. Knowledge and action are linked; when both occur there is illumination of the external and internal ᵇ*li*.

"When things are investigated in relation to that [the external world], then knowledge is completed in this [the self]" (*wu ke yü pi, tse chih chin yü ts'e*).[31] This means that the more thoroughly an external phenomenon is examined, the more completely it is *reflected* in our internal understanding. To become enlightened about the objective principle of a thing leads to inner illumination. The relation is reciprocal. In his commentary to the *Great Learning*, Chu Hsi put it this way:

> Surely there is no human mind whose active spirit possesses no knowledge; and all things in the world have their principles. Only when some principles have not been exhausted is knowledge not complete. Thus, when one begins to teach the *Great Learning*, [one] must cause the learner to approach all objective things in the world by exhausting their principles, basing himself on the principles that he already knows. In this way he can reach the summit of learning. When one exerts effort on this matter for a long time and, suddenly, holistically understands all things, there is nothing that one cannot understand inside and out, in whole and particular. There is nothing in the great substance and function of one's mind that is not illuminated.[32]

The process of internal illumination has both sudden and gradual aspects. In conversation with a disciple, Chu Hsi described the attainment of comprehensive knowledge by pointing to a candle. He said that if a candle is placed in the middle of a room, it illuminates everything in the room and there is no place for something bad to hide. When knowledge has not been completely extended, it is as though the candle (lamp) has a shade over it. One sees as far as the light reaches, but where the light does not reach, all is dark. Anything evil that may lie beyond the reach of the light cannot be seen. Chu Hsi pointed to a candle and said:

> It is like lighting a wax candle in the middle [of the room]. The light penetrates so that no spot is left unilluminated. Although one wishes to bring a bad thing in, there is no place to put it [where it could not be detected]. Naturally there is no place for it. When knowledge is not completed it is like putting a shade on the lamp. Then you can see as far as the light reaches. Where the light does not reach, everything is dark, and you cannot see. Although there is a bad thing or affair beyond it, you cannot know it.[33]

Chu Hsi states that knowing is a two-stage process. No final internal-external union is afforded by the first stage, which is "the investigation of things" (*ke wu*). A person investigates a physical object by observing it and investigates a social or ethical matter by practicing it. But what is learned in this manner remains limited to the principle of some individual thing or event. Only when the light that brightens the principle of an external thing (the first step of stage one) brightens, in turn, its counterpart principle or mirror image in the mind (the second step of stage one) and *then* goes on to reveal connections with other internal principles (stage two) does integrated knowledge become possible. Internal-external union requires such integration. (There are really three discrete levels to the process, two in the first stage and one in the second.)

The transition from the first to the second stage is termed "the extension of knowledge" (*chih chih*). Stage-two illumination involves seeing how knowledge of an individual object relates to other matters already known, that is, seeing things holistically instead of particularistically.[34] Polishing, in the sense of removing prior prejudices and selfish interests, helps clarify the matters already known, especially intuitive moral rules or goals.[35]

Actually, Chu Hsi has both cosmic and down-to-earth ways of speaking about stage two. Both approaches share the notion that the completion of particularistic knowledge in stage one enables the individual to expand his knowledge by seeing linkages between discrete principles that are known and others that are not known. On a cosmic level, stage two is awareness that all knowledge is integrated and that gradual enlightenment about all principles is possible: "The light in the mind can penetrate everywhere."

On a less abstract level, stage two is linking knowledge of some particular objective principle to an innate moral rule concerning social role duties. The principles shining forth most directly in the human mind are moral principles in the ordinary sense of social sentiments and social duties and expectations, not the principles of ships or carts or rivers. In sum, the individual's moral sense reveals itself to intuition. One of the concerns of this book is the status of that moral sense in Chu's work and its later influence.

Chu Hsi says that when a person is trying to regain his lost mind (good nature) by carefully watching over it, "the *moral* principles shine forth by themselves" (*i-li tzu ming*).[36] Human nature (*hsing*) is itself defined as the four *moral* minds identified by Mencius (humaneness, righteousness, good form in conduct, and moral knowledge). When Chu Hsi gives examples of constant principles, he almost invariably refers to the social role duties. When talking of the principles that "shine through," albeit dimly, in ants, bees, and wolves, he refers to righteousness and filiality. When talking about humans, it is filiality from the son, kindness from the father, and so forth, that shine.[37] Everything (including ships and carts) has its ᵇ*li* (principle), and these are all in the mind, Chu Hsi argues. But his examples are almost always on the order of "the obligation of the prince to be humane, the minister to be respectful, the son filial," and the like.[38] When the clouds in the mind thin out, the essence of humaneness can be seen.[39] The core of humaneness is social role duties, through which life-sustaining compassion is expressed. The principles of external objects or situations are moral, too. The principle of a given tree explains both how it will grow and how it should grow. But the innate moral principles with which a person eventually should integrate the objective ones are a more specific set, namely, those governing the duties of basic social relationships. All these examples serve to illustrate the presence of the innate moral sense. Such a mind stands as Chu's answer to the "empty mind" of the Buddhists.

"The extension of knowledge" thus involves relating a "fragmented" piece of knowledge about the principle of some objective phenomenon to some moral principle. Seeing how everything fits together in an integrated way is integrated understanding (*kuan-t'ung*). Chu Hsi describes the result as the increasing of light, as when one widens a hole through which light flows.[40] By completing the two-stage process, the second form of internal and external union is achieved in a manner that goes beyond contact with and knowledge of a single thing, entailing action appropriate to a normative conception of that thing. This conception of integrated knowledge is another medieval Chinese contribution to the ongoing Confucian fusion of facts and values. Here, as well, is a hierarchy of knowledge; integrated knowledge that entails ethical rules is more desirable than particular descriptive knowledge of individual objects.

The following passage explains clearly how a person can relate an external fact and an internal moral sentiment, thereby revealing the union of self and thing as a cognitive and affective exercise:

> Everything before your eyes has its ultimate principle. For example, each plant, tree, bird, and animal has its own principle. Plants and trees grow in the spring and wither in the fall. Animals love life and hate death. In midsummer one cuts wood on the southern side of the hill, and in midwinter one cuts it on the other side. All of this involves following the yin and yang principles [applicable to compass direction]. . . . All things share the same material force and form part of the same body. If you see something alive, you cannot bear to see it killed; if you hear an animal's cries, you can't bear to eat its flesh. If you do not cut even one tree and do not hunt even one animal when the time is inappropriate, and if you do not kill pregnant females, the ungrown young, and chicks or eggs in a nest, then you have unified the internal and external principles.[41]

The external fact is the relation between seasons and the growth of living things. The internal sentiment is the Mencian emotion of compassion that finds suffering, especially killing, intolerable both emotionally and as a moral rule. The individual who unites the external and the internal finds killing trees or animals intolerable (the internal) when the objective season of the killing is inconsistent with the natural rhythms of life (the external). Another example is investigating the principles of food. Knowledge of the principles of grain (something external), when linked with existing insight about the rules and feelings clustered around filiality, respectfulness, and so forth (the internal), unifies the internal and external. A person who has unified the two has also extended his knowledge. Such a person knows how to use food to nourish his parents and elders.

Chu believed that moral rules are natural to humans, just as Newton believed natural laws of motion are the natural behavior of matter. According to the mental illumination theory, the link between moral rule and objective fact also reveals the action that is appropriate to the situation (not cutting a tree, feeding one's parents). Making the correct response deepens the level of knowledge. It is another way of "brightening the bright virtue" (*ming ming-te*), or brightening what is already bright.[42] There is an interesting contrast here with the position of many Western rationalists, who believe that after illuminating innate truths in the mind (counterparts of Chu Hsi's subjective moral principles), the light within goes on to illuminate not the proper actions but steps in a deductive process of reasoning from those truths. Knowledge is extended through deductive inference and by obedience to the rules governing that reasoning process.

Chu Hsi's prescriptions for increasing knowledge involve studying books, practicing what books and one's enlightened mind reveal as correct action, and expanding the range of physical objects with which one sympathetically identifies. In his writings on the extension of knowledge there is a place for logical inference, but it is not a central or systematic procedure. The terms used by Chu Hsi are *lei-t'ui*, *t'ui-lei*, and *t'ui*,[43] all of which refer to the act of inferring from one member of a class of things to another member of the same class. In the case of the class "superiors," one can infer from knowing how to serve parents to knowing how to serve a prince. Chu Hsi does discuss what might be called turning a specific instance into a general case, as a characteristic of "extending knowledge." The examples he uses, however, suggest that when this happens thought disappears rather than plays an important role. For example, if a person not only knows a specific instance of loyalty when he sees it but understands loyalty itself, his behavior is always naturally or spontaneously loyal in the proper circumstances. Obviously, Chu Hsi made important inferences; there is, for example, the major role of the inference from clear stream to clear source in his use of the water image. Like many Confucians, he approaches moral problems by searching both for an analogous historical case and for the applicable constant principle. But he did not claim the ability to infer on the basis of reason as a uniquely human characteristic.

Unlike the Western rationalists, Chu did not select the ability to infer as a significant category in his portrait of mind and its associated values. For Chu, knowledge is not extended primarily through the process of deductive inference. His writings propose no clearly identified steps or rules in a reasoning process, as Aristotle worked them out in the *Posterior Analytics*. His light within the mind does not illuminate steps or rules in an argument so much as it illuminates courses of action.

The very idea of a mirror as a structural image for the mind suggests something that responds. Chu Hsi says that the individual must ensure brightness in his mind, because a dark mind cannot respond properly to things. "The sage's mind is like a pool of still water. When it encounters and responds to something, it only sees a clear image and so it can respond properly. If the mind is dark, then in responding to events, how can it properly hit the mark? [What image is there that could not be reflected?]"[44] A bright mind is to acting without error as bright sunshine is to walking without stumbling. And when brightness does exist in the mind, there is complete correspondence between the external object and the way the mind deals with it:

> Therefore, before the mind is moved by externals, it shines clearly like an empty mirror, as even as a balance scale, truly taking its position before the Lord-on-High with all principles established inside it. As soon as a thing moves it, the grace or abruptness, the very magnitude of the response, all are a function of that external thing itself.[45]

"Empty" means empty of prejudices, not of innate principles. When the principle in the mind is bright, the responsive action is appropriate to the objective thing that presents itself. If the occasion calls for joy, that is the reaction that occurs.

In the following passage, the minds of insects and animals are compared with darkened mirrors in which, unlike the human mind, only a few points of light shine. It is impossible for the reader of this passage to separate illumination of the principles of social relations from practices in accordance with those principles:

> The dissimilarities in principles are evident in the fact that in the case of the relation between prince and minister, among ants and bees, there is revealed only a small light of righteousness, and in the case of the relation between father and son, among wolves and tigers, there is revealed only a small point of humaneness. The other principles are more undiscov-

erable. It is like a mirror in which all the points are dark except for one or two light spots in the middle.[46]

Chu Hsi categorizes principle among things that are tranquil (i.e., static) and feelings and actions among those that move. The two categories "tranquility" and "movement," or those of "principle" and "feeling," cannot be divided so as to separate tranquility from movement or principle from feeling. Each category contains both items in the set, in different forms. The application of this rule to the mind reinforces the fact that brightening of innate principle and a corresponding action go inseparably together.[47] One and the same function of mind both contains the principle and implements the action. This function is cognitive awareness, which can be brightly illuminated or not: "The term 'human nature' is principle; the term 'feelings' refers to its flowing forth into practice. The mind's cognitive awareness is that by which the principles are contained and the feelings are activated."[48] When the mind is clear, the proper action emerges.

The term "feeling" (ᵃch'ing) is a general term that covers both covert emotions and overt actions; thus, when a response to an objective thing is described as feeling, the description may include either of these or, more likely, both.

Values: Knowing and the End of Separation

The image of light provides the structure that makes the concept of subjective-objective union intelligible. This is because light projected from a source establishes verifiable contact between source and object. The mirror image provides a familiar additional factor, required by Chu Hsi's portrayal of second-stage knowledge as integrated: the round trip made by the light goes from the mirror light source to the object, from which it is reflected back to the mirror mind, brightening and clarifying the image already there. Mind and things can remain different, yet the mind is capable of contacting the object, thereby gaining direct knowledge of it.

If the image provides the structure for a resolution to the mind-object gap, the immediate impetus to bridging that gap probably came from the ethical intuition that Buddhist-like separation from worldly things is wrong. An ethical interest therefore underlies the epistemological doctrine of Chu Hsi. This interest required that Chu characterize the mind not only as a passive receiver of images or of information but also as capable of actively projecting itself into the objective world. The knowledge of things or empathy toward them that results from such contact enables humans to contribute to nature's nourishing processes, and this is the ultimate ethical goal. The image of light is intended to generate in the reader an emotional reaction to his present state of understanding. Self-awareness is a distinctively human trait.[49] To be conscious of dim light or partial vision is to be aware of the possibility of unobstructed vision. The image creates a sense of concern to rectify the state of understanding through knowing.

It would be inaccurate to claim that only the image of light provides the emotional stimulus for the reader's acceptance of the theory of subjective-objective unity. The term [b]*li* (principle) had the meanings of pattern and order as early as the Chou period. In Chinese thought these are quite positive connotations. To make the purely philosophical statement that there are patterns ([b]*li*) accessible to the mind that are counterparts to those in nature is to make a claim that is descriptive and emotive. The beauty of the proposition may stimulate belief, as well as action in an attempt to solidify the links between the realms. But the problem lies with the method for ending the division. The philosophical theory based on [b]*li* and [a]*ch'i* relationships does not adequately guide the reader toward action. The light-source image does. It provides him with optimism: you already see with partial clarity, and your mind can project its light. And it tells him how to proceed: clarify your mind further through study. He will associate reading texts such as the *Four Books* with this clarity.

If knowing is a value, it is itself also a means to an additional value—namely, the end of separation from other people or, put positively, an active engagement in the world of things. A person can make contact with objects, understand that their principles have counterparts in him, and become practically involved with them. Later, after considering the image of body, the analyst will find Chu saying that when knowing and concern for things are properly broadened, the value of impartiality has been attained. Impartiality refers to the final goal—the sagelike knowledge of and affection for a wide range of persons and creatures beyond the family boundaries—a goal envisioned by means of the water image explored in Chapter Two.

Chu Hsi used the image of projecting light, or mental perception, to harmonize two polarized concepts: the "all in One" idea from Hua-yen Buddhism, developed by Ch'eng Hao, and the demarcation between mind and the world of things that both Chu and the Ch'engs saw in Buddhism. The light image was well adapted to aspects of each theory, and so formed a mediating bridge between them—a technique Chu used in applying process images elsewhere.

Under the influence of the former theory, Ch'eng Hao said, "The humane man forms one body with heaven, earth, and all things." In Ch'eng's case, the expression "forming one body with all things" includes the idea that distinctions between the self and things are ephemeral and disappear in the mind of the sage.[50] While Chu Hsi sometimes employs similar terminology, he opposed the idea that human beings are all present in a single mind of heaven and earth. First, the idea of "forming one body with all things" is too vague.[51] Second, ordinary people who think of the self only as an inseparable part of One Mind will become negligent about their own needs. They may decline to eat, because other parts of the self are eating, or they may feed themselves to a starving tiger, because it is part of them.[52] These are psychological implications of the elimination of distinctions. The contrasting thesis to the Hua-yen "all in One" was the supposed claim of other Buddhists that humans should "hate things," feel estranged from them, and retreat to a monastic life.

The process of outward mental projection and empathy provides the means of keeping the distinction between self and things (in the spirit of the latter thesis), while attitudinally forming one body with all (in the spirit of the former). In sum, the image makes a place for both the retention of difference between self and things and their periodic reunification through knowledge and empathy.

The usefulness of projecting light in explaining the mind's ability to reach out and bridge the gap between it and objects is clear from the examples given. The utility of the image in simultaneously maintaining the difference between self and objects is no less important to Chu Hsi's philosophy. It is worth noting that the image was still serving this purpose centuries after Chu Hsi. Tai Chen (1723–1777) employed the structural image of light to make a point with which Chu Hsi would agree: even though someone can mentally reach out to things, they remain distinct from him.

> All creatures have an inner light [*ching-shuang*]. Its quantity in the mind varies. It is like a firelight illuminating something. When the light is dim, it illuminates only what is near. That which it illuminates can be known with certainty. We must acknowledge our uncertainty of all that it fails to illuminate. Certain knowledge may be called "grasp of principle."[53]

The eyes distinguish colors and, like the other sense organs, bring one in contact with the external object. But it takes the inner light to grasp the principle of the colored thing (such as a bamboo plant). Like Chu Hsi, Tai Chen was committed to the position that minds and the objects of knowledge are different and separable things: yet, in spite of the difference, the mind can know things with certainty. The idea of a light projecting from the mind to an object underscores the fact that the two are different. As a contemporary Chinese study puts it, "His [Tai's] use of the analogy of firelight illuminating things has as its goal explaining that the objects of knowledge are external."[54]

In one respect, then, Chu Hsi and Tai Chen use the same image and agree. But, rejecting Chu Hsi's contention that there are principles in the mind that can be brightened, Tai Chen never made use of the image of the mirror, with its important addition of the return of light to the mind to illuminate images (the innate principles, not prejudices) in it. Light projecting from mind to principle in external objects ensures the possibility of knowledge—and the one-way nature of the process underscores the absence of innate ideas in the acquisition of knowledge. According to Tai Chen, there are no principles in the mind, only in objects as their structures. The difference between him and Chu Hsi highlights the appropriateness of the mirror image for Chu, with its references both to the projection of light (making possible mental illumination of an objective principle) and its possession of an image. The mirror is far more consistent with this account of knowing than the lamp, which conveys only the idea of light source.

EMBODIMENT AND EMPATHY

Although the image of the mind containing its own light source plays a crucial role in Chu Hsi's quest for a means to unify self and things, it is insufficient by itself to explain cognition. This is because, thinking holistically, Chu Hsi conceived of the experience of knowing as deeply affecting the entire self. An additional image used to expand the scope of his concept is that of a skeletal framework or a body (*t'i*). Chu explained that the term *t'i* basically means static structure, from which movement can emerge: "*T'i* is like this fan, with handle and a frame, with paper attached to it. When people employ it, that is functioning [i.e., the structure in operation]."[55] When used as a verb in the context of relating the self to things, *t'i* means to make things part of the body or of the self (see note 65)—in short, to "embody" them. The compound *t'i jen* suggests that "embodiment" involves an expansion in one's relation to something, expansion in the sense of exceeding mere routine knowledge of the thing. *T'i jen* means to understand something personally. The good student will try to understand "with his body and his mind," that is, with his whole self.[56]

In the case of abstractions such as proper duties, embodiment involves repeatedly practicing what the light reveals as a proper response. As one of the Ch'eng brothers put it, "When true principles are realized in one's mind they are different. If one merely hears them or talks about them, he does not truly understand them in his mind."[57] He understands them only if they are manifest in his acts. Embodiment means providing one's body as the framework (*ku-tzu*, lit., "skeleton") in which the abstractions can take on a concrete form affecting one's entire self.[58] Embodiment has strong implications for action when a duty is made part of the self. Embodiment thus pertains to matters both of feeling and of practical action.

Simultaneously, knowledge of the thing becomes qualitatively different from knowledge that does not involve personal experience. Chu Hsi says, "To embody humaneness [the abstraction] is similar to embodying a thing. Man stays within humaneness as its framework. So we say 'to embody humaneness.' Humaneness is a principle and must have a human to embody it and implement it."[59] A person adopts the patterns of humaneness as the rules of action of his body or self. And, with regard to ideas in books: "When you study something and grasp [the principle] in your mind, you should embody it in yourself."[60] In short, investigating things goes beyond looking at static objects—it means getting involved with the affairs of the world.

There is additional dramatic confirmation of the role of the image of body in Chu Hsi's account of empathic cognition. It lies in the frequent use of the secondary image of eating to describe the processing of what is absorbed from the objects of knowledge. Just as eating helps to transform physical nutrients into parts of the body, so practice enables an individual to make things that were separate from him ultimately a part of him: "If we only hold a bowl of fruit [without personally tasting it], we cannot know the flavor of the fruit, as sweet, sour, or bitter. So, we should taste it to know its flavor."[61] There is no knowledge of kindness to neighbors without practicing such kindness. Knowledge remains something external to the self unless it is practiced and incorporated into daily life. Just as the individual eats primarily for his own sake, so the primary end of study should be self-transformation, not the accretion of knowledge simply for the sake of impressing others.[62] Such procedures are as natural on the path to sagehood as eating when hungry is to sustaining life. The process of assimilating the principle studied or the text being read is like eating. One must "bite" it into small pieces and "chew" the pieces slowly.[63] The taste and nutrients register gradually. As one might expect from a theory that uses the digestion of food to explain the processing of knowledge, the treatment for the sick spirit is the "medicine" of self-control (*k'e chi*).[64]

The other category of objects that are subject to embodiment as the individual unifies self and things is that of concrete physical things, or "instruments" (*[b]ch'i*), as Chu Hsi sometimes calls them. In this case, embodiment is a combination of cognition (the light) and empathic projection of the self to the object:

Someone asked, "In the statement [of Chang Tsai], 'If there is a single thing that I have not embodied, then my mind has something outside of it,' what is the meaning of 'to embody'?" The answer was, "It means to put our minds into things and to investigate their principles, just as in investigating things and extending knowledge. It is different from the *t'i* meaning substance that is paired with function [substance and function constituting a set roughly describable as static, nonempirical potentiality and its moving, observable actualization]."[65]

The text goes on to say that "having something outside the mind" involves the existence of an obstruction between the internal and external, "and all things are treated as not having any relation to the self."[66]

Embodiment is elsewhere explained as like "humaneness permeating [lit., embodying] affairs" (*yu jen t'i shih*).[67] This means that a nurturing affection runs to and through them (Chang Tsai had stressed this). The projection from self to things that was initially understood as cognitive now clearly also involves affective empathy. One can think of projecting the entire self into objects in order to empathize with them: "Someone asked, 'Does *t'i* involve putting our own selves into affairs and things in order personally to experience them?' " The answer was yes.[68] Chu Hsi's idea of empathic projection can be traced back to Ch'eng Hao, who said, "The humane man feels all-embracing, forming one body with things."[69] But the roots go back even further, to the idea of reciprocity (*shu*) in the *Analects*.[70] The latter involves using one's assessment of one's own feelings about a situation as a guide to treating other people. The ability to do this lies at the core of the comprehensive virtue, humaneness.

Like the early idea of reciprocity, the notion of embodiment focuses on attributes of persons that are identical. The two ideas are similar, though reciprocity applies only to humans and is narrower in scope. It is a guide to specific action, whereas embodiment is both a guide and the beginning of an enduring relation between the individual and the other entity. Reciprocity assumes that people's feelings about major situations will be similar. *T'i* assumes that when the individual empathizes with others, he can use his

own feelings as a guide because people are similar, because he recognizes that the crucial function of roles makes all husbands or all
wives similar. But, from a twentieth-century perspective, this is a
factually inaccurate assumption and indicates a weakness in Chu
Hsi's notion of empathic embodiment. In essence, Chu is giving a
defense of the traditional view of empathy, which is flawed. I examine in Chapter Five the implications of shared human characteristics for the promotion of behavioral conformity.

People in fact have different personalities, and, as a result, their
motives and feelings about the same things may differ consider-
ably. Some individuals dislike their parents, others love them. In
a situation involving parents, therefore, two people may have
vastly different reactions. I cannot correctly empathize with someone unless I understand his particular state of mind.[71] It is not
enough to use my own feelings as a guide, because on the most
fundamental issues they may be different from the other person's.
I must be able to imagine how the other feels. In spite of the cognitive and affective sense of union, it is necessary to remain mindful of differences.

On the positive side of Chu Hsi's discussion of this subject is his
recognition that empathy must include knowing something about
the object in order for the empathic state of mind to be moral (i.e.,
one that produces the correct response). Chu is thus a long way
from Mencius, for whom spontaneous empathic feelings dominate. Chu's mistake is in thinking that such knowledge need be
only of the humanity that two persons share and in not equally
stressing unique characteristics. If Chu had noted this problem
and wanted a solution, he could have distinguished empathy in
the abstract from empathy as a useful first step in a relationship.
As a first step, it would allow one person to become sufficiently
engaged with another person so that he would be able and willing
to advise or help in accord with his standard. Chu might then have
replied to the critic that proper sympathy for a person's situation
is that which is defined by the rules of conduct (^{a}li). The response
to an individual whose hated father has died would be to try to
correct his indifference or joy at the event.

The closest Western philosophical counterparts of Chu Hsi's
idea of feelings for others are the German terms for "fellow feel-

ing" (*Mitgefühl*) and "empathy" (*Einfühlung*). These terms also involve the retention of individual identity at the same time that there is, in imagination, a re-creation of the other person's state of mind. But there is this crucial difference: for Chu Hsi, all living creatures, plants and animals alike, should be the eventual object of one's sympathy; Western moralists, in weaving sympathy into their ethics, generally restrict its objects to humans.[72]

Another difference reflects the Confucian tendency to cluster together psychological states that Westerners treat as independent. As noted earlier, the Chinese term for feeling ([a]*ch'ing*) covers both covert emotion and its overt expression in acts. A person able to empathize with another person would thus be expected to reveal those feelings in concrete ways. David Hume is among the Western philosophers who have put forward influential discussions of empathy. His position on this matter would seem either unintelligible or outrageously immoral to Chu Hsi, as it does to some Westerners. Hume divested his idea of empathy from any motivational or action components, defining it as merely an involuntary reaction: one can empathize with the beggar but have no difficulty in regarding him as disgustingly dirty and avoiding him on that account.[73] Chu Hsi's idea of empathy, in contrast, translates into activity on behalf of the beggar.

Values: Impartiality

Chu Hsi used the family image to explain his theory that *all* things in nature have their allotted places (*fen*), akin to social roles. A major value justified by the family image is the absence of selfishness (*wu ssu*), which has the sense of disciplined obedience to social role duties. Duty on behalf of the whole takes precedence over transitory personal desires. The absence of selfishness is also the central value justified by the two images of light projection and embodiment. As in the case of disciplined obedience, the term "impartiality" (*kung*) often denotes this value. But its meaning is different in this new context. Yeh Ts'ai says, "When impartiality prevails, all things form one body, but when partiality or selfishness prevails, the self and other become multiplicities."[74] In contrast with selflessness as obedience to role duties, at the core of which is an acute sense of social place, impartiality suggests the transcendence of such bounded positions. Chang Tsai said that selfishness means "being spatially bounded" (*yu fang*), meaning that there are things outside the self. Chu Hsi put it this way:

> The extension of [the principle of] the mind penetrates all. . . . If there is a single thing not yet embodied, the reaching is not yet complete, and there are things not yet embraced. This shows that the mind still excludes something. For selfishness separates and obstructs, and consequently, one and others stand in opposition.[75]

Selfishness is quite commonly described as the state in which the mind still has something outside itself (*hsin wei yu wai* or *yu wai chih hsin*). A person can be impartial and still observe personal role obligations; however, the idea of impartiality places the stress on expanding concern beyond those limited duties.

This second kind of impartiality is a way of looking at the world and feeling about it. Chu's way of conceiving it echoes descriptions by the Ch'engs, and it blends into the picture of the interpenetrating water. "Impartial [*kung*], then everything is one with myself. Selfish, then all things are different from each other."[76] For impartial persons, all things form one body, provided one remembers that for Chu Hsi this is only a way of looking at and feeling about things. There is no literal biological organism based on the human organism as a model of nature or society.

Concretely, impartiality takes several different forms. One is compassion. "The way of humaneness is difficult to describe; only the word 'impartiality' [*kung*] comes close to it."[77] "The humane man regards heaven, earth, and all things as one body; there is nothing not himself."[78] Commentators treat the Mencian mind of commiseration as the mind that views all things as one body. Another form consists in knowing the principles of all things. Ch'eng I says, "When one has no selfish subjectivity, there will be no occasion when he is acted on in which he will not respond to every stimulus with understanding."[79]

Commentators describe the mind that has embodied all things as "vastly impartial" (*ta kung*).[80] "Although one can *kung* all the affairs of the world, if one does it with selfish intentions, it is not *kung* at all."[81] This means that if the intention of someone attempting to remove selfishness from the affairs of the world is self-centered, the end result will not be the removal of such partiality at all. In addition, the impartial person, empty of prejudice, is responsive to the influences of all things, properly and without purposive calculation. If "the end of separation" describes negatively the value supported by the images of light source and body, "impartiality" is the way to refer positively to the same thing. And so three ideas converge to refer to the same value: the end of separation, selflessness, and impartiality.

LIGHT AS SOLUTION AND AS PROBLEM

Faced with what he considered to be Buddhist claims about the desirability of man's withdrawal from the world, Chu Hsi formulated a competing theory using two structural images. Together they pointed to the possibility of bridging the gap between self and thing by using knowledge and empathy, thereby realizing the value of impartiality. They made plausible the ideas of projection beyond the immediate self and assimilating things to the self. In the West, there is a genealogical tree of philosophical rationalists for whom bridging a state of separation through knowledge is an equally fundamental problem. They, too, employ the analogy of light and sight in their solution. Their problem, however, is the separation of man from something they consider divine, not from the mundane world; hence my phrase "vertical separation." Light is a property both of God and of quasi-divine ideas within the mind. Man's introspective preoccupation with such ideas is his means of bridging the separation. Virtue is knowledge. A glance at a few of these Western rationalists highlights the contrasting use to which Chu Hsi put the light source (mirror) and the body in solving his philosophical problem.

The core idea of the Western position is that sublime activity for man consists in discovering and reasoning from innate ideas of eternal truths planted in the mind by God. In this activity lie simultaneously the paths to knowledge and to reunion with God. Knowledge is increased by deductive reasoning, in contrast with Chu Hsi's claim that it is augmented primarily through its integration with moral principles and practical application.

Study of the light image reveals the Western rationalists' preoccupation with inwardly directed intuition and its role in deductive argument. Analysis also reveals a contrasting Chinese rationalist interest in matching intuition with outwardly oriented study, affection, and action. And it shows what the consequences of these varying preoccupations are for the rationalists in both cultures. In brief, some Western rationalists, using the same light analogy as their Chinese counterparts to explain cognition (intuitive truths are bright; people are illuminated by them), were left with a form of estrangement from the objective world. To treat the innate truths as divine was to suggest that contemplation, not worldly engagement, is noble. God left his bright traces only in minds, not in objective things. In spirit, that separation places a Cartesian, for example, close to the Buddhist position as Chu Hsi understood it. It places him far away from Chu Hsi, who believed that he had a method for overcoming the separation from things.

The origins of these doctrines about divine traces in the mind and the light metaphor go back to Plato, who, in his orphic mode, has Socrates say, "It really is proved to us that if we are ever going to have pure knowledge of anything, we must get rid of the body and survey things alone in themselves by means of the soul herself alone."[82] The innate ideas of which an individual has "visions" are the soul's recollections of the divine and transcendent Ideas among which he once dwelt. "Idea" comes from *eidos*, related to visual perception, referring to the common look of all members of a class of things. Through thinking about the eternal truths in life, the individual assimilates himself into what is divine, returning, in effect, to that from which he has been separated:

> [T]he man whose mind is truly fixed on eternal realities has no leisure to turn his eyes downward upon the petty affairs of men, and so engaging in strife with them to be filled with envy and hate, but he fixes his gaze upon the things of the eternal and unchanging order, . . . he will endeavor to imitate them and, as far as may be, to fashion himself in their likeness and assimilate himself to them.[83]

On many of these issues, Aristotle was a Platonist, too. His "mind" (*nous*) is a ghost ("Mind in this sense of it is separable, impassable, unmixed [with matter]").[84] Its highest activity is *theoria*, meaning "contemplation" or "intuitive reason" (from the verb *theorein*, meaning "to look"). What people look at is first principles.[85] These are divine things, to be contemplated by the most divine thing in people, reason:

> If happiness is activity in accordance with virtue, it is reasonable that it should be in accordance with the highest virtue; and this will be that of the best thing in us. Whether it be reason or something else that is this element which is thought to be our natural ruler and guide and to take thought of things noble and divine, whether it be itself divine or only the most divine element in us, the activity of this in accordance with its proper virtue will be perfect happiness. That this activity is contemplative we have already said.[86]

Knowledge advances by adherence to the rules that govern the making of inferences from premises, some of which are intuitive or not demonstrable. All of this was worked out by Aristotle in the *Posterior Analytics*.[87]

Augustine wove the Greek themes into a Christian pattern. A human moves toward God by virtue of a light within his mind that illuminates the eternal truths within it. These "truths" are the counterparts in man of the *rationes aeternae*, "divine ideas," that exist in the mind of God. Man's highest activity is intellection (*intellectus*), knowing these ideas.

> But we ought rather to believe that the intellectual mind is so formed in its nature as to see these things, which by the disposition of the Creator are subjoined to things intelligible in a natural order, by a sort of incorporeal light of a unique kind; as the eye of the flesh sees things adjacent to itself in this bodily light, of which light it is made to be receptive, and adapted to it.[88]

Illumination explains certainty. And he who contemplates the eternal truths is thereby simultaneously in touch with God. Just as Chu Hsi's epistemological theory of the mind's projecting itself out to "touch" objects reveals the value of ending horizontal separation, so Augustine's contemplation of eternal truths reveals the

105

value of ending vertical separation. Theories of knowledge reveal value commitments.

Augustine borrowed a "ray" theory of sight from Plotinus: "And so it is, for sight goes forth and through the eyes shines far to light up what we see."[89] He could have patterned his explanation of intellectual illumination by analogy with this theory and thereby approximated the projecting light theory of Chu Hsi. His problem, however, was reunion with the divine, not with things in the phenomenal world. Separation from God could be resolved by lighting up quasi-divine ideas; there was no need to go beyond them to the objective world.

The basic structure of the problem—and its solution—remained in place for the rationalists at the dawn of the modern period of philosophy in the West. One could plausibly argue that the chief interest of some of these thinkers lay not with God but with science and nature. On the surface this would seem to be the case with Descartes's concern. But a thorough reading shows that even his explicit philosophy fits into the structure I have been describing.

The eternal truths are "clear and distinct" in the mind, says Descartes, employing the sight image. Intuition is the "natural light of reason" (light as a property of mind as well as of truths). Knowing is seeing, not also doing and feeling, as it was for Chu Hsi. The ultimate objects of knowing are entirely internal truths, including mathematical ones, and these stem from God:

> For it is certain that God is the Author of the essence no less than of the existence of creatures; and this essence is nothing else than these eternal truths. . . . I say that I know Him . . . for knowing a thing it suffices that we touch it in thought.[90]

> In my view, the way to reach the love of God is to consider that He is a mind, or thinking substance; and that our soul's nature resembles His sufficiently for us to believe that it is an emanation of His supreme intelligence, a *breath of divine spirit*. Our knowledge seems to be able to grow by degrees to infinity, and since God's knowledge is infinite, He is at the point towards which ours strives.[91]

Knowing Descartes's consuming interest in scientific truths, it almost comes as a surprise to find that his philosophical writings do include an ethics. It does not come as a surprise to find that "the moral life of man then consists essentially in his thought-life" and that moral error emerges because people sometimes are wrong or *intellectually mistaken* about what is good.[92] In any case, knowledge for Descartes is extended as a result of following the right rules of thinking or of arranging data, not by linking it to moral principles and acting on it, as it was for Chu Hsi. Thinking starts with the innate ideas, which have God as their author.

Obviously, a less controversial example would be Spinoza, who wrote about the intellectual love of God. One of the most famous passages in *The Ethics* declares, "The mind's highest good is the knowledge of God, and the mind's highest virtue is to know God."[93]

By portraying the individual mind as capable of projection beyond the self so as to contact empathically the variety of things external to and different from it, Chu Hsi gave the individual an active role in the world. Instead of merely passively receiving images from without, the individual can contribute to nature's creative process. Moreover, Chu avoided any sharp split between what we call the private (subjective) and the public (objective). In contrast, as long as the Western rationalists focused on breaching the man-God gap through the illumination of "divine" ideas within the individual's mind, they were opening the door to the charge of creating another gap—the one between the self and the external world. Nowhere is this problem more apparent than in Cartesianism.[94] Descartes dropped a veritable curtain between the individual's mind with its ideas, on the one hand, and the physical objects making up the external world (including the eye, the brain, and their images) on the other. Man's mind never directly makes contact with external things. It knows them only indirectly, through copies of them in the mind, a fact of which it is aware. This curtain thus enforces a firm separation of the private, subjective world and the external, objective one. The consequence for conceptions of knowledge was the addition of another issue to balance intuition of eternal truths and deductions from them, an issue that concerns the ideas of external things; thus, knowledge also requires that ideas adequately represent things, and the only guarantee of that happening is the soundness of one's proofs that God exists.

In effect the Cartesian rationalists, in bridging the gap between the human and the divine, laid the groundwork for a new chasm, this time between the self and the external world from which it had been curtained off. The response in Europe to this new separation of man from things was remarkably similar in nature, if not in historical significance, to that of the Southern Sung Neo-Confucians to what they regarded as Buddhist withdrawal from the phenomenal world.

The instruments of the European response were the Cambridge Platonists and romantic poets of the early nineteenth century such as Wordsworth and Coleridge. They maintained that the mind can project life and feeling into the world. This can transform the world of dead matter, whose only Cartesian qualities are quantifiable extension and motion, into a living universe. They explained the mind by using the image of the lamp projecting light. In *An Elegant and Learned Discourse of the Light of Nature*, the Cambridge Platonist Nathanael Culverwel wrote, "Now the *Spirit of man* is the 'Candle of the Lord', he says, for the Creator, Himself 'the fountain of Light', furnished and beautified this *lower part* of the *World* with *Intellectual Lamps*, that should shine forth to praise and honor in his Name."[95] As Meyer H. Abrams explains it, the motivation of these thinkers was to end the estrangement between the self and the external world created by the Cartesian curtain between the mind and things:

> The reason for this common concern of the early nineteenth century philosophy of nature and of art is not hard to find. It was an essential part of the attempt to revitalize the material and mechanical universe which had emerged from the philosophy of Descartes and Hobbes. . . . It was at the same time an attempt to overcome the sense of man's alienation from the world by healing the cleavage between subject and object, between the vital, purposeful, value-full world of private experience and the dead postulated world of extension, quantity, and motion. To establish that man shares his own life with

nature was to reanimate the dead universe of the materialists, and at the same time most effectively to tie man back into his milieu.[96]

There is a significant difference between the projection from self to world advocated by some of the romantics and that described by Chu Hsi. The former would regard enlivening the world with a rich variety of one's own feelings as desirable. Chu Hsi would insist that the individual cleanse his mind of all morally neutral sentiments first and project only love and the inner light that grasps principle into the world.[97]

Conclusion

The central philosophical problem I have discussed in this chapter is psychological separation and the method by which it can be overcome. A single structural image, visibly perceptible light, has served differing attempts to link polarized entities that are estranged—those of the Neo-Confucians, the European rationalists, and the early nineteenth-century romantics. This suggests that to some degree the image is a tool in the service of a thinker, rather than a constraining mold that fits only one theory.

Study of the light image serves to disclose other important philosophical issues on which the Chinese and the European rationalists are divided. In the case of the modern Western rationalists, for whom the light is confined to the mind and its ideas, the central problem that they inherit from Descartes is the relation between appearance and reality. This problem concerns questions of the correspondence between ideas in the curtained-off mind and the things to which the ideas refer in the external world. In the case of Chu Hsi, for whom projection beyond the self is so important, the problem is how to attain breadth of empathic union with things. In short, his theory focuses on attaining the virtue of impartiality (*kung*).

Finally, had Chu Hsi been presented, as were the Cambridge Platonists and romantic poets, with the Cartesian subjective-objective cleavage, he, too, would have found it ethically intolerable, and for the same reason they did. He would sense immediately its psychological impact on people, namely, the intensification of the individual's felt and practiced separation from the natural world. Confucianism provides powerful reasons for the preferential treatment of family members. And the family is the ultimate anchor of social stability. Social order can be disrupted, however, if that care stops with the family, because heaven and earth are concerned with the nourishment of all living things. Order will exist when humans cooperate with heaven and earth to that end, because it is a natural consequence of that broadly oriented nurturance. Any doctrine that seems to encourage estrangement is dangerous, first, because it threatens the anchor and, second, because it calls man away from the cooperation with nature's nurturing activities directed at all living things through which he ensures harmony with natural processes. It is clear, then, that Chu's theory of knowledge can serve to oppose any perceived threat either to the anchor or to the nurturance that extends beyond it.

For the twelfth-century Chinese and the nineteenth-century Englishman, the matter of subject-object cleavage is simultaneously epistemological and ethical. This suggests that, some of the time, there is an emotional commitment to an ethical value embedded in what appear to be straightforward epistemological positions. From classical Platonism down to the modern period, the Western rationalists reveal in their theories of knowledge a special prizing of bright, innate ideas as traces of divinity. Their ethical commitment is to reunion with God. In contrast, Chu Hsi, like the early modern Cambridge Platonists, takes pains to value both subjective truths and the things of the phenomenal world, to the life and vitality of which every mind should learn to contribute. In short, he prizes the reunion with things.

The explicit topic of this chapter, then, has been the value of ending horizontal separation between mind and the phenomenal world, a value that can be realized by the person who remains mindful of Chu Hsi's epistemological theses. In terms of the structure of this book, however, the topic is what Chu's ideas on ending separation reveal about the method whereby an individual can overcome any competition between his obligation to those with whom he has basic social role relations and his duties to others: knowledge and empathy.

Clearly, the complexities of the issue of ending separation are greater than this chapter's consideration of knowledge and empathy discloses. There is the problem of how the individual can get either himself or others to exert the effort required to know and to empathize with other people and things. This means that the door to character development must be opened. As will be seen in the next chapter, the person concerned with such character development will take care to nurture both other people and himself. Self-nurturance includes introspective self-discovery of the principles within the individual's own mind. The phrase "honoring the moral nature" from the *Doctrine of the Mean*[98] refers to this nurturance. But character development also involves reliance on objective authorities. Part of this idea is covered by the textual study mentioned in this chapter and symbolized by the rest of the phrase from the *Doctrine of the Mean*: "follow the path of study and inquiry." But clearly Chu expects people to take account of a broader range of external authorities than just texts as they move gradually toward the virtues of sagehood. I will probe the nature of man's relation with these other authorities in Chapter Five. The next two chapters flesh out the complexities involved in the character development that makes possible the unity of self and things and a harmonious relation between love of family and love of others.

FOUR

THE PLANT AND THE GARDENER:
SELF-CULTIVATION AND
THE CULTIVATION OF OTHERS

From time to time serious people in any society ask the question: What kind of person do I want to be? The answer is largely a function of the idea of the self that the person already entertains. For Chu Hsi, the answer is someone with ever maturing and expanding sentiments (especially love rooted in kinship affection) and a mind clear enough to ensure that actions always properly fit situations. In short, it is to be a sage, someone sufficiently enlightened to make his actions effective in guiding and caring for others, within the family and beyond it. The method by which to achieve this goal involves nurturance of sentiments, study, and the conquest of selfish motives. Chu Hsi's answer rests on the view that the most significant aspect of the self is the seedlike repository of sentiments and innate principles contained in the mind, which serves as their "husk." I refer to them as the innate moral sense, the basis of man's social nature, supplementing thereby the earlier term ªi.

In contrast, many a Western philosopher, influenced by Plato and Aristotle, would answer the same question by saying that he wants to be someone who leads the examined life—that is to say, a person who is not dogmatic or narrow and not imprisoned by thoughtless acceptance of the customary beliefs of his society. Instead, he would be a person who thinks things through, his beliefs the result of logical analysis based on objective facts. His method would be to examine the evidence, or to review the legitimacy of premises and conclusions, or to see if various beliefs simultaneously held are consistent with one another. His answer is a function of believing that the noblest part of the self is the reasoning faculty, or intellect.

Chu Hsi's theories of cosmic or natural action or movement pro-

112

vide support and background for the idea of the self as a seedlike repository. He applies his general theory of movement to the particularities of the individual human self. In this connection, his explanatory image is the plant. In applying principles of cosmic movement to the human mind, he pictures action at the individual level as akin to cosmic growth patterns, which are revealed in the seasonal growing cycle of plants. The mind, along with all living things, participates in staged and gradual processes of change. The plant image provided Chu Hsi with a justification for the value of endless growth, or self-realization. This image was meant to elicit, from readers who accept the lessons of the plant image, the acceptance of new values: completion of growth and nurturance. Nurturance should be directed first at the individual's own mind and extended from there to the minds of others, starting with family members. Nurturance facilitates the transition from one stage to the next in the growth process, conceived as a cycle. This chapter focuses on the introspective side of the individual's nurturing efforts, and it thereby complements the outward-directed study practices described in the previous chapter. Chu Hsi, in fact, contends that introspective attention facilitates such study practices.

Chu prizes someone capable of extending love beyond the family. Yet within his philosophical system there is a potential incompatibility between family-centered role fulfillment and duty to the public. There is no inherent philosophical contradiction between the two values, or any reason why they cannot coexist. To say there is a potential incompatibility is to say two things. First, it is modern analysts who identify the problem, not Chu. Second, Chu's message is framed in universal terms. But the slant that he often gives to altruism, as an act between superiors and inferiors and as requiring some economic means, may make it impractical for ordinary people who have no hope of becoming superior men (*chün-tzu*). In addition, in the modern analyst's view, even an audience of literati would have required a detailed and compelling account of how any individual can accommodate both family and public values; otherwise, they would not have had adequate practical instruction with which to combat family-oriented priorities popular in their social class. They would not themselves have sought such instruction, assuming that self-cultivation, as Chu described it, was sufficient preparation for public-spirited action. I will suggest reasons for these and other gaps in Chu's conception of altruism, including those attributable to his explanatory image of the plant.

In sum, Chu's understanding of natural movement as a staged process in which the mind participates serves to preclude any incompatibility between role-based preferential affection for kin and expansive love. More specifically, he treated both values as appropriate to different stages of the growth process. In so doing, he developed what is, for the Westerner, a remarkable portrait of the mind. And yet, the very structural images of the plant that he applied to the theory of the mind and of the family, and which he in turn applied to all things in nature, helped to sustain a blind spot in his idea of altruism as an aspect of psychological growth.

The matter can also be summed up in terms of differences between today's perspectives and that of Chu and his audience. Today the term "altruism" suggests an ethical position that advocates selfless concern for others and that promotes this as a value at which everyone should aim. From a purely textual standpoint (and the present work is based on textual analysis), Chu does in many passages take these positions. Basic to his philosophy is the claim that the seed of humanity containing the possibility of expansive love is present in all persons, and that the material force that obscures it can be clarified. Against the background of these expectations, it is surprising to learn that Chu's altruistic message was in fact often directed at a relatively small group, a fact that will be discussed later in the chapter. Moreover, it was bound up with an idea of reciprocity absent from the modern popular notion of altruism. I will then point to a few historical facts that place this matter in perspective. They concern the actual values of Chu's literati contemporaries, for whom altruism of any kind may have ranked as a rather low priority, far below looking after the family and its property. The conclusion is that in arguing for any form of altruism, Chu stood out admirably from his peers. Yet from today's standpoint, his case lacks persuasiveness.

In trying to accommodate family and public love, Chu Hsi simultaneously helped to foster another polarity in his philosophy, one between moral intuitionism and reliance on external authority. This second polarity emerges from the first because growth stages assume a period of cognitive and affective immaturity early in the maturation process. During this period, the individual may appeal to his own intuitions, but he should refer to the rules of the sages in any conflict between those intuitions and the wisdom of the sages—that is, he should defer to the ritual rules devised by the early sages and issued or taught in his own age by the emperor, officials, or teachers. This second polarity will be revealed gradually in the course of this chapter and will become the focus of Chapter Five, in which I will consider the place of objective authorities in Chu's philosophy.

One of the many advantages afforded by the study of Chu's explanatory images is a clarification of the type of philosophy he set forth. It has been popular to describe it as a form of organicism, ever since Joseph Needham wrote,

> But I am prepared to suggest, in view of the fact that the term *Li* [principle] always contained the notion of pattern, and that Chu Hsi himself consciously applied it so as to include the most living and vital patterns known to man, that something of the idea of "organism" was what was really at the back of the minds of the Neo-Confucians.[1]

There is no problem with this, provided that the analyst remembers two things. First, Chu's philosophy is plant organicism, not that based on the image of the human organism. The human organism as explanatory image was rife in Western classical and medieval philosophy, emerged again in the nineteenth century, and seems to be what Needham had in mind in referring to Chu. Second, Chu's metaphysics relies on other images besides the plant, namely, the family and the stream of water. "Organicism" is therefore an incomplete account of it.

The plant image explains the mind as something alive that exercises its vitality in regular emotional responses. This picture complements the image of the mind as essentially cognitive, as suggested by the image of the light source discussed in Chapter Three. Along with the family image, the images of the plant and light work together for Chu Hsi to form a coherent theoretical sys-

115

tem. The family image in nature establishes the system of roles. The patterns of vitality indicated by the plant image establish the feelings appropriate to those roles. The light of the mind guides the growth of those sentiments into correct expression. Such light is crucial to the gradually maturing self, which is one theme of this chapter. Self is both the seedlike repository and the idiosyncrasies resulting from physical endowment that set individual problems of attaining moral perfection.

The Theory of Movement

The facts addressed by Chu's theory of movement are the commonplace ones that had long appeared in Chinese works, including the *Book of Changes*: the young grow old, the light becomes dark, the firm becomes yielding, and so forth. Chu's abstract theory of cosmic movement that purports to explain change has two aspects. One is that change occurs in a cyclical process with stages that go in sequence, so that going through all stages constitutes completion (*ᵇch'eng*). In nature as a whole, the process of change is cyclical and unending since the vital energy (*ᵃch'i*) forever expands and contracts. In individual humans, the life process has a beginning and an end, although within a given life there are repeated, even daily, predictable changes from tranquility to motion and back.

An individual's particular vital energy dissipates after he dies. But to the extent that he is a member of a clan, he participates in the more prolonged vitality of the clan unit. The clan *ᵃch'i* endures even though individuals die. Although it, too, will eventually dissipate, returning to the undifferentiated *ᵃch'i* of nature, clan energy may endure over many generations.[2] The *ᵃch'i* of the deceased, at times amorphous, can be contracted and revitalized through sacrifices performed by the living. The identifiable clan *ᵃch'i* that is subject to the constant process of change remains an essential element in the description of the clan. In sum, if we speak precisely about the cyclical life process, individuals go through the ultimate process once, although they pass daily through its subordinate phases from tranquility to movement. Within a limited time span (clans die out), clan units are cyclically repopulated (as are plant and animal species) and their energies are revitalized. And nature's processes, of course, go on without limit.

The other aspect of the theory of cosmic movement is that the initiation of the process is a transition from a state of being "hidden" to a state of being "revealed." What is hidden (ts'ang) reveals or manifests itself (ᵇhsien), or what is "subtle" (yin—the term combines the ideas of refined and hidden) becomes extensive (ᵇfei) in its function. The basic idea of transition, or movement, from the one to the other was known long before Chu Hsi's time. During the early classical period it had a specialized application with respect to mental states. The complementary concepts "hidden" and "revealed" occur, for example, in the Doctrine of the Mean: "There is nothing more visible than what is hidden, nothing more manifest than what is very small. Therefore the superior man is watchful over himself when he is alone." Hidden thoughts manifest themselves in action. And "the Way of the superior man is extensive [ᵇfei], yet hidden."[3] An indirectly related idea from the field of divination appears in the Tao-te ching. The prudent person will attend to early stages of a process that later might have an impact on people, and so the beginnings of action are like omens: "Deal with a thing while it is still nothing; keep a thing in order before disorder sets in."[4] There is an inevitable linkage between the two stages, the hidden beginnings and the manifest activity; barring obstructions, the one necessarily gives way to the other.

For Chu Hsi the hidden and the revealed take their places as fundamental metaphysical categories—two of the modes in which the tao of nature manifests itself. They are two aspects of the natural pattern of change: "Tao combines substance and function and also what is hidden and what is revealed."[5] The two categories are roughly comparable to the Western ones of potentiality and actuality, although there is a difference. For Chu Hsi, "hidden" and "revealed" are both attributes of a transcendental object, principle, rather than attributes of states or dispositions. Moreover, they are involved in an ongoing cyclical process, which is not necessarily the case with potentiality and actuality.

Chu Hsi often associates the set containing hidden and revealed and the set comprising principles and affair or thing (ᵇli and ᵇshih or wu). The principle in a thing that accounts for its patterns of change is its nature (*hsing*).[6] Sometimes the nature of a thing is hidden, but it can reveal itself as a developmental process, affected by the matter that constitutes the particular thing. The manifestation, however, will be in accord with the pattern. Or, thinking in the aggregate, the Great Ultimate is the hidden source of the patterns of movement of all things. But without some indication of its nature and direction, the idea of movement is far too abstract. And so the need arises for an explanatory structural image. Chu describes ideas that are too abstract as "empty," like the idea of [b]*li* that Buddhists employ to describe the Buddha nature. He believes that the latter does not adequately identify the specific types of activity that classes of things should perform.

The Plant

At this point, the plant image enters to explain and make concrete the abstract process of movement. Illustrating the categories "hidden" and "revealed," Chu Hsi refers to the tree. The vitality for growth and reproduction present within a seed during the winter (in dormant buds) is the hidden aspect; the bursting forth in spring of branches, leaves, and flowers is that which is revealed. Roots are hidden; branches are revealed. The former is "the nature [*hsing*] that makes the thing complete itself."[7] Strictly speaking, this nature is a feature of the entire process, for in every stage there are always the "hidden" seeds of the next.

Both Ch'eng I and Chu Hsi characterize the Great Ultimate—[b]*li* in the aggregate—in terms of the structural image of the tree. Ch'eng I writes "[b]*Li* is like a tree one hundred feet high that constitutes one continuous whole, from its roots to its branches and leaves."[8] And Chu Hsi, who speaks of "the thousand branches and myriad leaves of the principle of nature,"[9] describes the Great Ultimate in the following way:

> The Great Ultimate is like a tree, which, in growing upward, divides as branches and divides again to produce flowers and leaves. There is production of life without cease. Furthermore, when you get to the point of the fruit's maturation, within the fruit there is the principle of the production of life without

cease. Developing life from here, there is again the limitless number of the Great Ultimate, which is even more ceaseless.[10]

The four-season growth cycle of plants (sprouting, development, fruition, and death and energy storage) characterizes all the myriad things that exist in the universe. As Chu would put it, Buddhists who attempt to escape death (that is, to go beyond the cycle) are therefore doomed. Chu Hsi tied this seasonal cycle to the stages described in the explanations of the first hexagram of the *Book of Changes*: "*ch'ien*: 'originating growth', 'prosperous development', 'advantageous gain', and 'correct firmness'."[11] At the cosmic level, matter has directional movement determined by principle ([b]*li*), also called the "mind of heaven and earth." By explaining movement as a growth process, the image of the plant helps to structure it.

> Movement also is not the mind of heaven and earth. It is only that through which we see that mind. After all, in the dead of winter, how can we think that there is suddenly no mind of heaven and earth [just because all growth has stopped]? It moves according to its spontaneous course. . . . Of [the four stages of nature] *yüan* [originating growth] . . . is the time when the young sprouts begin to come up, *heng* [prosperous development] is the time when leaves and branches grow.[12]

The second aspect of the theory of movement, the transition from hidden to revealed, is thus explained in terms of the image of dormancy and budding. The vitality for growth and reproduction that lies dormant in the winter seed buds forth in spring as observable activity.

In introducing the value component of his theory of cosmic movement, Chu Hsi drew on an idea from the *Doctrine of the Mean*, an idea expressed through the elusive term [a]*ch'eng*, or "integrity" (sincerity). That text says that "integrity [[a]*ch'eng*] is that whereby things complete themselves; its way is that by which all things direct themselves."[13] One form of being complete is having a beginning and an end. Going through all the stages for which one is prepared is therefore a form of completeness. Things that go through such a process are thereby complete and can be said to have integrity. The person who has integrity "completes himself" and is able to "complete other things."[14] Being complete and having integrity are therefore ways to describe a person who completes a process. (My translation of [a]ch'eng as "integrity" rather than "sincerity" comes from the term's sense as a completeness that contains all natural attributes, none of which is fraudulent or missing.)

For the thing with integrity, correct actions come without effort because they are natural.[15] In the *Mean*, integrity, as the principle of completion, applies to all things in nature. It "covers all and contains all."[16] Chu Hsi accords integrity the same status: "Integrity flows forth and each thing has its own niche [lit., 'settling place']. When it is a person, it is this integrity."[17] It will become evident that a thing's "settling place" is all that is required for its completion, which may include the actions or duties expected of something.

As one would anticipate, given the explanatory impact of the plant image, the ideas of [b]li, of integrity, and of plant growth begin to converge. By drawing on the image of the plant, Chu Hsi was able to structure a process from start to finish, and then he could apply the term "integrity" to the whole of it.

> "Integrity is something's beginning and end." Its origin is integrity, and its final point is also integrity. If there is integrity, then there is something substantial, and if not, there is no substance. . . . For example, a plant from its germination until it withers, dies, and falls to the ground is following a real principle [*shih li*].[18]

Chu Hsi identified the fact that this process has a fixed number of stages as a primary example of a quality that makes a thing complete in itself (self-contained, possessing all its attributes). A plant with four seasons of growth is an example of something that has such stages. Chu then ties in the *Doctrine of the Mean*'s idea of integrity, which is the principle of something being complete. "Integrity is a state of being self-complete. It is like these plants having all these roots, branches, leaves, and twigs, and thereby being self-complete. It is what you actually have."[19] For any object, this makes going through all the stages of a process a good or natural event, because the object thereby manifests its completeness. The plant image explains what completeness is, thereby giving Chu an example with which to explain completeness in any other object, namely, the quality of having a beginning and an end and all the stages in between.

The "settling place" or niche for any individual thing will include whatever is needed for it to achieve completion. This concept overlaps with the idea of role fulfillment (*fen*), discussed in Chapter Two. Part of what brings completeness or integrity to a thing is the exercise of its proper activities or duties. In a living thing, these correspond to stages of growth.

Application to Humans

As part of a single cosmic whole, humans are subject to the same principles that govern all living things. When applied to man, the plant image explains man's mind as the repository of the life principle at the individual human level, and thus as the container of the principle that controls his development.

A disciple asked about the difference between the mind, the nature, and the feelings. Chu Hsi replied, "Ch'eng I said, 'The mind is like the seed of grain; the principle of life in it is the nature; the yang material force in bringing forth life is the feelings.' "[20]

A disciple asked, "The necessity that the seed of grain will grow is like the necessity for man to be humane. In this way we take growth as like humaneness. The life of the seed is the principle of growth. So then it follows that the principle of growth is humaneness." Chu Hsi replied, "It definitely must be this way."[21]

By speaking of the mind as like a seed of grain that contains the principle of life, *jen* (lit., "humaneness"),[22] Chu Hsi was making the point that the growth process is present in the mind as potentiality, just as life lies hidden or dormant in the plant during winter or hidden in the seed before branches and leaves blossom forth.[23] The cosmic categories of "hidden" and "manifest," having been fleshed out through the plant image, can now also be applied to humans. In the case of persons, two groups of ideas become linked through association in their respective sets: dormant, hidden, tranquil, and prestimulus (with *wei fa*); budding, revealed, active, and poststimulus or response (with *i fa*). But to avoid confusion, one should keep track of these terms by their literal meanings: *wei fa* is "not yet released," and *i fa* is "already released."

In using the seed image, Ch'eng I and Chu Hsi once again drew on an image familiar to their Buddhist opponents. The Consciousness-Only school that flourished during the Sui and T'ang dynasties spoke of pure and impure seeds in the *ālaya* consciousness. This notion, picked up by other Buddhist schools, refers to the existence of something like erroneous ideas (impure seeds) in the subconscious that construct the way a person perceives the external world. The resulting perceptions are products of these impure seeds and, as such, are not indicative of the true nature of the world. In a never-ending cycle, they then defile the pure seeds lingering in the subconscious, trapping the individual in new illusory constructs of the world. For Chu Hsi, however, the germ in the mind is only good, and there is no such cycle of defilement.

In any case, one ingredient in his theory that precludes conflict between duty to family and duty to the public is recognition of the plantlike qualities of mind, which allows the linkage of respective duties with different stages of growth. I turn now to what something plantlike needs in order to grow.

The value of completion or integrity applies to any cosmic process, so it naturally characterizes the sagelike maturity of a person's mind. This value in turn generates the value of nurturance, which is the activity necessary for the realization of integrity. It is particularly appropriate that Chu chose the image of a cultivated, rather than wild, plant to explain his theory. Psychologically, it suggests to his audience the obligation to nurture. The mind contains the potential for undergoing a process of growth similar (but not identical) to that of a plant. Although associated with all four stages, humaneness (*jen*) as the principle of life, whether conceived cosmically or in man's mind, is identified specifically with *yüan* (originating growth), or spring, the beginning of life and the first stage in the process. Passing through the stages successfully is not automatic, however; it requires nurturance.[24]

Nurturance applies to two different sorts of recipients—the individual himself as the subject of self-cultivation, and other people in a progressive sequence from within the kinship group to outside it. Nurturing others is an essential component of self-completion. The process of growth implied by the image enables Chu Hsi's theory to harmonize apparently incompatible positions on the objects of nurturance (family and public), thereby defusing conflict between potential advocates of either one.

VALUES: NURTURING ONESELF

I have noted that there is a difference between the awareness of the method for bridging the gap between duty to the family and to the public, and the ability to implement it. The method, detailed in Chapter Three, involves knowing and empathizing with all things. The present chapter, in turn, introduces Chu's position on how to put the method into practice, which involves the individual's treatment of the transition from family to public as a growth process. He must begin by applying the technique of nurturance to his own mind to promote its growth.

Loosely defined, self-cultivation includes the cognitive processes described in Chapter Three, the introspective, self-disciplinary procedures that I will now begin to address, and the reliance on authoritative models to which I will turn in Chapter Five. Using the structural image appropriate to each, one may speak of the first as polishing the mirror, the second as nurturing the seed, and the third as helping the Tao mind rule.

More narrowly defined, self-cultivation refers to practices of meditation and mental concentration (seriousness, or reverential concentration [^{b}ching]) that enable the mind to move directly into its proper role upon encountering any environmental stimulus. It refers to the practices through which the person discovers what he is as an individual and as a human being, and how he fits into nature's cyclical processes of change. It is the "internal" aspect of becoming a sage, the method by which the mirror is "polished" so that its light can project forth.

The application of the plant image to the mind and its content reinforces that strain in Chu Hsi's thought that treats the individ-

123

ual as a source of moral truths. The individual grasps, preserves, and cultivates the original nature, which rests like a kernel in its husk, the mind. He uses it as a standard against which to compare motives or desires in deciding if they should be allowed to "bud" forth in action. This Mencian-spirited moral intuitionism conflicts with the case Chu makes for reliance on objective rules and rulers, to be discussed in the next chapter.

In characterizing the mind as a seed, Chu Hsi was building on a Mencian base. Mencius had described the mind-environment relation as similar to that between barley seeds and variable soils and rains.[25] And he noted that humans need to nurture their "vast material force" with righteousness.[26] For Chu Hsi, the image of the seed became a central explanatory device rather than an incidental illustration. It is at the core of efforts to "preserve and nurture" the original nature (*han yang*). *Han yang* is used by both Ch'eng I and Chu Hsi to refer to the cultivation of the "sprouts" of goodness within the individual's mind. Such nurturance involves, among other things, meditation and reverential concentration. Chu formulated a theory of self-nurturance that, for the purposes of this study, contains five important points.

Feeling as Action

The topic of self-nurturance forces the analyst to consider the categories in terms of which daily human life was understood by Chu Hsi. Within the context of self-nurturance, the most basic categories are tranquility and activity. These are associated respectively with the states prior to the intrusion of stimuli (*wei fa*, or "not yet released," meaning no psychic activity is manifest) and after response to stimuli (*i fa*, or "already released"). Their most mundane forms are, respectively, sleeping and being awake, conditions of the absence and presence of cognitive awareness (*chih-chüeh*). But they also refer respectively to "latency" (as in the latent presence of the original good nature) and to emergent activity, which is the state in which moral effort is required. The relation between these two states can be explained in terms of the plant growth process. Central to that process is the relation between the stage in which the life force is hidden (the seed in winter) and that in which it becomes manifest (springtime budding). The significance of juxtaposing the stages of seed growth and the cycle of budding and withering is that complementary stages are potentially in one another; they alternate as growth continues. One of Chu Hsi's students received the master's approval after describing the relation between tranquility and activity, hidden and manifest, and winter and spring in the following manner:

> When the spirit moves, the substance of the intelligence is clearly manifest, and the spirit's budding can be viewed, as when the yang force returns and all things have the vital principle of spring. . . . When the spirit is not moving, then the substance of the intelligence is hidden (ch'ien-yin), and the spirit is quiet and makes no trace, as in the months wholly under the force of pure k'un [i.e., winter]. The living nature of all things is undetectable.[27]

Thomas Metzger has described the importance to Chu of breaching the gap between the states of tranquility and action. The former, as the latent original good nature, is the source of noble and creative feelings that emerge as action. Anguished about the relationship between the two states, Chu discovered in reverential concentration ([b]ching) the key to tapping the tranquil and hidden source on behalf of the emergent activity that is the focus of moral effort.[28]

There is a further subdivision of basic categories, derived from the distinction between sleeping and waking, which includes stillness and movement as aspects of the stage of being awake. Stillness (or "tranquility two," in contrast with sleep, which I will call "tranquility one") encompasses states akin to sleep in that there is an absence of normal conscious thought: for example, meditation; being in an environment without intrusive stimuli; and postawakening moments. Movement, in contrast, occurs when purposive thinking occurs, or when objects impinge upon and elicit responses from the individual. All psychological reactions, such as feeling, desiring, knowing, and having motives, belong to the category of movement or activity. Westerners think of movement or action as overt behavior. In Chu's doctrine, however, "movement" includes both the psychological responses to externals (feelings, motives, goals) and the overt conduct to which they lead. It includes what the analyst would consider both subjective and objective dimensions.

And so all subjective stirrings, such as feeling and having motives, belong in the category of action. Where human *action* is his concern, whether in his capacity as an individual, parent, official, or educator, the Neo-Confucian includes both overt conduct and subjective stirrings in this category. He assumes that they are interrelated, that feelings or motives generally manifest themselves as public behavior. Through nurturing action while it is still not overt, one can help ensure the propriety of its eventual manifestation.

The general term for the nature in action is ᵃch'ing, which most translators render as "feeling" or "sentiment."[29] As just noted, however, it encompasses the behavioral manifestations of feelings as well. The feelings come in two sets. The ethically positive set consists of the Mencian four: compassion, shame, modesty, and the ability to discriminate between right and wrong. The core feeling in this set is compassion or love, which is the active form of the principle of life. The sentiments in the other set—pleasure, anger, sorrow, and joy—are value-neutral.

ᵃCh'ing refers mainly to what the modern analyst would call affect or emotion. Cognitive activity is included in the list of emotions, not separated out as a different kind of activity.[30] The target of education and self-cultivation is feeling, not simply the exercise of reason, which is the concern of so much Western rationalist thought. Self-cultivation in the broad sense thus focuses on both the cognitive processes described in Chapter Three and the sentiments that are the target of self-disciplinary procedures.

Much Western rationalist philosophy explains why reason, rather than will or some sentiment (as in the Confucian case), is the focus of educational effort. Two of these explanations have religious origins. One is that reason is divine. It is either a nonmaterial faculty, godlike in its immaterial nature, or it is capable of intuiting God's traces in the mind. The second religiously oriented explanation is that reason constitutes what is especially human and sets man above other creatures. A third explanation is sociological: the exercise of reason is the domain of the elite (priests,

scholars, aristocrats), and its exercise by them gives them a justification for rule over lesser persons who use mere practical skills.

It is not that the sharp division between subjective and objective
or private and public, with which the Westerner is familiar, does
not exist for Chu. On the contrary, Chu expresses this separation
as *nei* (inner feelings) and *wai* (outer conduct). It is also familiar in
injunctions to ensure that one's internal sentiments, like filial affection, correspond to external deportment, thereby achieving integrity in the ordinary moral sense and avoiding hypocrisy. There
is in addition the ethical maxim that one should use reverential
concentration to straighten the inner life and righteousness to
square the external. The distinction between inner and outer aspects of the same trait was drawn early in Chinese thought.[31] But
these are not the primary categories by which Chu Hsi seeks to
explain the details of human action. The educator concerned with
nurturing human action would find it incomprehensible to ignore
subjective stirrings. They are both the source and the central focus
of action. If a categorical distinction is made, it is between, on the
one hand, subjective or psychological stirrings (a form of action)
and, on the other hand, the individual's tranquil state (tranquility
one or two), not between subjective stirrings and something outer
or public.

At the moment that the inner stirrings begin, one can observe
(*kuan*) them.[32] Ideally, just as a person constantly "nourishes" his
nature through the attitude of concentration, so should he constantly be alert to his emerging thoughts, asking if they are consistent with the moral rules.[33] The attitude of reverential concentration, says Chu, is like a doorkeeper.[34] The doorkeeper image
suggests an ever-alert state in which one is always mindful of the
prospective mesh between an emerging sentiment and the demands of the rules of conduct (ªli). Ongoing study and the extension of knowledge are required to help in striking the proper balance. In fact, the image of the balance scale occurs frequently in
Chu's writings to describe the unprejudiced mind that achieves
such coordination. The "doorkeeper" approach to reverential concentration contrasts with that of self-conquest (*k'e chi*), a technique
to apply after the fact, when an improper relation already exists
between motive or sentiment and the moral rules.

Eager to oppose the Buddhist theory that in contemplation the individual can "observe his mind" (*kuan hsin*), Chu Hsi argued that such a doctrine assumes that there are two minds, one to observe the other,[35] but he maintained that mind is one. In fact, Chu's own position is only slightly different from the Buddhist idea. It rests on distinctions between mind and feelings, and observation and control. The mind can observe and evaluate the feelings. Strictly speaking, Chu Hsi can distinguish the mind (*hsin*) in its cognitive capacity from the feelings (ᵃ*ch'ing*) and say that denying self-reflection applies to the former. But he makes no regular, formal separation of the two, and the cognitive and affective are generally linked in the vague uses of the term "mind." Although the mind cannot observe itself, it can control itself; that is, it can allow its inner life to be dominated by the attitude of reverential concentration (ᵇ*ching*) and permit its overt behavior (sentiments actualized) to be governed by rules (ᵃ*li*). I shall return to this topic in Chapter Five.

Members of the Chu Hsi school were fond of a maxim summarizing the capabilities of the mind that is nurtured with reverential concentration: "The mind encompasses and controls [ᵇ*t'ung*] the nature and feelings."[36] The character ᵇ*t'ung* means both to encompass and to control, so a more elegant translation would be that "the mind brings into conjunction the nature and feelings." The maxim means that the mind is capable of taking in or knowing both the original nature and the morally positive feelings through which it manifests itself. In addition, the mind can control both the original nature and all the feelings by ensuring that those feelings which are carried through to action are consistent with the original nature. As Chu Hsi says, "We have reverential concentration to control the whole matter. Then, when events happen and things present themselves, the font of goodness within manifests itself clearly in response to them."[37]

Since the time of the *Analects* and the *Mencius*, Confucians have advocated control of people through attitudinal transformation rather than through fear. This means stressing education and self-cultivation more than penal law, although not to the point of totally rejecting the latter. Chu Hsi is no exception. The path by which he arrives at the centrality of self-cultivation in transforming the individual, however, reflects the influence of two ideas that, in combination, are peculiar to his brand of Neo-Confucianism. One is the idea that "the mind is a living thing," like a plant seed, as Ch'eng I said. Consistent with the image, every stage of the mind's growth, including the initial, unobservable phase, requires nurturance. The other idea is the set of basic categories Chu devised to explain the mind's growth. If growth is action or movement, the explanatory categories applied to it are such that all kinds of inner events—like feelings, motives, and desires—are included under the umbrella of "action." Recourse to penal law is appropriate if the "action" to be controlled is only overt behavior. But because the concept of action, unlike that to which Westerners are accustomed, includes so much of the "inner" life, self-cultivation and education directed especially toward the inner part of the individual must play a central role. This brings me to the second important point in Chu Hsi's theory of self-nurturance.

Solitude

Solitude refers to withdrawal from routine daily stimuli as the individual calmly sits, concentrating on one thing only, namely, his original nature. It is not surprising that there is a place for solitude (an aspect of tranquility two) in the thought of this anti-Buddhist thinker, who was so concerned with the inner life. It is not an occasion for discovering what is unique about the self and cherishing it, and it is not an end in itself; instead, solitude is a means to more substantive growth along the lines shared by all persons.

The role of solitude as a means to future growth emerges from a comparison of changing interpretations of the mind as not yet released or premanifest (*wei fa*), and as already released or postmanifest (*i fa*). The crux of the matter is the idea of mutual implication, which underlies the categories of hidden and manifest and tranquility and activity suggested by the plant analogy.

Ch'eng I treated *wei fa* and *i fa* and tranquility and activity as separable *states* of being or even as things; it was theoretically possible to concentrate on one to the exclusion of the other. *Wei fa* and tranquility referred to the original nature (*hsing*), whereas *i fa* and activity referred to the mind.[38] Concretely, this meant that it was both possible and desirable to spend protracted periods in med-

129

itation[39] as a means of experiencing the original nature and "the disposition" (ch'i-hsiang) in which the sentiments have not been aroused. For Ch'eng and Chu's early mentor, Li Yen-p'ing (1093–1163), self-cultivation focused on discovery and observation, akin to the practice of some Buddhists in discovering the Buddha nature within.

Chu revised this position under the influence of Chang Nan-hsien (1133–1180), who pointed to the impossibility of separating the two states.[40] Chu then moved beyond even Chang's position to treat them as distinct yet related. Tranquility and activity are found in each other. Each gives rise to the other.

> If we comprehend the idea that activity and tranquility are each other's roots, and that, supported by reverential concentration and righteousness, they cannot be separated, then we know that the word tranquility was never meant to denote a lifeless thing. Within the extremity of tranquility there is the font of movement. This is what we call "seeing the mind of heaven and earth." . . . This is not escaping from events and things and sitting upright in a rigid manner and being biased in favor of tranquility.[41]

The mind contains both aspects. They are therefore best thought of as distinct but mutually related stages, each being the "root" of the other, instead of as entirely separate states of being. The language of the plant image informs the analysis, as Chu explains that the wei fa stage is one in which thoughts have not yet "budded forth."[42] Meditation, therefore, is a prelude, transitional, flowing into the moment when the budding occurs and presenting opportunities for controlling the flowering. When tranquil, one "sees" the nature that one shares with other people, the mind of heaven and earth. This perception is followed immediately by an attitudinal commitment to honor it, to be true to it. I shall give some consideration shortly to how significant it is that what one sees in solitude when encountering the mind of heaven and earth is something common to all people. One does not discover a trait unique to oneself that is intrinsically worthy of preservation.

With the appropriate attitude of reverence, the individual gains from the wei fa stage a sense of the continual renewal of life:

"When reverential concentration is preserved, thoughts and wor-
ries have not budded forth and cognitive awareness is not blurred.
This is the state of activity in tranquility, which is what is said of
'the hexagram *Return* as illustrating the mind of heaven and earth'
[concerned with the perpetuation of life]."[43] Activity is an inseparable part of life and requires control.

In the mature theory, the focus has shifted from discovery and
observation as intrinsically valuable goals to discovery as a part of
nurturance, meaning as a part of control. The control consists of
maintaining an unwavering attitude toward the original nature so
that all inner stirrings, when they do arise, are consistent with it.
Ultimately the aim is to attain a state similar to that of Confucius
at age seventy when his desires were spontaneously consistent
with propriety. Nurturance (or *han yang*) must be preceded by
some knowledge of the good nature that the person will experience in that state.[44] That knowledge is obtained through the investigation of things and the extension of knowledge—in short, by
study.

Understanding that actuality resides in the state of potentiality,
that activity resides in tranquility, one can understand why Chu
Hsi, while approving of some degree of solitary meditation, came
to disapprove of half-day meditation. The half-day form had had
the approval of some of his predecessors, still influenced by the
Buddhist practice.[45] Chu says that some moments of silent sitting
are useful to remind a person of his good nature.[46] But he must
proceed from this technique to action in line with his social role
obligations.

The Moral Attitude

The third significant point in Chu's theory comes to light when
one considers the nature of the control required by nurturance.
Chu Hsi quotes approvingly the statement of Chou Tun-i that "the
effort of reverential concentration [bching] pervades activity and
tranquility."[47] Control centers on bching, and the appropriateness
of its association with tranquility means that it must be a general
attitude rather than a particular thought or a rule. It is an attitude
of respect for the original nature. And the important thing about

it is that it provides the individual with a means by which to moralize any act. An attitude, like the sun, can shine on anything.

Concentration as an aspect of self-cultivation refers to keeping the mind focused on doing properly whatever may be required. It is related to but differs from single-mindedness, discussed in detail in the next chapter. Single-mindedness refers to goal commitment. It is dedication to an ideal in the selection of life's priorities. For the Confucian, the ideal is sagehood. Reverential concentration is daily practice that helps sustain one's single-minded goal commitment.

Reverential concentration follows naturally upon the vision of the good nature. It is necessary because of the mind's tendency to stray, like a rudderless boat, from the patterns that are natural to it. The patterns are primarily the behavioral acts associated with the basic social role relationships. Concentration in the tranquil phase maintains one's attitudinal commitment to honoring those patterns. Ideally, the commitment should become so ingrained that all actions spontaneously reflect it. It should pervade the active phase, governing the emergence of feelings, motives, cognitive awareness, and desires and their manifestation in conduct.

In essence, this means that all actions should reflect one's mindfulness of the heavenly principle that structures everyone's nature, mind, and feelings. This is why Chu Hsi so often comments that "preserving and nourishing [the good nature] are involved in the daily activities of watering [the dirt], sweeping, answering people, and advancing to or receding from them."[48] He says that reverential concentration is not just a kind of silent sitting, because even "in raising our feet, moving our steps, we need our mind here."[49]

This doctrine echoes but does not repeat entirely a Ch'an Buddhist position, specifically, that the Buddha nature (here in the form of principle) can be found in all human activities, even the most ordinary. Ch'eng Hao, a Neo-Confucian, worked the idea into his thesis that the tao is present in all aspects of human life. The psychological implications are that ordinary activities have as much moral worth as traditional pietistic acts and obvious virtues. In Chu Hsi's case, although there is principle in all action, acts become morally significant only when infused by the proper attitude.[50]

Believing that the mind as a living thing requires nurturance and that its "actions or growth" include the internal or subjective aspects of life, Chu Hsi hit upon the proper control technique for humans. Though he admits the need for penal law, he does not stop with it. The best control is not fear, which nourishes nothing. It is cultivation of a specific attitude. Hence his statement that "reverential concentration is like cultivating the land and irrigating it."[51]

Weeding Out Desires

The road to sagehood is not easy. The decent buds in the mind are surrounded by weeds. They are a source of anguish, and combating them requires maximum effort. Growth is not unproblematic. If the good sprouts are to thrive, the "weeds" must be removed, and this brings me to the fourth point. Until the doorkeeper is trained, meaning until the individual has perfected his attitude of reverential concentration, there is a place for "weeding," which is literally how Chu Hsi describes eliminating selfish desires in commenting on a phrase in the *Analects*, "Conquer the self and return to obey the rules of conduct."[52] It follows upon self-examination (*hsing-ch'a*) of the emerging feelings. Ch'ing-dynasty Evidential Research school scholars (focusing on philological matters) disputed his interpretation of the passage, saying he wrongly attributes a Buddhist ascetic interest in denying the legitimacy of all desire satisfaction to Confucius.[53] In other words, he is wrong to equate "self" with "selfish desires," as if that were all there is to the self and its desires. Chu's actual position is that the individual should reduce desires quantitatively and, more specifically, that he should eliminate those which cannot be fulfilled in accordance with rules. He should eliminate, for example, all instances in which he desires to eat at the wrong time or the wrong food. Chu makes this point in commenting on Chou Tun-i's repressive interpretation of Mencius' statement that "to nourish the mind there is nothing as good as reducing the number of desires."[54] One of the functions of introspective self-discovery is therefore to identify which desires or motives to pull out by the roots. The decision is made by comparing the desire in question with the dictates of the innate moral sense or by consulting the objective rules (see Chapter Five).

While exploring the solitary and introspective aspects of self-cultivation, the analyst should note in passing a disquieting implication in the linkage Chu Hsi makes between weeding out selfish desires and the instruction in the *Analects* to "return to obeying the rules of conduct." It is disquieting because, in Chu's thought, as will be shown, this opens the gate to objective authorities who establish the rules in the period before people's minds are as clear as those of the sages. To use the image of the ruler studied in the next chapter, Chu Hsi thereby charges external authorities with assisting the better aspect of the self to conquer the less stable one. Overall in Chu's works, the optimistic tone set by the recognition of man's perfectibility and the efficacy of positive nurturance outweigh the anguish at the weeds. But there is no mistaking the presence in Chu's doctrine of this other aspect and its ominous implication.

Endless Growth

The fifth and final feature of Chu Hsi's theory of self-nurturance is directly related to the theory's portrait of cyclical growth, which involves patterns of activity and rest. The significant idea for ethics is the thesis that good or natural action involves endless movement through stages—continual growth, rather than the attainment of a final, static goal. In sum, what stands revealed through the image is endless growth as a value in itself, not merely as a means to other values.

This fifth point can best be explained by noting a remarkable convergence between the Neo-Confucian cosmological picture associated with the plant analogy and that which was dominant in Europe from the Greek age until the Renaissance. One form of classical Western organicism employed the image of the human organism to explain society and nature. In this construct, a life force (*psyche*, or soul) permeates nature, providing motion and life, which are identical. Mind gives order to the motions of the life force, serving as the source of the regular, intelligible, quantitative changes in it that make natural sciences possible. Plato described this world as "a living creature with soul and reason."[55] Life and mind exist in the organism and in nature. In medieval Europe, more complex correspondences appeared. Distinguishing in the organism and in society the head that rules and the body that obeys, John of Salisbury (twelfth century) spoke of the prince as head, the senate as heart, the soldiers and officials as hands, the financial officers as stomach, and the peasants as feet.[56] Plato's organic image was descriptive: the universe is an organism. John's was functional and normative: the state should be organized like a human body.

During the Renaissance, the organic image faded from many cosmologies, to be replaced by the machine. The world came to be seen as a machine (Newton) and so did the human being.[57] Some of the most influential theories of the state in nineteenth-century Germany, however, went back to the human organism for explanation: the state possesses the attributes of human personality, or it goes through developmental stages similar to those characterizing human life, or its beginnings and development are similar to the birth and developmental biology of the animal. Writing in the 1840s, Karl Salamon Zacharia figures prominently in this approach.[58]

In France and England, in contrast, nineteenth- and early twentieth-century organicism had something of the flavor of a romantic reaction against the world and society as machine. Whitehead (1861–1947) and Bergson (1859–1944) are among the well-known figures in the movement. Its ideas were not restricted to theories of the state but applied to all nature. They differed from classical organicism in avoiding claims about near identity between parts of the universe or society and parts of the animal organism, as well as claims about an omnipresent vital force (Bergson is an exception).

The most dramatic convergence with Chu Hsi's organic plant image, however, is provided by Aristotle, in the theories worked out in the *Physics*. These overshadowed Platonic physics through the Middle Ages. Early in the *Physics* Aristotle takes as his theme the "nature" (*physis*) of things. He says, "For those things are natural which, by a continuous movement originated from an internal principle, arrive at some completion."[59] His account, he says, per-

135

tains to animals, plants, and the elements earth, air, fire, water, and their inorganic compounds. "Each of them," he says, "has within itself a principle of motion or of stationariness (in respect of place) or of growth and decrease, or by way of alternation."[60] That principle of motion can also be called the thing's nature. Motion is the fulfillment of what exists potentially, the process by which the thing's end or incipient form is realized. The key ideas in Aristotle's account of the nature of things are growth, an internal principle of motion, and teleology. The whole theory is inspired by the picture of something material that grows. In speculating about the underlying image, the choice seems to be between plants and living animals. The stronger case can be made for the latter, that is, for living animals as things that move themselves and grow to a point of completion.[61]

The plant image serves two of the same functions for Chu Hsi that the animal image does for Aristotle. One is to provide psychological security to anyone who accepts his metaphysics by explaining that change is neither sudden nor unpredictable; rather, it is part of an intelligible process that moves from potentiality to actuality. The second is to establish a standard against which to measure every object that is subject to the process, namely, its distance from actualization, or its progress in growth from the original state of potentiality to being "complete."

There is a crucial difference, however, between the theories of the two philosophers. Chu Hsi's theory of the hidden and the manifest includes a heavy stress on the stages of growth, an idea relatively absent in Aristotle. When the concept is applied to humans, the emphasis for Chu is on continued cyclical growth, on movement from one stage to another. This might simply be willing participation in daily transitions from tranquility to movement and back. Or it might be a lifetime's development. Human development is a manifestation of ceaseless cosmic change. Chu focuses attention on the unceasing effort of the student, rather than on static contemplation of integrated knowledge, of which a sage would be capable. There is a passage in the *Analects* in which Confucius, standing by a stream, says, "It passes on like this, never ceasing day or night."[62] One of the Ch'engs commented on it, and Chu wrote, "The general idea of the passage is that things in the past have been unceasing just as the operation of the universe is unceasing. The Master wanted to warn the student to be similarly unceasing in his effort. For the mind of the sage is characterized by purity which is unceasing."[63] Chu's writings stress the gradual cleansing of the mind, or incremental illumination, through constant study, a message appropriate for the vast majority who will never be sages. He did admit that a sudden enlightenment about the integration of knowledge is possible at the end of protracted study.

Chu believes that in the expansive development of the mind's capacity for love, the beginning stage of a process—for example, love of kin—may have an intrinsic value that places it above a simple means to an end. In contrast, Aristotle treats *full* actualization as the end (*telos*), and it is intrinsically more valuable than any earlier point in the process. This concept tends to diminish the intrinsic worth of activities leading to the end, reducing them to mere means. Both of these positions have important political implications.[64] Of more immediate concern to fellow Confucians, Chu's position suggested that there is never any end to studying for sagehood. To Wang Yang-ming and others, this was a tiresome and demoralizing thought. Few people would ever be able to finish the task of study and become sages. After a famous 1508 experience of enlightenment, Wang determined that there is already in the nature of each person sufficient intuitive basis for sagehood, a condition into which one can quickly enter through action.

The difference between Aristotle and Chu on this matter boils down to the degree of emphasis each places on the *telos*. Aristotle's model functions largely to support a teleological view of cosmic development (in which cyclical development conceivably might occur). Chu is largely concerned with cyclical processes, which may (or may not) have realistic teleological implications for the nurturer (the ideal state being one in which a person fully nurtures his nature and has the sudden enlightenment of all knowledge as integrated). But the initial stage is intrinsically valuable itself, not just a preliminary stage. And nurturing others, which occurs with maturity, is also a means for completing the earlier stages of growth. Maturity does not mean coming to a golden static state. Early stages have intrinsic worth. Final stages serve also as means. Means and ends share each other's traits.

VALUES: NURTURING OTHERS

As has been described, the water analogy makes a case for equality of worth. The $^b li$ "flows" through all things. It is clear now that $^b li$ is present also as their "seed" of life. All humans and, indeed, all living things need and are worthy of nurturance. The immediate implication is that the noble thing for the individual to do is to practice some kind of Mohist universal love (see Chapter One) or Buddhist compassion for all creatures by trying to nurture them all. At the same time, however, the family image justifies the value of social role fulfillment, and the most important roles are kinship ones. The implication is that family members have first claim on an individual's affection and nurturing resources.

There is no logical necessity for a belief in equal worth through equal possession of the mind of heaven and earth to lead to a universalistic rather than a small-group or particularistic loyalty or concern. But this egalitarian aspect of Chu's theory does make the linkage: all living things have the principle of life, and so the sage has a duty to aid the mind of heaven and earth in nurturing them (though not in the same order of priority). Nor does hierarchy require particularistic or limited loyalty. A person can still care about his race or country in its totality. As I will argue, however, when the hierarchical kinship positions occupy such a numerically prominent place in the sets of approved social roles, it is likely that people who think in terms of these categories will be particularistic in their priorities when it comes to caring for others.

The plant image as applied to the individual's mind reconciles the two values of family and universalistic love, making a place for both preferential and universal nurturance of others by treating the values as appropriate to different stages of the person's own growth. In the early stages of development, the individual's efforts will be focused primarily on himself and his family. Assuming that development continues, the individual's capacity to nurture will expand beyond his family to other humans and creatures. As will be discussed, despite the individual's expanded concern, he must continue to function within the context of his various social roles, which he will never transcend.

With the proper nurturance, the individual's mind may grow progressively from love of kin to love of other people to love of other things in the world:

> For instance, [the process] is like a grain of millet sprouting forth. Humaneness is the seed, filiality and brotherly love are the sprouts. Then humaneness is the root of filiality and brotherly love. ["Humaneness is the nature, filiality and brotherly love are the functions."] That is, it is like a tree having roots, a trunk, branches, and leaves. Loving one's parents is the root. Being humane to people is the trunk. Loving creatures is the branches and leaves. So practicing humaneness is based on taking filiality and brotherly love as the beginning.[65]

All cardinal virtues grow simultaneously from the same seed. And such growth is as necessary to the completion of the individual as becoming an oak is to an acorn. The person whose own mind has been suitably nurtured is able, as a consequence of his own growth, to nurture other people and things. Within the Ch'eng-Chu school this takes the form of educating family members, comforting elderly persons and being gentle with the young, protecting pregnant animals and saplings, hunting animals only in the proper season, and empathizing with lower creatures.

In addition to implying the mind's ability to expand through love to gradually embrace all things, the plant image suggests a few concrete ways in which the individual can "form one body" with, or participate in, the cosmic family. Realizing that, like a seed, he is part of an endless cycle, he can produce and nurture offspring in the same way that he was produced from a prior seed. If he attains an official position, he can nourish the minds of others (through educational and economic policies). Education is the key to dislodging selfish thoughts that impede the flow of the vital forces, which are the stimulus to growth. The plant image thus suggests actions that make somewhat intelligible the theory of forming one body. By alerting his audience to the paths just mentioned, Chu goes a little way toward clarifying the vague description in the *Doctrine of the Mean* to which the Sung writers refer in speaking of the individual who is able to effect this union: "Able to assist the transforming and nourishing powers of heaven and earth, he may with heaven and earth form a ternion."[66] I will return to this issue of vagueness about the content of altruism.

Chu's preemption of value conflict between family and public love rests in the expansive growth capacity of a self that is at the start bounded. Though locked in his immediate social network, the individual's mind need not be private and permanently bounded by family roles any more than the vital force need remain hidden within its seed or root. Mentally transcending immediate family roles and duties is a realistic ideal. The image provides an argument for mental expansiveness by structuring it as a known natural process: the principle of life is contained in a shell; life emerges from within the shell; and staged growth follows. The reader can thereby comprehend that through his mind he can go beyond the actual family or other limited network bonds. "Someone asked: '[In the statement] "Man's mind should be alive, flowing everywhere without end and not located in just one spot," how should we understand "alive"?' Chu Hsi replied, 'When the mind is unselfish it can thrust out. By "alive," we mean undying.' "[67] That which is alive expands, "thrusts out," like the sprouting seed. If love and life are viewed as one and the same, it is possible to conceive of love expanding. The image provides the framework for thinking in these terms. In the end, the individual realizes that the mind awaits only the proper nourishment or cultivation to grow. To grow outward, to thrust outward, means that the self expands as it embraces more and more people and things. The individual comes to know these things (their principles) and to love them, and so they become part of him. The boundaries that previously limited him fall away as his mind "grows," projecting itself beyond his physical person to embody all things that lie outside him. The bounded self becomes transformed into an expanded self.

In essence, Chu Hsi took an old idea from the *Mencius* and added to it. The old idea is the extension of an individual's sentiments toward others: because a person cares for his own parents, he assumes that other people care for theirs, and he has a duty to enable them to do so. He must create conditions making it possible to maximize the affection of all children for their parents. This is a key point in the Confucian response to Mohism. (Mohism advocated that the individual love all persons in the same degree, avoiding preferential affection for kin.) What Chu added is the metaphysical justification for such an obligation: there is one principle that interpenetrates and unites all (the basis of equal worth), and there is a process of growth inherent to the individual mind (caring for others is a process of growth).

The fact that the growth process occurs in stages solves the problem of preferential treatment for those in the immediate family. Filial and brotherly affection within the family network are the initial sprouts, to be followed by increasing affection for other people and things. Chu Hsi explicitly says, however, that kinship love should not be treated as a mere means to altruism. It is not to be cultivated only as a step. It is itself intrinsically natural and proper. The later stages of growth (love of other people, love of things) develop when kinship love exists. The *Classified Conversations* says,

> Chu Hsi was asked if the statement that "filiality and brotherly love are the root of humaneness" means the following: having served your parents and elder brothers to the utmost, you have established this root, and then you expand it to loving other people and things; thereby your loving is practiced according to principle. Chu Hsi replied, "It is certainly so. But filiality and brotherly love are proper in themselves. It is not because you want to love people and love things that you then start with filiality and brotherly love." K'e-hsüeh said, "Would it be like a plant having its root, then the branches and foliage can be lush?" Chu replied, "It is so, but where there is a root, the branch and foliage will naturally be lush. It is not because of the desire to have lush foliage that you then go to cultivate the root."[68]

This passage contrasts with the Aristotelian theory of the process from potentiality to actuality, which reduces the early stages to mere means. A clearer, perhaps more accurate, description of Chu's own view than he himself provides in the above would be that kinship love is intrinsically valuable yet simultaneously serves as a means—that is, cultivation of kinship love enhances one's ability to love others. The progressive outward extension of affection to others is as natural as the stages from seed to ripened grain.

If one function of the plant image is to suggest the mind's expansive capabilities, another is to provide optimism and an argument for cultivation. The virtuous life is possible because it is a manifestation of a real potentiality, the living seed or root; actual compassion derives from the innate principle of humaneness. And compassion is to be valued, because it represents the fulfillment of something natural.

The Problem of Altruism

Having identified those aspects of Chu Hsi's philosophy which reconcile the competing demands of family and universal love, the analyst should pause to consider the adequacy of the effort. Gaps in the attempted reconciliation would be indicative of weaknesses in the philosophy as a whole. Such lacunae would totally undercut its panhuman or humanitarian textual formulation, showing it to be meaningful to only a small audience and not very practical even for that group.

There are many possible contributing explanations for Chu's failure to explain adequately how altruism is made concrete and practical. But one of these reasons is the misuse of images discussed in Chapter One. There are negative consequences of his use of the explanatory image of the plant to clarify his theory of self-development and of his use of the family image to explain social relationships. Explanatory images may inhibit the thinker from considering adequately facts that have no precise counterpart in the image. In this case facts about which Chu is obscure concern the details of altruistic action and the nature of the "public" to which it should be directed.

To explain mental maturity in terms of the growth of a plant is to focus attention on the individual self (plant). Altruism is a characteristic of the complete or mature mind. But the plant image explains it as an inevitable byproduct of self-growth and can blind the thinker to the details of the needs of a public beyond the self and how to meet them. The thinker focuses on the plant first and only cursorily on what lies beyond it. He knows that completion of the process occurs in a social setting, but he has been taught to think of that as naturally occurring in a proper manner when prior development is satisfactory. He does not think sufficiently about what specific method of outreach will work since he believes his effort in the prior stages ensures satisfactory progress. The mind will naturally be "lush."

There are difficulties, too, with the way the family image influenced Chu's description of the public that receives humanitarian attention. He refers either to the vague group "people and creatures" or to relational sets informed by the family image.

Ch'eng I and Chu Hsi never abandoned their criticism of Mo Tzu's doctrine of universal love as a position that "ignores role distinction" (*wu fen*).[69] It must be remembered that at every stage of the mind's expansive growth process, social roles continue to govern nurturance of others. Roles may change, but they do not disappear. There is no anonymous educational or economic philanthropy; rather, a person always nurtures in the context of his role as family member (actual or imagined), as magistrate, or as father of the people. The need for nurturance may be universal, but the obligation to supply it is role-specific. The influence of the family image continues to affect the nature of compassion as it extends beyond the nuclear family.

The family image encourages people to think in relational terms centering around role categories and the boundaries that shut out those persons beyond the relational links. Normally, the family image causes someone to think of individuals as involved in reciprocal ties between two principals, as in the sets known as the "Three Bonds" (ruler-minister, father-son, and husband-wife) or the "Five Moral Paths" ("paths" refers to the duties linking occupants of the sets of "Five Relations": father-son, prince-minister, husband-wife, elder brother–younger brother, and friend-friend). The order of the first two sets of the Five Paths is Mencian; later writers often reverse them.

When the idea of equal worth suggested by the water image is positioned next to the sets suggested by the family image, there seem to be two opposing ways of thinking about person-to-person connections. One is that the individual fits into one of the standard categories and tends to be restricted in his duties to those with whom he has specified reciprocal relations. The combination of hierarchy and a limited number of social role categories into which to fit a relationship makes it likely (not necessary) that the individual's love and loyalty will be focused on particular individuals to whom he has ties by virtue of his role within the hierarchy. At the other extreme is the utopian individual in his role as sage, who makes no distinctions between himself and others. He does not feel bounded or partial only to those with whom he has standard role relations, although he does have special affection for his own kin. Mindful that the Great Ultimate (or the mind of heaven and earth, or originally pure water) is in all living things, the sage feels an obligation to show his compassion by nurturing universally. What is missing between these two poles is clarity and specificity about the situations in which most people find themselves most of the time. This concerns the relationships between the imperfect individual and mankind, groups, and individuals outside the family.

A search for specificity uncovers Chu's restriction of the size of the population capable of being altruistic, and this is a surprise for the Westerner expecting to find something like his own idea of altruism. Altruism is love that transcends immediate family. When Chu describes how it is made concrete, he speaks of nurturing people educationally and economically, as well as preserving the lives of other people and other living things. This is a case of structuring humanitarianism according to the parent-child image. Now, in fact, although many people are capable of not killing animals so as to avoid interfering with seasonal pregnancy cycles, or of saving sapling trees, few have the position or means to nurture others educationally and economically. In its broad sense, therefore, altruism cannot be a universal prescription for people at all stages of development. There are different expectations for people at different stages of growth, and altruism is an expectation for people at an advanced stage, namely, a small group of potential "parental officials" (*fu-mu kuan*). This is clear from the way Chu describes loving people and creatures as akin to the *mature* state of plant growth. It can also be inferred from the audience for which he wrote. Chu's explicit audience is composed of literati or people who are actually or potentially superior men (*chün-tzu*). That is to say, it includes his scholar friends and officials on active service who are in a position to serve as parents to the people. Implicitly (and here is an example of vagueness on a crucial issue), the group of potentially superior men may also include all those who study and obey the teachings in Chu's *Elementary Learning* (*Hsiao hsüeh*), which he completed in 1176 as an instructional guide for daily life. Needless to say, only a small number of people could have identified with an audience of scholar-officials aspiring to *chün-tzu* status. The low literacy rate would already have restricted the size of this group. Neither group would have included women, since according to Chu they are not capable of digesting the complicated curriculum leading to advanced learning. Limited to studying the easy sections of the Confucian *Analects* and the *Commandments for Women*, they would lack the education needed to practice *chün-tzu* altruism.[70]

Further, nurturing others educationally or economically is justified more as a way for the superior man to develop his own nature than as a duty derived from rights to which all humans are entitled. People, like children, may expect nurturance, but nothing specific or equally distributed.

Through Chu's application of the family image to all societal roles, such roles are presented in terms of reciprocal duties.[71] Realistically, very few people ever will be in a position to have a relationship with others of the kind Chu describes in his account of altruism. It is clear that reciprocity is essential to picturing the relationship as plausible, and that there are five sets of relationships in terms of which the individual finds his identity. Of these, the superior party in each of the first two sets constitutes the potential altruist. He is prince (*chün*), and he is father of the people—a parental official. He stands juxtaposed with the recipients of his nurture, from whom he may demand that they live up to the expectations of their subordinate social roles. In Chu's terminology, the recipients are expected to comply with the *Analects* injunction "let the minister act as a minister" (*ch'en ch'en*) and "let the child act as a child" (*tzu tzu*). The latter means that they should be receptive to this educational or transforming activity. If they are ministers, they should work hard on behalf of their superior. If they are commoners, they bend before their superior's commands like grass bending before the wind. Whether it is a case of children with parents or of officials with the emperor, people should remonstrate if they think the master is wrong.[72] Even if the *chün-tzu* is out of office, the relation remains. He exists as a role model for the people, who in return owe him the duty of emulating his virtue. The point remains, however, that very few ordinary people will ever be in a position in which they can expect obedience from the recipients of their generosity. Altruism is presented in terms that make it remote from the actual circumstances of most people. The result is that they will likely attend to the sets of roles they realistically can occupy, namely, the actual family roles.

In the list of five sets, the only one that provides a plausible egalitarian structure as an alternative for the relation of altruist to people is friend-friend. Family and hierarchy color all the other relations in the five sets, a prominence reinforced by the family-based cosmology. No wonder Chu leaves the altruist primed to think in terms of the father-child relation. Obscured by that image are the limited resources of most people that prevent them from nurturing others economically.

Occasionally, in his educational materials and memorials, Chu discusses altruism outside the family, such as in his comments on the Lü family community contract (*hsiang-yüeh*), on which he did editorial work. The contract was an organizational model discussed or used at various times and locales in China to foster mutual encouragement for moral development among various families through periodic ceremonies, lectures, and public praise and criticism. Chu says, for example, in the *Elementary Learning*, "When there is a calamity, all members of the community contract show sympathy for each other [*hsiang-hsü*]."[73] Showing sympathy is "aiding the sorrowful and needy"; however, sympathy is not shown to people in general but to those with whom a person has established a formal relationship within the contract, that is, people who participate in the ceremonies of the contract. In a "public proclamation" (*kung-i*) when he was a magistrate Chu enjoined the people to show sympathy for members of their community in time of death, but, again, he was not promulgating a general ethical principle that was to be treated as universally applicable.

Chu's doctrine of loving people and creatures requires practical detail in order to become a realistic supplement to the value of fulfilling role duties, but he has little to say in his philosophical works about how to accomplish this. Even in his many memorials and letters, there is little guidance other than general comments of an official nature about reducing taxes, educating the people, and preventing famines.

The educational and economic content of altruism can be inferred from scattered remarks about the principal duties of kings and officials. Confucians as far back as the Chou period defined nurturance as fostering growth and thereby aiding the nourishing powers of heaven and earth. The purpose of such education is to teach proper relationships. But although Chu has much to say about the *chün-tzu's* introspecting on his own faults and starting his self-cultivation with family duties, he has much less to say about the nature of philanthropic activity. If his philosophical works lack concreteness about the activities of the accomplished altruist, they also lack specificity about the step-by-step measures by which a person develops as an altruist. The reader looks in vain for guidance about the incremental steps that an ordinary person may realistically take to manifest such love. In this connection, Western counterparts include the idea of charity.

The idea of "groups outside the family" or "people and creatures" toward whom the individual Confucian has obligations is unclear. Perhaps this reflects the assumption that they are the concern only of sages, and either sages are enlightened enough to know who they are or there are too few sages to bother talking about the issue. Or, perhaps Chu assumed that the literati to whom his message was directed already knew that they had duties to the family, the community (*hsiang*), and the state, and those were the only categories that mattered. But often none of this is spelled out, and the analyst is left with the question: how are "people and creatures" identified (in terms of what interests or needs)?[74] How are the competing interests of different groups to be balanced? If it is not possible to relate a group somehow to a familiar region, occupation, lineage, or other cohort with which an individual can identify himself or his family, it may be too much to expect the individual to treat the group seriously. In fairness to Chu Hsi, this is the least challenging of modern Western difficulties with his philosophy. Clarity about the nature of groups and their competing interests did not begin in the West until the advent of the social sciences. Of course, altruistic acts are directed not only at groups but also at individuals outside the kinship organization.

Historical Considerations

Some factual background serves simultaneously to lessen surprise at the difference between Chu's idea of altruism and contemporary expectations and to support a positive evaluation of Chu as an individual. Chu himself was a person of compassion. He once even advocated forcing the wealthy to help the poor in times of emergency.[75] As an official, he compiled an admirable record in famine relief and the establishment of communal granaries. In a memorial he advised the emperor to issue an edict encouraging granaries in other areas.[76] Chu left a fine legacy of support for schools and the design of curricular materials, the details of which are outside the scope of this study.[77] Robert Hymes has argued that in supporting the community contract, local academies, and communal granaries (no interest charges on loans to farmers at planting time), Chu and others were trying to fill a gap left by a weakened central authority. That authority had lost strength fighting and paying off the invaders from the north.[78] Such voluntary organizations would certainly go beyond the family to serve the community (*hsiang*). The infrequency with which the community granary and contract are topics in the memorials and letters does perhaps raise a question about the priority that Chu gave this level of society.[79] But in fairness to Chu's genuine contributions in these areas, criticism should be generous, repeating that the vagueness about the content of altruism lies principally in his philosophical works, and, to some degree, in his memorials and letters. His practical educational writings fill in some of the gaps quite nicely.

The problems with Chu's account of altruism just addressed focus on the limited audience to which it had a realistic appeal. There is an additional problem even within the restricted population of literati. This is partially historical, not philosophical. It lies in the fact that after centuries of Confucian teachings about humaneness, there is no evidence of any widespread acceptance among the elite of humaneness as a high-priority value. The family role fulfillment values seem to have dominated. This means that Chu was not making a case for improving humaneness outside the family to the already convinced. The need to persuade therefore required Chu to formulate a doctrine sufficiently clear and compelling to overcome powerful social attitudes among members of his class. This he did not do.

Robert Hymes has presented evidence of charity in one region of Sung China where local elites were exhorted by officials to sell grain in times of famine. But he has also described the content of arguments that several persons used to justify charity. For example, the brother of the philosopher Lu Chiu-yüan argued from utility that one should give to the needy rather than risk conflict with those who expect that one should do it. Charity was nevertheless a consideration for Lu, although it ranked far below preservation of family property. There does not seem to have been any general acceptance of a principle of altruism in this region. Speculating about such reasons for charity as its utility, Hymes writes, "The use of such arguments from self-interest suggests that there was considerable disagreement as to the ethical basis—or more broadly, the basis in general rules of social behavior—of charity in general and relief grain sales in particular."[80]

Historically speaking, members of Chu's own scholar-official class went far beyond Chu in treating the prosperity and preservation of the individual's own family as the ultimate value, rather than altruism. This is revealed in Patricia Ebrey's study of Yüan Ts'ai (fl. 1140–1195).[81] Chu valued a mind with a broader capacity for compassion. And he condemned acts that involved profit seeking and indulgence as immoral, no matter what their beneficial effect on the family. Further, he was more interested in genealogical lines than in nuclear families. In going as far as he did in advocating an altruistic attitude, he was remarkably outside the mainstream of his social group. From the perspective of time, he was an exemplary symbol of what he preached.

Considering the actual value placed on the family throughout subsequent Chinese history, along with the theoretical deficiencies in Chu's position, it is no wonder that his iconoclastic move to broaden the individual's perspective was so ineffectual. In rural

China, the power of rich families within clans acted to fragment even a clan organization, when one existed. The lines of responsibility were therefore already tenuous within the one unit of society in which there was some presumption of cohesion, and this was so because of the tighter ties of each rich and powerful family within its own network. Writing about nineteenth-century rural China, Hsiao Kung-chuan describes the problem this way:

> Perhaps there was something in the nature of the clan that made it act and react as it did. It was an outgrowth of the family; it was theoretically based on the same natural relationships that gave reality to the family. But since the family group was extended far beyond its natural dimensions, whatever natural sentiments or affection existed in the family were found to be diluted to the vanishing point in the clan. The clan was therefore held together more often by utilitarian considerations than by sentiments among its members. As our survey of clan activities shows, a good deal of the behavior of kinship groups was not motivated by unselfish principles. In many instances the clan organization was promoted and maintained to advance or protect the interests of a minority of clansmen. And even where the interests promoted were those of the entire group, these were selfish in that the clansmen assumed that their welfare was paramount to that of the community in general.[82]

Of course, the behavior of actual clans varied. Hsiao also discusses the self-interest involved in the nominally altruistic practices of preparation for famine relief by gentry and scholars: these groups often were trying to save their own lives by avoiding confrontation with starving mobs.

While in the realm of historical fact, it would be quite reasonable to ask what evidence there is that Confucians even managed their own families well. My attention has focused on the altruism that comes with maturity, but what about the ordering of family that occurs early in the mind's development? This is a subject about which the scholarly world knows little; it needs investigation through the type of historical sociology applied to the European family.[83]

The Moral Sense: Chu's Legacy

Today when an analyst thinks of the Confucian roots of the idea of the innate moral sense that is shared by all persons, he reflexively traces it to Wang Yang-ming and other Ming thinkers. But it is so prominent in Chu's ethics that one may legitimately go farther back, to the Sung reactivation of Mencian moral intuitionism. After all, the philosophical figures of the Ch'eng-Chu school enjoined their audience "to preserve and nourish the original nature." It reveals itself as the intuitive moral sentiments and principles by which a person enters into proper relations with other people and things.

At the same time, note should be taken of the special features introduced in the Ming conception of self-cultivation. The contrast between Wang Yang-ming and Chu is mainly one of priorities. Chu treated the study of books and the study of social affairs as more worthwhile than did Wang. While not ignoring books, Wang felt that their status in Chu's ladder of importance distracts people from the inner orientation that alone leads to understanding of the unity of things. The two men were different temperamentally; the pleasure Chu found in books, Wang found in participation in political problem solving. He was by choice an activist.

The final chapter in this book examines the meandering yet vitally important path of the idea of the moral sense in the modern period. In claiming that this is a descendant not simply of Wang Yang-ming's doctrine of innate knowledge (*liang-chih*) but also of Chu Hsi's idea of man's awareness of the original nature, I have in mind in particular the following points: the moral sense is innate and is universally possessed by all persons, and it reveals itself in emotional and cognitive ways (that is, as a mind that discriminates right from wrong and loves the former while hating the latter), summed up with the phrase "the four minds" (first discussed by Mencius); love, the most important of the social sentiments, is the manifestation of the principle of life, and it first reveals itself in filial affection; when stimulated, the four minds respond as feeling, which, rather than being something forever subjective and private, belongs to the category of action (and action flows from a hidden to a manifest state); the moral sense requires cultivation to promote a course of development akin to that experienced by all cosmic life processes; and the mirrorlike mind must be "polished" to remove selfish thoughts in order for the moral sense to properly enter the consciousness. Finally, certain structural images, such as the plant, are embedded in descriptions of the moral sense. All of these points were inherited by Wang Yang-ming. As T'ang Chün-i argued, Wang accepted important aspects of Chu's doctrine of moral cultivation, such as self-care in solitude and self-examination that leads to weeding out bad desires.[84]

Chu's interest in the study of books in no way diminishes his contribution to the formulation of the concept of the moral sense. The question of the relative importance of book reading remains a separable issue. Wang Yang-ming certainly enriched Chu's idea of innate knowledge of natural processes and objects; in so doing, what he called innate knowledge (*liang-chih*) is coextensive with the principles of heaven that permeate the universe. Wang therefore gathered more under this umbrella term than Chu Hsi ever did under what I call the moral sense. Wang also refused to distinguish the substance of the mind or the mind in a state of potentiality from the mind in operation. Where there is knowing, there is mind, just as where there is the perceiving of color, there is eyesight.[85] In this respect, Wang saw himself as differing from Chu. While granting differences on such issues, it is still possible to identify Chu's contribution to Wang and the continuity between the two thinkers. The final chapter picks up the theme of the legacy of Chu's idea of the moral sense.

CONCLUSION

Self-nurturance is an introspective enterprise, and it is useful to sum up what an individual will discover about himself by practicing it. He will uncover facts about his particular motives and desires that are unique to him. This includes knowing which ones he must weed out. He will discover the moral sentiments (compassion, shame, modesty, and the ability to discriminate between right and wrong) that he shares with others. Especially in moments of solitude, he will have a sense of the mind of heaven and earth, or the principle of creativity within himself that gives rise to those sentiments. He will be aware of his capacity for honoring those sentiments and that mind. Finally, he will be mindful of his passage through stages of change, from daily alternations of tranquility and movement to a lifetime's growth process. The significant thing is that introspection and solitude are not in any necessary way associated with the discovery of traits worth preserving because of their uniqueness; rather, the individual's particularities make him aware of his own special problems in attaining sagehood and suggest that his path to it may be different from someone else's. The traits worth preserving as intrinsically desirable are those which he discovers he shares with others, namely, the moral sentiments, the capacity for creativity, the ability to honor his moral nature, and his participation in nature's regular processes of change.

Modern Westerners are accustomed to associating introspection, solitude, and self-effort with marching to the tune of a different drummer—with the pursuit of unique goals and adherence to one's own particular values. My study of self-nurturance in Chu Hsi's writings reveals that no such association should be assumed for this Southern Sung thinker. What his views of self-nurturance do reveal is a capacity for altruism that in theory is available to all persons.

If Chu Hsi wants to be a person with ever-expanding love and a mind so clear that the propriety of acts always matches situations, that is because he already has a certain view of the self. The plant image plays a significant role in that view and in the procedures whereby the self can reach the ideal he seeks for it: the self as social nature, possessing universal moral sentiments through which the principle of life is manifest and requiring effort and the right educational environment to mature. The growth thesis colors those nurturing procedures. All of this is background to understanding how the individual can resolve the competing claims of family and public for love: he must regard fulfillment of the duties to each as stages in a growth process and proceed to nurture his mind to ensure its growth. As I have indicated, however, Chu's position on the ordinary citizen as altruist has flaws.

There is a powerful emphasis on self-effort that runs through

Chu Hsi's discussions of cultivation. The focus in this chapter has been on the individual's own role in achieving self-discipline through introspective means and on the individual's reliance on the original nature in his mind as his moral standard. This tilt toward self-discovery is balanced by the authoritarian strain in Chu Hsi's teachings that is the subject of Chapter Five. The individual must be mindful of authorities other than the texts mentioned in connection with brightening the mind through study. Living in imperfect societies and with inadequate knowledge, individuals should submit themselves to those who know the Way. Chu Hsi saw no tension between these approaches. He introduced no new process image to attempt a resolution. Perhaps one reason was his expectation that what is discovered through self-effort will be the same as the rules promulgated by sagelike rulers, officials, and teachers. Modern Westerners associate solitude and self-discovery with difference, and difference with the questioning of authority. But for Chu Hsi, introspection, solitude, and self-effort do not suggest the pluralism of values that would constitute a direct threat to authority. In other words, Chu Hsi did not see the potential tension between the two themes that today's analyst identifies as yet another polarity, this one between self-discovered moral intuitions and external authority. In traditional Confucian terminology, this conflict is between the dictates of the moral sense (*i, or *liang-chih*) and "returning to the rules of conduct" (*fu li*).

In Chapter One, I referred to the possibly dangerous implications of Chu's Confucian tendency to fuse matters of fact and value. The dangers are intensified by his treating the significant characteristics of the mind as moral principles and feelings, whether self-nurtured or educated by others. Having this view of mind, the Confucian then speaks as though any event in which a person plays a significant role may therefore strongly reflect that person's standards, and assumes that morally cultivated minds generate successful events. This approach may ignore the other variables relevant to the situation, including the availability of technical skills and economic and organizational factors.

FIVE

THE RULER AND THE RULED:
AUTHORITARIAN TEACHERS AND
PERSONAL DISCOVERY

Chu Hsi's writings have an authoritarian strand that coexists with the stress on self-cultivation. That strand is broader in scope than the study of classical texts containing fundamental truths with which scholars of Chu are familiar. It centers on the importance of rulers and teachers to the nurturance of people and on the attitude that one should have toward the texts.

Many analysts have noticed that Chu is often critical of existing rulers. Few have noted that he still treats them and their office with the respect due models and regards their social role as essential. It is a commonplace that Chu emphasized the importance of the investigation of things in classical texts. It is less frequently mentioned that he treated the texts as limiting personal explication, and that he regarded some Confucians who interpret these books and who personify their contents as authority figures on whom people should model. One of the most influential modern Chinese studies of Chu describes the core of his teaching in terms of the self-development of the excellent traits that are inherent in the individual's nature.[1] The analyst infers disregard of Chu's authoritarian strand in this work. Leading Japanese scholars of Chu correctly recognize the place of textual study in his doctrine, though they differ on its importance in comparisons with intuitive concentration. They fail to note at all the legitimate place of rulers and teachers.[2]

There are ways of accounting for the authoritarian strand that are matters of history, not philosophy. A historian would doubtless attribute the status of emperors to the rise of imperial authority during the Sung. Chapter One referred to the thesis that during the T'ang and early Sung, the emperors were beholden to aristocratic clans in north China.[3] Leaders of the clans were instrumental in determining who became emperor. The person selected was a successful competitor from their midst who then owed favors to the others. Those favors might include appointing them to high office, where they could influence the emperor. Eventually in the Northern Sung, however, the power of the clans faded. With the rise of a meritocratic examination system, the emperor could choose his advisers from officials recruited without reference to clan ties and to whom he was not beholden. Fan Chung-yen, who led reforms in 1043–1044, was an example. In short, the ruler's authority increased. Sung emperors demonstrated their independence from their highest advisers and advertised it with symbolic acts, as in the case of the Sung emperor who refused to drink tea with his premier and made this chief official stand while he sat.[4] In his own attitude toward imperial authority, Chu Hsi could not have been unaware of the changed historical position of the emperor.

Individual Confucians had considerable authority, as shown by the stature of those without any official position. The analyst can offer different explanations for Confucians' declining to serve, depending on the dynasty and time: fear of inquisitions directed at advocates of certain intellectual positions, loyalty to a fallen dynasty, or the view that the integrity of the examinations had been compromised.[5] For some Confucians, separation from officialdom was a path to status. Dating from the Northern Sung, persons from newly rich families in southeast China sought prestige that they could not claim through their bloodlines. They found it in a claimed association with the teachings of the early Confucian sages and in their mastery of texts said to contain these teachings. Their Confucianism gave them authority separable from the occupation of any office, though it could also be used to argue their special qualification for governmental work. It was their answer to the inherited status of the old northern families.

A related consideration, more relevant to the Southern Sung, is John Chaffee's finding cited in Chapter One concerning the increasingly small number of officials actually recruited into the bureaucracy through the examinations, among other reasons because so many jobs went to relations of existing officials. Many students spent their lives studying for the examinations, and so there was a large cohort of educated literati without government jobs.[6] Cynicism about the methods of recruitment drove some to criticize the examinations and the bureaucratic system. At the same time, many of these individuals regarded themselves or were regarded by others as exemplary Confucians, capable of leading the moral life apart from official position. Their stature did not derive from passing the examinations or from proximity to the emperor but from embodying the teachings of the sage. This attitude emerged against a background of increasing elite attention to local regions and away from aspiration to the official bureaucracy. Robert Hymes has identified three factors in the Southern Sung that helped encourage the elite families to reorient their interests: the weakened control of central government officials over the application of policy in local areas, making leverage with officials irrelevant to a family's local interests; factional struggles in the middle and late Northern Sung that may have made high office appear to local elite families to be a dangerous career for their sons; and Southern Sung disorders that encouraged preservation of family wealth and property as a primary goal.[7] These historical conditions reinforced the goal of individual Confucians to seek sagehood at home, rather than as part of the bureaucracy. One of the reasons for stressing this is to avoid confusion between the several authoritarian aspects of Chu's doctrine discussed here and the claim that Chu is an advocate of imperial autocracy. Chu believed in a number of legitimate external authorities, including exemplary local Confucians.

My task in the present work, however, is to identify and account philosophically, not historically, for the authoritarian strand in Chu's writings. There is direct evidence for the strand. Accounting for it is more difficult. To do so requires a thesis that draws on elements in Chu's known doctrine that most easily explain it. Herein lies the relevance of Chu's theory of the mind that uses the political image of the relation between ruler and ruled. The key elements in this search for an explanation are the idea of a ruler inside each person, the cloudiness of most minds, and the existence of external authorities.

THE POLITICAL IMAGE

Dealing with conflicting desires, sentiments, and motives is a routine process for everyone. Chu developed a theory that he applied to this process, namely, that there are two different levels of awareness in the mind, differentiated in terms of the things of which a person is aware, and that each level is tied in with different grades of action that follow upon the awareness. He called consciousness of the heavenly principles or of the original nature the "Tao mind" and consciousness of desires the "human mind." "When the mind's intellectual ability becomes conscious of principle [^{b}li], it is Tao mind. When it is conscious of desires, it is the human mind."[8] There is but one mind, focused alternately on different subjects. "If we say that the Tao mind is heavenly principle and the human mind is human desires, that would be to create two minds. Man has but one. Cognitive awareness of the heavenly principles is the Tao mind; cognitive awareness of sound, sight, smell, and taste is the human mind."[9] In order to describe its superior worth as compared with matter (^{a}ch'i) and its ability to account for the patterns in the world, Chu sometimes refers in his metaphysics to ^{b}li (principle) as Lord (ti).[10]

If among their various functions structural images provide an account of the structural relations between facts to which a theory applies, then in applying the political image to the mind, Chu Hsi was concerned with the relations between such facts as the conflicting motives within the individual's mind. In the classical Confucian political ideal, there is a strict division of roles between ruler and ruled, with the ruler maintaining an ordered harmony among the occupants of all social roles. The principal goal of those seeking utopia was to find one good ruler who, through the example of his own upright mind, could unite and transform people into tranquil occupants of their roles. As applied to the individual, this image suggested that a person can identify rulers and ruled within his own mind, and the goal should be to enable the ruling element to control and transform all psychological phenomena within its subjective domain. The effect of this portrait on the reader was to magnify the significance of internal conflict and to cause him to think of competing motivational alternatives as respectively allied with the ruling and ruled aspects of mind.

Mind has two "aspects." And, in Chu's formulation, the Tao mind can and should dominate the awareness of bodily desires, sensations, and certain sentiments collectively called "the human mind." The political image is thus applied to explain the relations between awareness of principles and awareness of desires. It is variously expressed in terms of parties involved in a ruling process, either ruler and ruled, host or master and guest, or general and soldier: "Someone asked if we can do without the human mind. Chu Hsi replied, 'How can we do without it? However, the Tao mind is the ruler and the human mind must obey its orders.' "[11] He also said, "The human mind is like soldiers, and the Tao mind is like a general."[12]

There are nuances in the individual's respective attitude toward external emperors and internal rulers. While sage-kings might be objects of reverence, actual rulers can be objects of less estimation. Although they should be respected for their position as teachers of the people, they themselves may be seriously flawed in character. The inner ruler is the object of almost religious reverence, suitable only for the sages.[13] Although Chu showed respect for existing emperors, he was often critical of them.

Chu's principal textual authority for the distinction between the Tao mind and the human mind is a passage from one of the Old Text sections of the *Book of History*. A mythological emperor, Shun, admonishes his successor-to-be, Yü: "The human mind is dangerous; the Tao mind is subtle. Concentrate [the Tao mind], be single-minded; sincerely grasp the mean."[14] For Chu Hsi, the Tao mind takes on a technical meaning that it did not have in this original passage, namely, awareness of the innate original nature or heavenly principles. And the choice of the political image to explain the relationship between the Tao mind and the human mind constitutes one of Chu's important innovations. It is an innovation that is consistent with the image suggested by the *Analects* passage that plays such an important role in his ethics: "Conquering the self and returning to obeying the rules of conduct is *jen*." The idea of one aspect of the self "conquering" another is present in both the *Analects* passage and Chu Hsi's treatment of the Tao mind as a ruler of the human mind. This language is historically significant for introducing the value of frugality without asceticism. For centuries, the related concepts of conquering the desires and frugality were a point of controversy among Confucians and rulers.

Values: Single-mindedness

The political image implies the value of single-minded concentration on finding, elevating the prominence, and preserving the internal ruler, akin to seeking the ideal king. There is also a double meaning here. First, the inner ruler consists of the innate principles, which are single in the sense of being a "unity" or an integrated whole. Second, single-mindedness means having only one motive and acknowledging only one standard, namely, finding this integrated "ruler" and obeying it. To do so is to be "unitary" and "single." Attainment of single-mindedness ensures dominance by the internal ruler over all thoughts, which in turn guarantees the tranquility of the individual. Tranquility follows upon the transformation or subjugation of thoughts. Single-mindedness is simultaneously a means to the goal of harmony of action and principle and a value to be attained for its own sake. Its relative presence or absence is an important trait in any description of a person.

A comprehensive description of a person, or his identity, begins for Chu with the social roles encountered in Chapter Two. As part of a family, whose structure reflects the tao of nature, the individual is born into a well-defined set of duties and mutual obligations with respect to members of his kinship group; he may acquire additional specific roles at any time thereafter as a function of his actual circumstances. He is the son of X, the father of Y, an official of town Z. The identity description does not stop there, however. It includes traits that are a function of the interaction between physical endowment and the self-bright cognitive principles; the most important individual trait to be influenced by the physical endowment is the capacity to see principle (considered in Chapter Three). In most people, this capacity is reduced, and a cloudiness obscures the view of principle.

With the introduction of goal orientation and single-mindedness ([b]*i*), the picture of what a person is and is capable of becoming is complete. The possibilities go beyond the continuous growth (see Chapter Four) in integrated knowledge and empathy (Chapter Three) already described. The participant in the world's affairs, whose sense of engagement arises from his involvement in an on-going process of self-cultivation, is also distinguished by his sense of purpose. This sets him apart from those who, to varying degrees, fall short of "completing" themselves.

Having a goal or direction (*chih*, lit., "aspiration," often translated as "will")[15] means having a sense of life's priorities. In Chu Hsi's eyes, it sums up much of a person's identity beyond what is encompassed in his social roles. Being single-minded means sticking to the goal. It is an attitudinal matter, and therefore it is under the individual's control to a much greater extent than most of the traits affected by his physical endowment.

In advocating single-mindedness and claiming that all people have an internal ruler with access to a single standard, Chu Hsi was expressing the desirability of uniformity of moral goals and judgment. Specific duties may differ in groups from different economic backgrounds, but the goal of role fulfillment is universal. One lasting effect of this appeal was the strengthening of a general belief among Confucians in the possibility of attaining society-wide consensus on ends and active popular commitment to them. This consensus in turn was thought to guarantee social reform and well-being. Herein lies the cultural significance of the idea of single-mindedness.

The value of single-mindedness has its textual basis in the statement of Shun to Yü cited earlier in this chapter, specifically, in the portion of the passage coming immediately after the reference to mind: *wei ching wei i* ("Concentrate [the Tao mind], be single-minded"). To be single-minded is to have only one goal in all thoughts and actions: locating and preserving the Tao mind with its unified principles, which is how a person becomes a sage. In his preface to the *Doctrine of the Mean*, Chu explains these words this way: " 'Concentrate' means to differentiate between the two [aspects of mind] and not mix them up. 'Single-minded' means to grasp the correctness of the original nature and not to leave it."[16] Narrowly speaking, to be single-minded means having only this single goal. More broadly, and referring to the content of the goal, it means to try to know and obey the role duties and other sagelike obligations grounded in the original nature, using the Tao mind to control all desires.[17] Among other things, the path to single-mindedness is "the investigation of things and the extension of knowledge."[18] This is a reminder that the pursuit of single-mindedness leads to the integrating of factual knowledge and innately understood moral principles.

I turn now to the authoritarian implication of a theory about the mind based on the political image of a ruler and the ruled. This will enable the fleshing out of the concrete personality manifestations of single-mindedness as a value. These manifestations include emotional constraint without the extreme of asceticism and, among all who are single-minded, uniformity of motive, feeling, and moral standards. The application to the mind of the structural image of a political relationship (ruler-ruled) produces associations that confirm the legitimacy of external authorities, though legitimacy is not logically derived from the use of the image.

Inner Masters, Cloudy Minds, and External Authorities

All persons are born with the Tao mind, which constitutes their inner master. The terminology of a ruler is there in the texts, from the terms for ruler and host and master (*chu, chu-tsai*) to the language describing the Tao mind's relation to the human mind. The Tao mind conquers; the human mind obeys (*t'ing-ming yü*).[19] Without a master, says Chu Hsi, man is like a rudderless boat. Chu's writings on a variety of topics warn of the dangers of a "mind that lacks a ruler."[20] And yet the images of water and a light source have already dramatically confirmed that most men's minds are turbid, cloudy, or covered with dust. They do not clearly perceive their master. Self-cultivation is the gradual process of enabling the Tao mind to become accessible to the individual. The conclusion is unmistakable. Until the inner master is clear, an individual must also look for a master externally, where other authorities exist. The content of what those outer authorities teach is identical to what the inner master would reveal were it clear. Teachings include the principles underlying the rules of propriety, to which a person must return if his human mind is to be conquered and transformed.

As early as the Chou period, there was a process by which traits of formerly external authorities, such as heaven and the king, were internalized. Man's mind possesses a sovereign, whose moral commands are like those formerly issued only by heaven and the acting sage-king. Mencius spoke of a heavenly nobility (*t'ien-chüeh*), certain innate moral tendencies that should be valued above human nobility (*jen-chüeh*), the actual occupation of a position of great rank. Hsün Tzu described the mind as the "heavenly ruler" (*t'ien-chün*), an expression that had been used exclusively to designate the reigning king during the Western Chou. The content of the innate moral sense as described in the *Mencius* is identical with the content of the commands (*ming*) formerly issued by heaven or the sage-king. He who obeys the commands of the external heaven thereby accumulates *te* (virtue) and ensures some kind of communion with heaven. In the Confucian works, he who obeys the commands of the inner moral sense also accumulates virtue and establishes such a communion.[21] In form, Chu's doctrine contains a justification for a reverse process, a reexternalization of the master that most men need. The inner sovereign continues to exist, however, and the justification lasts just until the inner ruler is clear.

Texts

Analysts predictably answer any question about the existence of external authorities in Chu's philosophy by referring the questioner to the classics, the favored objects for studying the principles of things—especially the *Four Books* and, among them, the *Great Learning*, the first book among equals.[22] The classics are properly treated as authorities because they contain the doctrines of the sages, and "in reading books we have as our goal grasping the ideas of the sages and worthies, and through the ideas of the sages and worthies we perceive the principles of nature."[23] The sages and worthies modeled on nature, and the reader models on the books containing their insights.

The *Doctrine of the Mean* is the source of that canonical set entailing an introspective value, "honoring the moral nature," complemented by an external prescript, "following the path of study and inquiry."[24] The latter is one of the principal ways whereby a person clarifies his mind through the investigation of things and affairs, especially as they are revealed in texts. As noted in Chapter Three, such action helps end the separation between self and other people or things. The concomitant self-illumination is then directed back toward the objective truths in the texts to reveal linkages between these truths. The texts in question are mainly the *Four Books*: the *Analects*, the *Mencius*, the *Doctrine of the Mean*, and the *Great Learning*. They also include some works dealing with ritual, such as the *Li-chi*.

But besides providing aid in fostering self-illumination, the classics play a less appreciated role. The analyst finds that the authority Chu gives them may impede individual interpretation of passages and individual judgment about the issues they address, thereby acting as a brake on self-discovery. The classics are not simply tools for self-discovery; they may become objects of intrinsic worth and veneration and nurture too much reliance on outside authority.

The student is not encouraged to persist in tampering with the traditional interpretations of their passages. If he regularly ventures his own interpretation, he may lose his heavenly principle and sink into the selfishness of human desires. And so the texts take on the status of outside authorities and rein in individual judgment.

> Generally speaking, when you read texts you should probe their meaning and savor them according to the explanation of the early Confucians, causing it to penetrate right into your mind, so you perceive the ideas and their beauty. If you find old explanations to be incorrect, and by chance come up with some other interpretations, then it is no obstacle. But if you must persist in wanting to seek some so-called self-discovery [*tzu-te*] beyond the traditional interpretation and focus on a new explanation, then maybe you were not able to understand thoroughly the explanation of the early Confucians and lost it. If you use your mind like this, the more you exert yourself the farther from tao you will get. I fear that you will soon

lose the correctness of heavenly principles and sink into the selfishness of human desires. This would not be the original idea of learning.[25]

If this caution holds for scholars, how much more must it hold for ordinary students. In sum, it must be remembered that the authoritarian side of the picture places limitations on the self-discovery discussed in Chapter Four when it comes to the texts.

The external authorities that seldom appear in studies of Chu Hsi are the emperor and living Confucian teachers. But the cloudiness of the mind coupled with the absolute need for a master makes their role not only legitimate but crucial.

Emperors

Chu often criticized the existing emperor. At the same time, he treats the emperor's mind as having an essential role to play in the transformation of the people.[26] In this connection he draws on traditional model emulation theory and on the assumption that all minds, when purified, will reveal the same values or goals to all individuals.

All of the Chou Confucian works teach that a person legitimizes his acts by copying the mind or the *te* (virtue) of an ancestor or sage. Here is the precedent for looking externally for a model's mind to imitate. Chu says, "We learn the tao of the sages so we can know the mind of the sages. When we know the mind of the sages and use that to manage our minds to the point that our minds are no different from those of the sages, this is what is called transmission of the mind [*ch'uan hsin*]."[27] In fact, the Northern and Southern Sung Confucian works routinely refer to this process as the means "for the world to be united in one mind," and assert that "the king, being high above, is the model of the world."[28] The emperor is pivotal in attaining the goal of a world with "one mind."

The ultimate models are the sage-kings of old, Yao, Shun, Yü, and the rest. Chu praises the sage-emperor Yü for reaching the high point of rule in which an emperor's educational transformation of the people is like a strong wind in the face of which nothing can avoid being bent.[29] He speaks of an emperor as "like a guidepost and the people as like its shadow."[30] When the post is up-right, the shadow will not be crooked. In commenting on a passage in the *Book of History*, Chu says,

> That is to say, all the people in the world will not dare follow their own selfish desires. Thereby they will comply with the transformation initiated by the ruler, and they will return to the highest standards. . . . That is to say, the ruler is the model of the highest standards, and he issues commands to those beneath him. That which he treats as constant and what he teaches all embody heavenly principles and are not different from the decrees of the Lord-on-High.[31]

From the fact that Chu finds the above *Book of History* discussion important enough to warrant explanation, one can infer that he regards the points just made as correct and as significant. The implication is that through imperial edicts emperors can convey the proper rules to the people. Learning those rules facilitates the people's transformation. The rules of the sage-kings can appear either in imperial edicts or in school texts. From Chu's standpoint the rulers in question are either the sagelike rulers of the pre-Han period or they are actual contemporary rulers, assuming they follow Chu's advice and act as their exemplars would (see below). Actual emperors who drew on Chu Hsi's doctrines obviously considered their rules to be in accord with sagelike principles.[32]

The current ruler is one medium whereby teachings personified by the sages can reach the mind (the other is a combination of books and teachers). The emperor does not need to be a sage, only a transmitter. Service as a medium between the teachings of Yao and Shun and the minds of the people is his justification for educating and punishing and otherwise controlling the people. Actual rulers are the people who interpret the standard (the ritual rules, ᵃ*li*, and the constant principles, ᵃ*ching*, used in transforming the human mind).

People have the natural ability to model on a present-day ruler who transmits the teachings of the sages, and they should exercise it. Such teachings are embodied in the ᵃ*li*. The people need an up-right ruler, says Chu Hsi, in order to be upright themselves.[33] As emperors take the lead from the early kings in revealing their likes and dislikes, it becomes evident that the people will learn what is forbidden.[34] In addressing the throne, Chu Hsi states that "the imperial mind is the basis of the world."[35] The ruler should be single-minded in ruling the world's affairs, following heavenly principle, which is the original nature.[36] Chu praises his current emperor for having been single-minded in pursuit of the essence of the tao.[37] The most efficient administrative device is the example of the emperor himself as he makes the proper decisions.[38] These statements serve two purposes. On one level, they are exhortations to the emperor to take his responsibilities seriously. On another level, they tell readers that there are those on whose minds they should model themselves.

Chu bolstered the legitimacy of appealing to an external mind with another argument. When it comes to values or to evaluating, all clear-minded people think the same. One and the same heavenly principle is in everyone, and everyone is aware of it as intuitive moral principles. The latter correspond to the natural order of things, so when affairs are evaluated in accordance with them, the evaluations coincide with the natural order. The minds of the sage-kings, as reflected in the ritual rules of conduct that they formulated, correspond with the hierarchically natural patterns in the cosmos: "The minds of the sage-kings are one with heaven. Therefore, in their issuing these rules of conduct [[a]li] there is not a single thing that does not coincide with heaven."[39] By copying the minds of the early sage-kings in promulgating rules, the actual rulers themselves become sagelike emperors, and their rules achieve legitimacy. When the people's own minds clearly perceive the principles that constitute the original nature, they will discover the same standard used by any sagelike ruler or authority to whom they submit (who uses sagelike rules of conduct). "The original nature of the sages and worthies is the same as that of ordinary persons. Since it is the same as that of the ordinary person, how can the ordinary person not take [equaling] the sages and worthies as his responsibility."[40] By obeying the rules of sages and worthies the people imitate them and act as their minds would have them act if their minds were purified.

Among the people today, Chu says, diversity of motivation is rampant. The emperor has a role to play in ensuring that the people do not follow their private motives when those would be inconsistent with the heavenly principles that a good ruler at this time can identify:

> Your servant has heard that in this wide world with millions of people, each has his own intentions and wishes to act according to his private perspectives. There already exist heavenly principles to hold and norms with which to spread them down. It is only because of these that the good rulers can encompass [the private intentions] and bring order to them and cause each person to follow principle and not dare to act contrary to our aim.[41]

There are textual justifications in Chu's portrait of the mind for conclusions that he would not accept. Such conclusions concern the elevation of emperors to the role of the highest moral authority. The self is split between Tao mind and human mind. This provides future external rulers an opening for taking over the law-giving that should be done by the internal ruler or Tao mind, on the grounds that they know what the ordinary person's higher self requires, even if the individual is too unenlightened to know it.[42] Of course, Chu would maintain that actual rulers must first model themselves on the minds of the sage-kings of antiquity in order for their own minds to have moral legitimacy. And there are competing authorities (texts and true Confucians). But there is a possibility here for actual rulers to, first, downgrade the importance of the ordinary individual's moral sense in any complex ethical situation and, second (another consequence not intended by Chu), to control people on the basis of self-proclaimed moral legitimacy or self-described imitation of the mind of a sage-king.

Chu Hsi likes to contrast reliance on self-discovery or inner-directed cultivation with other authorities in sets of bipolar categories, such as "honoring the moral nature" and "the path of study and inquiry." In this set both poles are legitimate. Another includes, on the introspective side, rectifying the mind plus making the mind sincere (*Great Learning* phrases) and, on the other side, considerations of practical utility (*kung-li*). In this set, the objective authority is the accumulation of state power and wealth stemming from institutions or policies. As far as Chu Hsi is concerned, this set differs from the previous one in that only the introspective side of the polarity gives the proper guidance for self-cultivation. Its external pole constitutes a negative example—something to avoid in the search for objective authorities. As Hoyt Tillman has demonstrated, Chu Hsi rejected such utilitarian considerations as reinforcing selfish motives or as tied with the use of force as a control device typified by the behavior of the hegemons (*pa*) in multistate Chou China.[43]

It is amusing and predictable that the objective authority "emperor's mind" does not appear in a standard bipolar set in which it is contrasted with inner discovery or cultivation. Chu was not prepared to announce the possible incompatibility of the emperor's authority with the dictates of the individual's own moral sense, though he himself often criticized imperial character and policy. Presumably he appealed to his own moral sense in doing so.

True Confucians

Confucians routinely believed in the strict authority of individual Confucian teachers without simultaneously believing in imperial autocracy. A famous example of another age, mentioned in the next chapter, is Huang Tsung-hsi (1610–1695). He condemned the notion that the emperor is the ultimate judge of right and wrong, but he would have rejected the idea that each student is his own judge. He believed instead that authority rests in individual scholars and teachers in the academies and schools. Chu Hsi criticized the emperor for his reading habits (Buddhist, Taoist, and poetry books), his foreign policy, his permitting a prince to be tutored in a certain way, his lack of filiality to his father, his attitude toward ceremonies, and his luxurious life style. And Chu directly criticized the emperor for dismissing certain officials without consulting others.[44] In these acts he showed that he believed in judges other than the emperor himself. One can therefore infer his belief that individual Confucians working alone do not completely depend on the emperor to point out the standards they should employ. As individuals, there is much that they can discover for themselves, and in the process they become external authorities for other persons.

The evidence that he depicted certain living Confucians as authority figures lies in his referring to some contemporaries by the traditional terminology—*chün-tzu*[45]—for a person who has attained moral superiority over others and should be emulated. Additional evidence is that he employs the traditional imagery of people bending in submission before the Confucian teacher like grass before the wind.[46] Within the Confucian tradition, the *chün-tzu* always serve as exemplars. According to Chu, the rectitude of some of these superior men even causes their imprisonment when it comes in conflict with the intrigues of corrupt officials.[47] Their traits include knowing the nature of heaven and earth and avoiding the taints of Taoism and Buddhism.[48] Though they wear common clothes, they rectify their minds.[49] These are the "true Confucians" (*chen ju*).[50] Their job is to transform and nurture the people and to be examples for other literati.[51] Such true Confucians may be found teaching in schools rather than serving as prefects, and the schools are models for the people.[52] The sages advocated setting up schools because of the wickedness into which people are led by their physical nature in general and material desires in particular. The Three Bonds and Five Moral Paths provide the rules the sages intended the people to follow.[53] Punishments to rectify the minds of those who go astray are a necessary supplement to education, although when all people are transformed, punishments will disappear.[54] In sum, the same principles of model emulation that justify treating the emperor as an external authority apply to true Confucians.

One of the intriguing symbols of this status as authorities for others was the emergence of a genre of literature called the "recorded sayings" (*yü-lu*). These constituted records of conversations that some Sung Confucians and Buddhist abbots had with their respective disciples. The existence of the genre suggested to some later Confucians that these individuals were treating themselves as masters. For example, Ku Yen-wu (1613–1682) criticized both Ch'eng Hao and Ch'eng I for introducing this genre, and thereby helping in the spread of the Ch'an thought that saturated their conversations. Evidential Research scholars of the Ch'ing rejected the genre, preferring writings based on "solid learning" that required some specialized knowledge.[55]

CLEARING VERSUS CHOOSING

The Western reader who encounters all these references to rulers and masters, and who finds that Chu Hsi advocates some reliance on external authorities, is likely to wonder if this means that Chu favors removing the individual's freedom. The issue is serious for some Westerners for whom morality requires that actions be free.

Western commentators have sometimes attributed to Chu the idea of free will or free choice and claimed that such choice plays an important role in the existence of good and evil.[56] In actuality, Chu would say that the individual does not choose to follow the heavenly principles (the supreme authority). He exerts effort to know them through study or model emulation or introspection, and they move him to act accordingly, to the degree that he perceives them. Exerting effort is not the same as "freely choosing" in a Western sense. Some writers refer to the famous phrase "to establish the will" (*li chih*) as an indication of Chu's belief in free will. But it means to adopt a goal for one's life, such as to be a sage; it suggests more an aspiration and a commitment to it.

In being a sage, the emphasis is on clearing the mind of obstacles, not on making choices. The obstacles are selfish desires. One can begin the difficult task of removing them prior to any actual conflict of motives. My previous discussions of "purifying" the nature and "polishing the mirror" addressed this procedure. The underlying assumption is that with the removal of selfish desires comes automatic clarity of moral judgment and proper response. The innate patterns of correct response are always present as potentialities, awaiting only the breaking down of the barriers that block their realization. Chu Hsi provides a good example in his description of the behavior of monks. Following innate patterns (*bli*), monks who leave their families and retreat to monasteries inevitably re-create familial relations in the temple. They treat abbots as fathers and new monks as younger brothers.[57] It is implied, however, that if the obstacles to their Tao minds were eliminated, they would maintain proper familial relations at home in the first place and never leave for the monastery. In contrast, many Western ethical doctrines have emphasized the centrality of choosing between reason and desire.[58]

171

As long as the issue is ends or ultimate values, the emphasis for the individual should be on learning to obey, not on judging for himself and then choosing what is good. If a person has not read or has not understood the texts, then he obeys the interpretation of the texts by external authorities. This places considerable power in the hands of interpreters or commentators.

As will be shown, there is a role for choice in Chu Hsi's ethics with respect to matters of means. Otherwise, the treatment of purposely chosen action by Ch'eng I and Chu Hsi reflects a Taoist influence. They like to quote the *Doctrine of the Mean* passage describing the sage who "apprehends without thinking and hits upon what is right without effort."[59] This passage is also consistent with the *Analects* reference to Confucius' condition at the age of seventy, when he could follow his heart's desire without transgressing the rules.[60] The preference is for obedience to proper authorities (Tao mind, teacher, father, ruler) until such time as the right actions spontaneously emerge, without deliberate choice making. The following illustrates the denigration of deliberation.

> Someone asked, "In his endeavor, a student should aim at becoming a sage. Why not set up a target?" Chu answered, "Of course a student should regard a sage as his teacher, but what need is there to set up a target? As soon as one sets up a target, his mind will be calculating and deliberating as to when he will become a sage and what the state of sagehood will be like."[61]

There is a difference, therefore, between many European ethical systems and that of Ch'eng-Chu Confucians on the matter of choice. The ramifications are enormous in both traditions for derivative ideas about the primacy of individual responsibility for acts or the primacy of the state's role in the nurturance or educational molding of its citizens. In addition, there are ramifications for the content of blame. In Chu's writings, the individual may be criticized or derided for not exerting effort. The Western advocate of free will blames the individual for abusing his God-given freedom, and blame represents a religious violation, along with other special features. What is curious about this particular difference is that it emerges from a background of profound agreement on related issues. For example, there is agreement among Neo-Confucians and many Western rationalists on selecting the conflict of motives as the aspect of the psychic life on which to focus in their ethics and on the use of the political image to explain that particular aspect.

The European position on free choice of the will has at least two roots. One is the Epicurean assertion of the individual's ability to select courses of action that can maximize his personal pleasure and help him to avoid pain. It was directed against classical materialists like Democritus and the founder of Greek Stoicism, Zeno (366–264 B.C.), both strict determinists for whom every action is dependent on prior physical causes.[62] According to the atomists, each event is entirely a product of prior physical causes in the form of the weight, motion, size, and other qualities of the atoms involved in the events preceding the one in question. This suggests that man is controlled by fate or, more precisely, by the random state of environmental and personal atoms prior to any possible act. In response, the Epicurean Lucretius (99?–55 B.C.) said that the individual can initiate action from his will (a material organ), thereby causing bodily atoms to change direction and freeing himself from the bonds of atomic causation. Perhaps the action of his will is itself uncaused.

> [W]hat is the source of the free will possessed by living things throughout the earth? What, I repeat, is the source of that will-power snatched from the fates, whereby we follow the path along which we are severally led by pleasure, swerving from our course at no set time or place but at the bidding of our own hearts. There is no doubt that on these occasions the will of the individual originates the movements that trickle through his limbs.[63]

In any case, later theories of indeterminism focus on the claim that aspects of some events in the world, such as human choices, are uncaused. By the fifth century A.D., Epicureanism was a dormant creed. The physical determinism of some Stoics was pushed from center stage by the different concerns of Christian philosophy. The Epicurean vision of how to deal with such physical determinism was noted once again in the seventeenth century, when the attempt of its proponents simultaneously to retain a materialistic metaphysics and a place for free will became influential.

A second European source of the centrality of free will is early medieval Christianity, principally the doctrines of Augustine (354–430).[64] Augustine's concern with free will as an entirely subjective and personal authority (the concern of so many later European moralists) has its root in the problem of locating the blame or responsibility for evil. If God is omniscient, does this not mean that He knows that people will do evil? If He knows and does not stop them, is He not to blame? The doctrine of free will is absolutely required in order to absolve God of responsibility. Otherwise, His goodness would be in jeopardy, because He sees that human beings will sin and does nothing about it. Moreover, by removing from God the blame for sins, one justifies the use of punishments and rewards as control devices for sinners by God's agents on earth.[65] Augustine wrote *De Libero Arbitrio Voluntatis* (On the free choice of the will) to clear God of blame for evil by showing that free will in man and angels is the cause of sin and evil.[66] Augustine was reacting against the Manichees, who said that God cannot be both omnipotent and perfectly good.

The modern formulation of the problem arises from the need to defend the sometimes irreverently termed "three-O" conception of God: omnipotent, omniscient, and omnibenevolent. On the surface it would seem that a three-O God would not want to permit evil, because He is good; He would know how to prevent it, because He is omniscient; and He would be able to prevent it, because He is omnipotent. Yet evil exists. Do we then deny that He has one of the "O" traits? Descartes gave the most popular modern answer: God gives humans free choice, which is intrinsically good. Human evil (in contrast with a natural evil, such as a tornado or typhoon) comes from erroneous choices in action or judgment. There could not be free choice without the possibility of error; otherwise, the will would choose only the good. Evil, therefore, comes into being when a person chooses on the basis of inadequate knowledge. Having free choice, the individual has the power to choose only when he fully understands a situation. In the end, evil results from his erroneous choices.[67] God is therefore absolved from responsibility for evil, because He could not give people free choice (an intrinsic good) without simultaneously making it possible for them to err.

The reason for this glance at two of the roots of the Western conception of free will is to pinpoint the concerns that underlie the centrality of free will in European ethics—uncaused choices, a God free of blame, responsibility and blame, and a thing called a "will"[68]—thereby underscoring their absence in Chu Hsi's Neo-Confucianism. According to Chu Hsi, evil has always existed on earth because of the material dust that darkens the self-bright light (within the mind as [b]li) and the material obstructions that impede the correct directional movement of motives and acts. No god is disgraced by its existence. Evil is simply part of the way things are, a given in the relations of principle to [a]ch'i (matter). For Chu Hsi, then, the crux of the issue has nothing to do with assigning blame; rather, the question is *how* to remove the existing dust and obstructions. Chu's proposed technique entails both the internal transformation discussed in Chapter Three and Chapter Four and the reliance on the teachings of external authorities described in the present chapter. Because people have the capacity to apply these methods, they can control their destinies: originally pure water can be cleansed; an originally bright mirror can be polished. But the hedonistic interest in maximizing personal pleasure through wise choices would be condemned as completely selfish and immoral in Chu's scheme of things. This Epicurean concern, whether classical, as with Lucretius, or modern, as with Bentham and Jefferson, is simply absent from Chu Hsi's formulation.[69]

As a function of these differences between the European and Confucian accounts of evil and responsibility, there are also significant differences with respect to the consequences of wrong acts. As might be expected of Chu Hsi, his references to such consequences do not focus on immediate rewards and punishments for good and bad choices; rather, failure to remove the obstacles to understanding carries negative consequences that are built into the natural system. These are a sense of disequilibrium, absence of tranquility, and separation from others. The individual may suffer such consequences long after morally wrong deeds are committed. The language of divination is appropriate to describe the penalty for the person who ignores principles: inauspicious future happenings. There are interesting implications here for a sense of psychological time. The span between committing an act and reaping its consequences may be long, perhaps generations. In contrast, in the case of those Western ethical systems that assume the existence of a three-O God, bad choices often bring a rapid, justified punishment from the external, judging God—if not a divine thunderbolt, then some rebuke from His self-appointed agents on earth.

For Augustine, the will mediates between reason and desire, ideally choosing to affirm the alternative identified by reason, not the one demanded by desire. Once the free will of the individual emerged as savior of God's goodness and locus of the individual's responsibility, there was already a place in the mind to locate it commensurate with its independent status (although Augustine did not utilize this place). The Platonic political image had provided a tripartite structure to describe the mind: ruler, soldiers (imperial guards who aid kings in implementing laws), and ruled and producers.[70] In this tripartition of the mind, High Spirit, akin to anger or courage (depending on the context), generally aids reason against the appetites or emotions. The essential point, however, is the preexistence of tripartition, which provides a place for a third faculty in addition to reason and desire or emotion. This place was eventually taken by free will, which edged out High Spirit in the process. The "will" then became a thing with a place of its own, whereas Chu's term $^c i$ (intention, volition) refers to the "outthrust of the mind," not a separate thing.

In contrast with tripartition, Chu Hsi's construct of the mind has only two aspects (Tao mind and human mind, or ruler and ruled). Not only was there no three-O God external to man to require that Chu Hsi highlight the free choice of the will; there was no legacy of a three-tier political structure to use as a structural image. Confucian hierarchical social sets come in pairs. Moreover, third parties do not intervene in the idealized relation between the two parties. There is no need for a middleman between a father (the emperor) and his children (the ministers or the people, depending on the context). Officials are extensions of the emperor's person, not a separate entity with motives that are different from the ruler's. In addition, proper rulers do not use force against the ruled, as Plato's High Spirit and soldiers do against the desires and the ruled. To the degree that the political image helps to structure the aspects of the mind in terms of bipartition or tripartition, Chu Hsi predictably employs the former. There is no important place for any counterpart of the conative will or High Spirit in his account of the conflict of motives as the individual solves an ethical problem.

One might infer from this discussion that Chu Hsi never brings up choice making at all, but in fact he offers some rather extensive remarks on the subject. And what he says is significant to an exploration of the value of single-mindedness because, through the exercise of choice, individuals might depart from the single standard that is presumed to be derived from the original nature. Hypothetically, people could make and act upon their own potentially unique moral judgments. His position reveals his fears about the reliance of ordinary people, with their unclear minds, on their subjective intuitions.

In discussing choice, Chu Hsi is common-sensical enough to recognize that the single principle of humaneness must be applied differently by different people in different situations.[71] People must draw on their intuitive moral sense ([a]i), which he explains through the image of a scale. To appeal to the moral sense is to choose in accordance with the specifics of a situation, or "to scale" (ch'üan). "When we use righteousness to scale something, and afterwards hit the mark, righteousness is like a steelyard, and scaling is using it to measure, and hitting the mark is judging the propriety of a thing."[72] Unlike Ch'eng I, Chu Hsi contrasts choosing, or scaling, with observing the constant principles ([a]ching). An analyst must note at the outset that following the constant principles differs from choosing (ch'üan) in accordance with the intuitions of the moral sense in that the [a]ching principles are recorded and objective and are thus available to officials or scholars who can publicly certify their content. As Ch'eng I says, "The Spring and Autumn Annals embodies many great principles. . . . It is the weight and balance for handling things and the norm [lit., model or pattern, mo-fan] for judging moral principles."[73] In contrast, relying on the moral sense, that is, scaling or choosing, is subjective and open to a plurality of individual judgments, some of which may not accord with an external authority's view of what the standard requires.

The term ᵃ*ching* covers customary ritual rules (ᵃ*li*), social role duties, and the broad theses governing both (such as the naturalness of distinctions between superiors and inferiors). A number of classical Confucians treated the ritual rules as human inventions, although it was generally accepted that the sages formulated them on the basis of certain cosmic principles, for example, hierarchy. An example of a ritual rule is the taboo against touching between males and females who are not married and are of different bloodlines.[74] As human inventions, the rules are not intuitive; they are recorded in texts. They are uniform for particular dynasties, though not for all time.[75] The social role duties, such as parental kindness and the child's filiality, are intuitive to the moral sense known as ᵃ*i*, yet they are also objective because they are recorded in the texts. In Chapter Two I referred to the "ten things that men consider right" as described in the "Li yün" section of the *Book of Rites*. They compose an example of rules that are intuitive and also objective, by virtue of their being recorded in this authoritative work.

Some instances of individual scaling by the moral sense are not problematic. They concern the choice of a particular means of exercising a duty (like filiality) in a specific family situation or where no clear-cut constant principle is applicable. The philosophically important discussion concerns those instances in which there is a conflict between obedience to the objective ᵃ*ching* and individual choice based on subjective interpretation of the situation. There is a common-sensical recognition that flexibility may be required in some situations because of the urgency or timing of an issue.[76] But even in these cases, Chu Hsi reveals his clear preference for the objectivity of the ᵃ*ching*, citing the situations above as abnormal ones (*pien-shih*) that should be kept to a minimum.[77] They are really counterexamples that only prove the general superiority of the ᵃ*ching*.

When the issue involves those ᵃ*ching* that pertain to social role duties having a bearing on the authority structure (the zone of some ultimate values), Chu's position is that the ordinary person had better entirely ignore individual choice based on subjective standards and obey the objective rules. A modern commentator might add that reliance on one's own standard could be dangerous. These are cases, for example, where the [a]*ching* require loyalty to the king and the individual judges that there is reason to kill him, or the rules require obedience to parents, who select brides, and the individual contemplates ignoring their wishes.[78] Only sages dare weigh the specifics (*ch'üan*) in such cases and risk choosing a course of action that is contrary to the predictable uniform code embodied in the [a]*ching*. "The constant principles are the ways to be applied all the time. The expedient is what is applied when you have no other choice."[79] The implication is that generally, one should not resort to the expedient. The minds of the sages alone are clear enough always to understand the moral principles (*tao-li*) that somehow transcend the [a]*ching*. The *Mencius* does contain a message to the effect that revolt against an illegitimate ruler is justified. In his treatment of scaling, however, Chu Hsi plays down the spirit of this idea, which seems to imply tolerance of self-discovery of the most serious moral answers.

It is ironical that Chu Hsi, a Mencian Confucian who believed in innate moral principles, generally prefers that people in any complicated situation do what the [a]*ching* say rather than follow their intuitions. The message for the ordinary person is that one must continue to investigate a lot more things and remove a lot more obstacles before one's own intuitions will be clear enough to be reliable. One must not be too quick to rely on such intuitions in a problematic and serious situation that may arise before the achievement of such clarity. The [a]*ching* contain explicit formulations of rules, many of which are also innate to the human mind. Being explicit, they reduce the possibility of erroneous transgression. Their existence promotes single-mindedness in the individual and uniformity of moral judgment in society. For anyone but a sage to open the door too far to individual subjective standards is to invite departure from the single standard and, therefore, chaos; as Chu Hsi says, "scaling" is difficult.[80]

True to the moral intuitionism of Mencius, Chu Hsi primes his audience to expect a great deal of the intuitive moral sense ([a]*i*). Chu says that it is a kind of internal scale that enables a person to make flexible moral judgments (*ch'üan*).[81] The image of the scale predisposes the individual to assume that his own subjective judgment is not capricious but has the same presumption of consistency with a real standard that is conveyed by looking at an actual scale. He can rely on $^a i$ in deciding on the routine means of realizing some principle (e.g., choosing food that is appropriate to give to parents as an expression of filiality). He can also rely on $^a i$ in determining the relative importance of people to him, this being in part a function of intuitive familial emotions for which there is some presumption of accuracy. And he certainly can appeal to $^a i$ when an objective ritual rule ($^a li$), part of the constant principles ($^a ching$), covers the same situation.

Chu Hsi takes the moral sense completely away from most people when the situation is not one of routine means or familial emotion but involves a possible conflict between the objective rules and the subjective intuitions. The explanation can only be that on serious, complex issues he is wary of diversity of judgment. Subjectivity opens the door to such diversity. Two people can have inconsistent judgments when they appeal to their respective moral senses. The moral sense of the hermit encourages withdrawal from family; that of the Confucian requires family participation. There is no way to choose who is right, and so diversity equals disorder. Chu Hsi remains a moral intuitionist only in those cases where there is no objective rule, or where the content of the intuition revealed by the moral sense ($^a i$) is the same as that revealed by an objective authority such as a classical text. Filiality is an example. Any suggestion of conflict with the objective rule is automatically decided in favor of the objective rule. The only exception is the moral decision making of the sage, and there are few sages.

In sum, insofar as the day-to-day life of ordinary people is concerned, the ethical focus is either on removing selfish thoughts, having a proper attitude, or obeying external authorities, whether they are the constant principles ($^a ching$), rules in texts, teachers, the emperor, or the penal code. These coexist with consulting the moral sense. The individual's main concern is removing obstacles to clear intuition, not on making a free choice based on knowledge or reason. And until the obstacles are cleared, he needs the external authorities.

Once again, as was the case with the plant image, it becomes evident that the use of images can obscure as well as clarify. Much of the discussion in this chapter concerns how people ultimately do one thing rather than another. The pertinent images have been ruler-ruled and the balance scale. Both help to reinforce an over-simplified view of human motivation. The ruler-ruled image suggests that people act either to satisfy selfish desires for comfort, food, sex, wealth, or the like, or that they act in order to do the morally right thing or achieve some life goal such as sagehood. In actuality, people routinely have mixed motives. They do something both because it satisfies a selfish desire and because it is consistent with a moral standard. The reason most people do not throw a brick through the window of a restaurant in which they have had a poor meal is because of their selfish desire to avoid the discomfort of a jail cell and simultaneously because they value orderly societies in which such anarchic violence is minimized. In the case of the balance scale, the image suggests that people balance a single potential act against a single intuitive principle to see if the act is appropriate. Actually, real people compare a host of changing alternatives to several varying principles. The images therefore obscure complexity. They perpetuate an either-or description of action: a person either follows a moral principle, or he follows a human desire.

The Single-minded Personality

Mindful that each person must defer to a master, either the internal Tao mind or an external ruler, teacher, or book of teachings and rules, the analyst should now examine what concrete difference such deference should make in how the individual lives and what he believes. Previous chapters have dealt with the implications for living of other aspects of the mind. Here I draw out those implications that follow from the authoritarian strand specific to this chapter. It should be kept in mind that the masters dealt with here are respected as the modern reader respects parents or teachers, not hated as oppressive overlords.

Emotional Constraint: The Root of Frugality

Rulers and ruled fall under the general precept that (except for "mind") "all things in the world come in sets of complementary pairs."[82] Complementarity is evident in the description of the relation between heaven and earth: "Heaven gives orders; earth completes them."[83] The ideal political relationship is the harmonious interaction of the occupants of different but mutually dependent roles within a unified state. The alternative would be conflict-ridden hostility between separate antagonistic classes. The ruler's main duty is thus to transform, or win over, the ruled, not to eliminate them.

There is no question about the dominance of the Tao mind, which conquers the human mind in a relationship originally inspired by the reference in the *Analects* to "conquering the self."[84] But the image of ruling means that there is more to the relationship than conquest. The Tao mind is literally the host (*chu* means either ruler or host); the human mind, the guest. The image for the Tao mind, then, is alternately civil ruler, military general, and host. The vaguely interrelated military and civilian functions permit Chu Hsi to shift from drawing on the idea of military conquest to drawing on the more benign civil ties of ruler to ruled when it suits his purposes; therefore, such a relationship need not be permanently antagonistic. The ruler transforms the ruled through education. By analogy, the Tao mind transforms the awareness of the physical desires and directs it toward meeting a particular standard or rule. "If the Tao mind serves as ruler, the human mind will be transformed into the Tao mind."[85] "Transformation" tilts the essence of self-discipline from simple conquest, which invites severe asceticism, to cultivation. The desires need a standard.[86] If, by means of cultivation, the satisfaction of desires is always consistent with the standard, then the human mind, that is, the awareness of those physical desires, has been transformed.

The difference between conquest alone and conquest plus transformation is subtle but important.[87] The self-cultivation advocated by Chu Hsi requires constant watchfulness to avoid backsliding, and continuing education, but not a life of bitter struggle between implacable psychic enemies. He says, "To nourish [the mind] is not to struggle bitterly. Rather, it is to let the mind be empty and tranquil. Then, after a time, the mind naturally will be bright."[88]

Although Chu Hsi avoids advocating the asceticism of the monk, his ethics falls short of actually encouraging an emotionally rich life. To the contrary, his doctrine trivializes a whole range of emotional responses that are part of common human experience. It does so by differentiating between the intrinsically acceptable, or valuable, moral sentiments (compassion, shame, modesty, and the ability to discriminate between right and wrong) and those which only become acceptable when under proper guidance (love, anger, grief, joy, hate, pleasure, and so forth).[89] The two lists parallel the division between Tao mind and human mind; the former involves awareness of the moral sentiments and the latter includes consciousness of the neutral ones. The suggestion is that only the moral sentiments are innate to man's original nature,[90] which places a high value on them as intrinsically good. There is room for the neutral sentiments only when they are properly expressed in specific situations,[91] for example, joy at parental well-being and hatred of disloyalty. This means that sentiments directed toward objects that are not on the "accepted" list should be treated as insignificant, for example, love of a concubine and fear of death.[92]

The important point here is that the range of legitimate sentiments, as revealed in the examples Chu Hsi provides, is not broad. It is generally restricted to the four moral sentiments mentioned above, or to the various forms of filiality. To the extent that variety among people is a function of variety in emotional life, Chu Hsi's division of the two sets of sentiments makes clear that the former is not his priority.

In describing the pure nature revealed to a cleansed mind, Chu Hsi often says it is like a bright mirror and balanced as evenly as a scale. The latter phrase means that the pure nature, being without partiality, responds to all things appropriately, as they objectively are. Once again, the hierarchical distinction between the pure nature and the feelings serves to trivialize a whole range of experience. This includes those experiences characterized by imbalance and disequilibrium. In other words, a consuming passion for any single interest, whether music or sex, calligraphy or mathematics, is wrong because it is "partial," without intrinsic worth, or trivial. It reflects imbalance rather than the harmony appropriate to the sentiments. The only type of single-mindedness that is valid is that which leads to sagehood.

The most important point of all with respect to the desires is that they must be exercised in accordance with the rules of propriety (ᵃ*li*). Eating a gourmet meal is morally correct only if undertaken in accordance with the rules (revealed by the Tao mind); otherwise, it is the expression of a selfish desire.⁹³ Because the rules assume different rights and duties as a function of social position, the individual is to banish any desires deemed inappropriate for his social position. Beautiful food is more proper for some people than for others. This is how the idea of "conquering the self and returning to the rules" (*k'e chi fu li*) links with the hierarchy of social roles examined in Chapter Two.

Earlier I referred to the description in the *Analects* of the state Confucius attained in his last years: "At seventy, I could follow what my heart desired, without transgressing what was right."⁹⁴ Self-cultivation aims at bringing about a convergence between what a person desires and what is correct and involves inhibiting or sublimating desires for all objects that do not fit the standards. A theme central to the *Hsün-tzu* is how to cope with the imbalance in the world between the material goods available for consumption and human desire for them. Hsün Tzu's solution is to habituate each person to want only those goods appropriate for someone of his social rank in given circumstances. "If a person focuses single-mindedly on the rules of propriety and righteousness, he will end by satisfying his passions and the rules."⁹⁵ According to Hsün Tzu, the innate moral sense (ᵃ*i*, to be distinguished from the innate moral sentiments, *jen*) reveals to the individual the desires and responsibilities appropriate to his social role. Chu Hsi accepted the premise that something like that moral sense is part of the original nature in everyone. To return to the favored example of elegant foods, the moral sense will reveal that for most of the people most of the time, the frugal repast is correct. His message was particularly addressed to emperors and others with wealth and power. To be frugal in one's dining habits is to conquer selfish desires; however, the moral sense, properly interpreted by authorities, permits elaborate meals for those obligated under the ritualized rules to participate in them.

These examples tell the analyst something about the "self" Chu Hsi had in mind when he spoke of successful self-cultivation. That self is not the hollow-cheeked arhat who rarely eats and experiences no sexual passion. At the same time, it is not the whole person as he exists before the masters (including the Tao mind as his own inner Confucian master) influence him and his varied passions or his compulsive partialities. That earlier person disappears, to be replaced by someone whose passions have been redirected to acceptable objects. The image of "conquering" at least part of the self inevitably lingers in the memory of anyone who reads Chu Hsi's ethics. Later writers focused on this aspect of Chu's teaching to argue for frugality as a principal virtue. Those who conquer the self and return to the rules of propriety do not want material goods beyond those necessary for subsistence. It is an aspect of Chu Hsi that Tai Chen (1727–1777) in particular severely criticized.

Uniformity

Single-mindedness is not the same as uniformity. The former refers to an individual's having a single goal; the latter, to an unnamed condition similar in all people to whom reference is made. Chu Hsi specifically discusses single-mindedness as a principal value. He rarely deals directly with uniformity. The analyst who examines his comments on single-mindedness and other relevant topics, however, can infer that Chu Hsi endorsed uniformity of a certain kind. He advocated sameness among people in goals and in moral judgments when they are faced with comparable situations. The structural images suggest this. There should be only one ruler, the same for all people. The Tao mind as ruler means the same standard for everyone. Water's movement is in one direction only, and water springs from its source in a pure, or unmixed, state. Single-mindedness, then, is dedication to one purpose (becoming a sage, or recovering the original nature). All people should have the same purpose. The possibility of achieving uniformity lies in the universality of innate sentiments.

This is not the same as believing in the possibility or desirability of uniformity of personality. Single-mindedness means dedication to finding and preserving the internal ruler; the general principles it reveals are the same for everyone. Until people find their internal ruler, social harmony is achieved by everyone's being of one mind with the external ruler, which requires obedience to the social regulations that he sanctions. Ideally, the emperor already has the sage's impartial mind (*kung-hsin*) and his single-mindedness.

185

The group of people Chu was thinking about in his exploration of these issues probably comprised males belonging to or realistically aspiring to the official class. Outside of platitudes about the need to observe social roles, there is little in his philosophical writing that would be meaningful for a large part of the population—in his time or any time. He does not face the potential problems confronted by women or "mean people" (*chien-min*), such as ya-men runners, actors, and slaves, in any attempt they might have made to seek sagehood or form moral judgments on issues faced by scholar-officials. One should remember this restriction on relevant groups in any discussion of uniformity.

Chu Hsi was certainly mindful of the ways people differ in significant abilities and character traits, a function of differences in their physical endowments. Nearly a thousand years before his death, Chinese writers had worked out theoretical classifications of people according to differences in abilities and traits. Liu Shao's work *Jen-wu chih* focused on what Liu judged were the only abilities worthy of consideration, namely, those manifest either in public service or in scholarship.[96] The abilities (*yeh* or *ts'ai*) are innate, functions of a person's material endowment. Liu Shao distinguished twelve "personality types" (*t'i pieh*), each with its particular defect; for example, "So [when a man is] severe, strict, sharp, and resolute, his ability lies in regulating others, but his defect is to stimulate their faults."[97] Chu Hsi was no less sensitive to similar variations among people. People's material endowment is "unequal" (*pu ch'i, pu chün-p'ing*). To varying degrees it is unbalanced (*p'ien*) or correct (*cheng*), muddy (*cho*) or clear (*bch'ing*). There is ready acceptance that people do, in fact, differ in all these ways, and that the path to sagehood will differ accordingly.

Many such differences among people are most accurately expressed in negative terms. In relation to an ideal standard of purity or balance, people fall short in varying ways. The differences are not traits worth preserving. Generally, these differences are seen as determining specific problems to be addressed through self-cultivation, which involves both preserving the original nature and transforming the physical nature. With the proper transformation, many (not all) of the differences will fall away. This is especially true of those that involve impediments to clarity of moral insight and supremacy of moral motive. Chu Hsi specifically states that "the purpose of study is to change the physical nature."[98]

The special interest of the exemplary individual is not in encouraging the preservation of uniqueness of any kind; rather, it is in attaining a state of mind that, in fact, will be the same in all perfected persons. To attain this state is what Chu Hsi refers to as "diminishing differences and returning to sameness" (*ch'u ch'i i erh fan ch'i t'ung*), where "sameness" means acting in accordance with the nature that is the same in everyone.[99] Role-related duties may differ, but the fact that they must be obeyed is common to all people. Rules that are uniform for all those in specific social role relationships are given in the rites.

If personality difference is not at the center of concern, the important thing is sameness in what people feel (especially the familial sentiments that emerge from the original nature), sameness in moral judgments (using the rules of conduct underlying the social roles as the standard, a standard intuitively present in the original nature), and sameness in motives or goals (to be a sage or to recover and activate the original nature). One of the Ch'eng brothers put it this way: "When there is impartiality there is sameness. When there is selfishness, there are differences. What is most appropriate belongs to the one sameness. The essential idea is no other. What makes the minds of people different like their faces is only having selfish thoughts."[100]

In utopia the individual's mind is impartial, as are the minds of all those around him. All people are sages, their minds the same in a commitment to the cardinal value of impartiality. And so people should fix their mind on how to attain this sameness: "People's natures are good; there are differences of good and bad among them because of bad physical habits. Therefore, princely persons provide education so that people can return to goodness."[101] "Returning to goodness" is returning to the condition in which the Tao mind that is the same in all is master of the human mind. Minds are all impartial in their knowledge and affection for living things, and they naturally observe the proper role duties.

The image of water that portrays the universality of certain human traits is described as a single source flowing into various channels. The sameness of people's original nature ensures varying degrees of sameness in their actual emotions and so offers the possibility of achieving complete uniformity as a desirable ancillary effect of the ideal of social harmony. Uniformity is both an effect and a subordinate goal.

Chu Hsi does not admit the possible value of a variety of motives, and he considers all non-single-minded motives selfish. The terminology that he uses to describe variety in motivation is revealing. Variation (*tsa*) means to have several different desires, and he describes it as a state of impurity. Single-mindedness, on the other hand, suggests purity.

> The sage and the ordinary person are the same. Where they differ is in the clarity of their yang material force or the turbidity of their yin material. [As far as] the cyclical interaction of activity and tranquility is concerned, the sage is completely single-minded [*bi*], with clarity and purity supreme. In contrast, ordinary people's desires are mixed [*tsa*] and uneven.[102]

Ideally, in every action all people should be motivated by the same, single-minded desire to be a sage or obey the Tao mind.

Additional evidence of Chu's favoring uniformity is his traditionally Confucian belief in the virtue of reciprocity (*shu*), which essentially means using one's own feelings as a guide in treating others.[103] It assumes that one can "infer someone else's desires from one's own" (*t'ui chi chi jen*), implying that people share some important emotional reactions.[104] If someone feels an obligation to treat the elders in his family respectfully, he can infer that others feel the same way, and so he should try to enable them to do so. Ultimately, the possibility of uniformity in moral judgments rests in the emotions or sentiments, especially those involving the family. The original nature is first presented as familial affection. Found in all persons, as it is nurtured it becomes involved in all other virtues. Through nurturance, this one emotion can be directed at persons or things other than parents. It comes to inform the actions through which individuals comply with the social role duties of which the Tao mind is aware. In short, basic emotions that spring from the original nature and the ultimate moral standard of the Tao mind are the same in all persons.

The terminology that Chu uses is the same to describe respectively the internal path to single-mindedness (in the case of individuals) and the external route to "one mind" in the whole country. This is suggestive of reciprocal influence between the portrait of the mind and the image of politics at work in the real world. The key terms are selfishness, ruler, impartiality (*kung*), and single-mindedness or unity (*ʰi*).[105] In the case of the individual, selfish desires divert him from single-mindedness. With the selfish desires removed, the Tao-mind ruler is spontaneously impartial, and single-minded commitment to impartiality is possible. The relation between the emperor and many political factions (*tang, p'eng tang*) is that between a good ruler striving for impartiality and selfish factions seeking to divide the mind of the country. With selfish factions removed, the emperor is spontaneously impartial and single-minded in commitment to the tao. All people, including the emperor, will be of one mind, *i hsin*.

In actuality, the idea of selfishness is itself so vague as to permit its encompassing almost any position or behavior with which one disagrees. Buddhists departing for an ascetic, monastic existence can be condemned as selfish, which seems on the surface like doublespeak. (Their behavior certainly is "for the self," though not necessarily selfish.) The vagueness of selfishness provides those who employ it with yet another tool to enforce uniformity. Any interest group opposed to one's own position on a political issue could be accused of having a selfishly mixed, as opposed to a single-minded, motivation.

On issues involving goals and moral standards, therefore, Chu Hsi's value of single-mindedness blends into the idea of uniformity. He believed that the natural possibility of achieving the latter lies in the shared innate sentiments of human nature, which makes the same principles accessible to everyone. The practical possibility lies in the mind of the emperor, the "basis of the world," whose goals and standards can be emulated by all persons.

CONCLUSION

Single-mindedness is intrinsically interesting in stressing purposiveness as a basic character trait that all persons should actively seek. At the same time, it is derivatively significant because of the idea of uniformity, with which it is associated. In terms of China's own philosophical tradition, single-mindedness and uniformity contributed to the belief that social consensus is possible and is contingent only upon the rulers' fulfilling their educational obligations to themselves and others. This Neo-Confucian idea of uniformity on goals and moral judgments is also consistent with the prevailing view in premodern Western ethics. In Europe it was not until the late eighteenth and early nineteenth centuries that the idea emerged that uniqueness was desirable in matters of judgment and life goals, especially among German romantics. As Arthur Danto has noted, Kant, whose glorification of autonomy has influenced so many thoughtful Europeans, expected that all rational people would come to the same conclusion in judging a single moral situation.[106]

The political image often provides the justification for either controlling or trivializing other emotions that, if cultivated, could serve as a basis for encouraging variety rather than conformity. In addition, Chu Hsi believed in uniform duties for occupants of the established social roles. In broad outline these were conveyed in the traditional Confucian rules of conduct or rites (^{a}*li*). Centuries earlier, the Neo-Taoist poet T'ao Ch'ien (365–?427) considered himself an outsider to the world governed by the rites. He described himself as one who "does not fit the common rhyme-scheme" (*wu shih su-yün*) and would be well advised to go back to his family farm and stay out of trouble.[107] Chu Hsi might criticize existing official behavior, but he never questioned the desirability of a common rhyme scheme.

Self-effort and self-discovery are important to the process of becoming a sage, as noted in Chapter Three's discussion of the investigation of things and embodiment and in the treatment of the cultivation of reverential concentration and examination of motives in Chapter Four. These activities coexist with the call for obedience to objective authority discussed in the present chapter. A possible incompatibility between them arises because of the implications of what Chu has to say about the long period when the mind is cloudy, and a person is only dimly aware of his inner ruler. During this time he needs models and winds to bend him.

But there is no consistent or clear answer in Chu's writings to the question of when an individual should follow the inner authority and when the outer ones, and if the answer should be the outer ones, there is no guidance on which of them should be followed. The doctrines in Chapter Four point to the inner ruler; those in the present chapter, to the outer ones. But the question of which and when remains murky. The stakes in this tension are not small. Concretely, the direction in which an individual tilts when considering the relevance of authority may affect his understanding of the good life. For example, the imperial authority may stress those elements in Chu Hsi that call for frugality and austerity through the conquest of desires. On the other side, the individual's own voice may permit a wide and rich range of activities so long as, like sweeping and watering the floor, he has cleansed them by his attitude of reverential concentration.

TWO POLARITIES AND THEIR MODERN LEGACY: THE MORAL SENSE AND ITS CONTENT

Chu's writings contain the key to Confucian explanations of how social order and personal tranquility are achieved. That key is the cultivation of what in common speech would be called the conscience. In the Confucian case, however, its content is innately fixed. Included in that content are the principles and feelings appropriate to personal relationships, especially family ones. Insight into the indubitable sentiment of family love is for Confucian ethics what Descartes's *cogito ergo sum* is for his epistemology. It is the intuitive first principle on which the individual builds all subsequent moral judgments. In this chapter I deal with the traces in the modern era of Chu's ideas about the moral sense. Many of these traces have been suggested by the two polarities in terms of which I have examined this moral sense, namely, self-discovery versus reliance on objective authority, and family love versus universal love.

Before turning to those developments, however, it is fitting to begin my concluding observations by considering the likely modern fate of structural images in Chinese theories about man, society, and nature. I refer not to the specific images that Chu Hsi selected but rather to the general question of the continued use of such images as explanatory devices. After coming to some conclusion regarding the technique's likely longevity, I will turn to this book's central themes and consider their destiny as China moves through the modern period.

STRUCTURAL IMAGES

There is every good reason to believe that theoreticians in modern China will continue to use structural images in formulating their doctrines. The best way of testing such a contention is to try to identify the strongest possible argument that could be made against it, which is that Chinese thought may be evolving toward a kind of positivism in which structural images have no place. In this line of thinking, even metaphysical theories have no place; only description of empirical regularities is relevant. The observations that follow thus constitute an attempt to develop this counterargument to my position.

I began in Chapter One with the observation that, at least in the case of Chu Hsi, structural images were often used in discussions of theories employing "explanatory fictions" such as heaven, tao, principle, and human nature. This positivistic term refers to unobservable entities that supposedly cause all kinds of observable regularities in nature, from seasonal cycles to human family behavior. The "fictions" need the support of pictorial images in order to describe how the things to which they (or theories about them) refer interact with each other. The two often, but not always, go together in Chu Hsi's works: discussions of such "fictions" as heaven, tao, principle, and human nature are paired with images such as family, stream of water, plant, and government. Either the "fictions" or the structural images can be called "explanatory devices." The former explain perceived regularities and the latter describe the integrated relationships among the facts to which the "fictions" refer.

Each type of device has its drawbacks. I noted in Chapter One the dangerous influence of the images on Chu Hsi's own thinking. From a positivistic standpoint, the "fictions," in turn, may be "thought terminating": they may encourage a person to believe that he has an explanation of the regularities when he in fact knows nothing more than he did before introducing one, namely, that there are certain patterns in nature.

The reader may well wonder if he should now expect the prediction that Chinese thinkers, as they become mindful of the drawbacks of these two intertwined explanatory devices, will abandon them both—in short, become positivists. A competing prediction is that Chinese thinkers will continue to use both types of explanatory devices, though perhaps for different reasons. When they use the "fictions," they will continue to require the structural images, and adjustment to the drawbacks of this technique may simply follow.

In considering the first prediction, I will assume the positivistic perspective and so drop the quotation marks around "fictions." There is at least enough evidence to formulate, for the sake of inquiry, a hypothesis that there is a trend in the history of Chinese philosophy toward the gradual reduction—and, perhaps, elimination—of the fictions. This is not a trend in which every school or figure can be said to have taken part. But there is a pattern, alongside the other movements, and its representatives are of some significance. By viewing the Chou-Han period as a time in which each of the explanatory fictions had a discrete meaning, it is possible to identify two subsequent, broadly conceived stages in the pattern: a reduction in the number of independent and discrete explanatory fictions and, sometime thereafter, their elimination.

One sign that the reduction stage has begun is the equation of many fictions, inevitably resulting in fewer of them. Indications of this trend can be identified in Ch'an Buddhism, before Chu Hsi's time. A disciple of the famous Southern Ch'an master Shen Hui has left these remarks:

> Someone asked, "What is the tao? What is principle? What is mind?" The answer was: "The mind is the tao, the mind is principle, and so there is no principle outside the mind and no mind outside the principle. From the standpoint of the mind's ability to classify we call it principle, from the standpoint of principle's being bright so it can be understood we call it mind."[1]

The general idea in passages like this, whether Buddhist or Neo-Confucian, is that different terms serve simply to highlight different aspects of a single entity. Consider the following discussion involving Ch'eng I:

> [Pai-wen asked again, concerning a *Mencius* passage,] "Do mind, the nature, and heaven refer simply to the single thing principle?" [Ch'eng I] answered, "When we speak from the standpoint of principle, we call it heaven; from the standpoint

194

of what humans receive as endowment, we call it the nature, and from the standpoint of what is preserved internally, we call it mind."[2]

In yet another example of the same kind of formulation, Chu Hsi interprets and elaborates on Ch'eng I's view:

Principle is one. From the standpoint of what heaven bestows on the myriad things, we call it *ming* [what is decreed]. From the standpoint of what they receive from heaven, we call it the nature.[3]

In the case of both Ch'eng I and Chu Hsi two formerly discrete explanatory fictions (here, heaven and nature) become equated with *li* (principle); each refers to a different way of thinking about it. Mind must be excluded because, although Ch'eng I equates it with principle, Chu Hsi treats it as the material container of principle. Let me consider how *li* explains each major fiction.

In the *Book of Changes*, the Great Ultimate (*t'ai chi*) was symbolic of origin, which gives rise to the symbolic sets of unbroken and broken lines and thereby to everything else. For Chu Hsi, *t'ai chi* refers to the aggregate of all the *li*, carrying over from its earlier usage the idea of something that encompasses everything.[4] Next, according to Chu Hsi's reductionism, use of the term "heaven" in place of *li* conveys the ideas that the *li* account for all changes that are natural and therefore unalterable and that the *li* are worthy of human reverence. Third, use of the term "tao" implies that the *li* are responsible for an order that incorporates morality. Accommodation to that order brings about ease of both mind and body; transgression creates difficulties. Fourth, *ming* means a decree, something fixed, and so, by extension, refers to the life span. As a substitute for *li*, it points to the timelessness or fixed nature of natural classes or orders of things. Such classes—and their characteristics—are fixed before the occurrence of events that are manifestations of them. Nothing happens unless there is a *li* that dictates its occurrence. The *li* of a thing is what is decreed for it, meaning its probable qualities and behavior. Finally, *hsing* (the original nature) points to *li* as something present in the individual thing at birth, sometimes called its *li-hsing*. And so during Chu

195

Hsi's stage in this hypothetical trend toward Chinese positivism, explanatory devices are reduced to a single one, namely, ^{b}li, to each different aspect of which the name of a previously independent explanatory fiction is attached.

The elimination stage of the hypothetical trend is an expression of the spirit of practicality prevailing in the late Ming and early Ch'ing. Stimulated in part by the fall of the Ming dynasty to the Manchus, one aspect of this interest in practical matters centered around questions of technical utility: how to build better forts, how to take better advantage of China's geographical attributes, and so on. The other aspect was a rejection of supposedly impractical speculation about the terms that provide a causal explanation of things, terms such as "heaven," "human nature," and "mind." Advocates of the practical approach favored concern with actual moral problems facing the individual or his country. Criticizing the Neo-Confucian legacy, Ku Yen-wu (1613–1682) said:

> Accordingly, we see that human nature, divine order, and heaven were topics upon which Confucius seldom touched per se, but present-day scholars are occupied with them every moment without reference to realities. Again, the questions of being in public service or staying out of it, of accepting or declining official appointments, were subjects to which Confucius paid much attention. But scholars of the present day are not interested in them at all.[5]

Ku Yen-wu favored avoiding discussions of what the positivists would call explanatory fictions, unless such discussions could somehow be tied in with solutions to practical problems.

Typical of the monistic materialists in this final stage of the hypothetical trend is Tai Chen (1723–1777). He continued to use some of the explanatory fiction terminology favored by Chu Hsi; however, he redefined terms so that they lost virtually all trace of references to any abstract, nonempirical entity. No longer did they denote something transcendental, superior to matter, separate from or "prior to" matter, and responsible for its ideal behavior. In Tai's discussions, ^{b}li means nothing more than the patterns of change or the order in matter. In humans, it is not something sent by heaven, residing in the mind and different from the emotions.

The tao is only matter, or the endless changes of matter, including its capacity for reproduction. *bLi* is found only in human relations and in daily life. There is no "original" nature of man (*pen-hsing*), only his physical nature, composed of blood, breath, and intellect.

The positivist's position would be that explanatory fictions exist because they supposedly explain natural regularities. His prediction would be that as a result of the developments in the final stage of the trend symbolized by the ideas of Ku Yen-wu and Tai Chen, such fictions can be expected to disappear. People will be content simply to know the regularities. For purposes of facilitating prediction or divination, instead of worrying about the role of the fictions they can be content with purely statistical guidebooks. And, with the disappearance of the fictions, the structural images that are their aids will pass away as well. People need only to describe, and thus do not require the services of a fiction or its supporting structural image.

Here again Tai Chen provides an apt example, that of the thinker whose doctrines are consistent with the elimination phase of this postulated trend. For example, in what may be his most important work, the *Meng-tzu tzu-i su-cheng* (Evidential explanations of the meaning of terms in the *Mencius*), his only philosophical use of a structural image is to explain mind. He says either that mind is to body as the emperor is to the people, or that mind is like a light ray (a concept discussed at length in Chapter Three). He is clearly mindful of the uses to which the most popular structural images in Chinese thought have been put, referring, for example, to the Taoist and Buddhist use of water to explain the original clarity of human nature;[6] otherwise, Tai generally abstains from mentioning structural images in his discourses.

The development of the hypothetical positivistic position is useful because it compels the analyst to deal with the question of why people use explanatory devices, whether "fictions" or structural images. Perhaps it is the idea that one is dealing with entities that explain genuine regularities, thereby helping in prediction. This might be called a "scientific" reason for using them; it is the most vulnerable reason, however, if statistical guidebooks can convincingly take the place of the explanatory devices. But there are also nonscientific reasons that have to do less with an interest in prediction than with other factors. To the degree that these other factors can be identified, one can be sure that the explanatory devices will continue to be used. This is because they will be unaffected by any positivistic currents or trends such as I have hypothetically traced for China. In other words, abstractions like (but not necessarily the same as) heaven, tao, principle, and human nature will continue to exist no matter how accurate the statistical guidebooks prove to be in forecasting the future. And, along with the abstractions, the structural images will also endure.

One of these nonscientific reasons is the contribution of such devices to psychological tranquility. For example, the abstract explanatory devices classify and thereby introduce order into the experience of phenomena. "Heaven" supplies a place for objective natural events; "mind" supplies one for subjective psychological events. Such concrete images contribute to peace of mind by providing all phenomena with a structure that seems to explain how they are related. Events do not remain chaotic when structured. Someone who takes these devices seriously receives *understanding* about the world, not truth. In understanding lies tranquility.

A second nonscientific reason is aesthetic.[7] In Neo-Confucian writings, heaven suggests height and requires reverential treatment. Water connotes purity, freshness, and clarity. Other images suggest other ideas. Depending on how they are worked into a description, images like these can have strong aesthetic appeal. People may construct their accounts of reality so as to incorporate things considered beautiful; inspired by those beautiful traits, they then characterize nature accordingly.

The third nonscientific reason, related to the second and pertaining to the structural images, has played a central role in this book. I have tried to show that, in addition to clarifying the relationships among facts to which theories apply, the structural images justify certain values. And they persuade the reader who is affected by them to act in a certain way. The images accomplish this in part because they are emotive, drawing out responses that are a function of Chinese society and the historical events of Chu Hsi's time. They are capable of eliciting fear, zeal, anger, or almost any powerful sentiment. The emotions generate responses that can imply specific duties, and these duties are associated with specific values or goods. If the examples of the preceding chapters have established that structural images do serve this function, the structural images will endure, among other reasons to support values that the author of a theory may want to justify. In this connection, they have both sociological and political uses. They are ready-made tools for rulers, effective sometimes for good—and doubtless equally as often for bad—ends.

One can therefore reject the positivist's prediction. Neither eighteenth- nor twentieth-century appearances of positivistic features in China are likely to mean the end of "explanatory fictions" or of structural analogies. These devices—even if they have no scientific merit (which has not been proved)—will continue to exist on other grounds. As older "fictions" disappear, new ones will rise to replace them. New structural images will appear, perhaps to explain relations among facts, perhaps to justify values. The plant image is probably gone for good, a victim of its conservative association with cyclical, rather than progressive, change.[8] In modern China, some of the "fictions" will belong to universally shared scientific theories on waves, particles, black holes, quasars. Similarly, some images will have universal quasi-scientific status, such as computer-based explanations of the mind: cognitive development as akin to increasingly sophisticated information processing by machine.

Other entities will be more specific to China's particular ideology and culture. Chinese Marxist theories concerning the forces of production and dialectic, for example, fit here. These, too, will continue to rely on structural images, such as that of the ladder used by Chinese Marxist writers to illustrate theories of social change. Rungs on the ladder correspond to stages of human development. Small wonder that, early in the People's Republic, such writers were already describing new institutions that would lead upward to a final utopia as China's "heavenly ladder" (*t'ien-t'i*).

As will be argued in the sections that follow, the "fiction" deriving from Mencius and reworked by Chu Hsi that is most likely to endure in modern China is the idea of a universal moral sense. I leave this discussion of explanatory devices with two intriguing questions: What structural image will emerge to support such a concept? How will it interact with the competing image of the mind as an information-processing machine?

The Portrait of Human Nature

A Menu of Choices

Moving beyond expectations about the future usage of Chu Hsi's type of explanatory image, the analyst is left with the future course of Chu's portrait of human nature. In that portrait, the moral mind and its obstructions are in the forefront. The preceding chapters have revealed how exceedingly diverse is the content of the mind: hierarchical social roles (justified by the family image applied to nature), pure principle (the stream of water), cognition (the light source), life principle or sentiments such as love that develop in stages (plant growth), and tension between heavenly principles and human desires (ruler-ruled). Though all of these are interrelated, they do provide Chu Hsi's reader with the semblance of a choice of what to emphasize about human nature. And, as I noted in discussing the self-discovery and authority polarity, Chu's vagueness leaves the reader with a choice of means to resolve the Tao mind-human mind tension.[9] He can opt to stress reverential concentration (ᵇching) and associated self-cultivation activities, or he can choose to emphasize one or more of the authorities (books, emperor, true Confucian models). He may speak about the individual who ensures that his desires are satisfied in accordance with the ritual rules. Or, he may focus on the authorities who, through education, bring uniformity to the minds of the people to help them conquer desires and abide by universal values. The range of these options is the starting point for this essay on Chu's likely long-term impact.

In imperial China, those who claimed to accept some or all of Chu's teachings were a diverse group: oppressive emperors, emperors who were strict yet benign, officeholders, aspirants to official position, and those who wanted nothing to do with officialdom. But they all believed in the existence of an innate moral sense possessed by each person. There was also some overlapping of their views of the mind, in particular, of their belief in universal values such as propriety in human relationships and selfless impartiality. In making distinctions among them, however, it is useful to think about what each of them chose to stress about the moral mind in his writings. The mind might primarily contain the Three Bonds (the social role duties); or principles of right and wrong; or sagelike wisdom (integrated patterns of order in the world, of which the sage has totalistic knowledge); or love between father and son that can extend to love of all people and things. Any such account of the content of the mind also included enumeration of the selfish desires that partially obscure the mind's moral content and may make some men evil.

Chu's influence extended over too long a time, and the fluctuating nature of that influence is too complex, to deal with here. Moreover, others have already eloquently told part of the story.[10] What can be offered here, on the basis of the preceding chapters, is some guidance on how to think about the legacy of Chu's concept of human nature.

The method selected to trace the legacy, then, involves looking for the relative weight that a later thinker gives to one or more of the possible components of the moral mind, while remembering the overlapping traits that were accepted by all. Also important to note is the degree of stress given to the obscuring desires and the particular technique selected for dealing with them. Chu's successors have a menu to choose from. The analyst can single out the distinctive characteristics of subsequent Confucian ideas while identifying their common roots in his writings that touch on the moral mind, although there is, of course, some variation in the different editions of his writings on which different successors relied. Using this procedure, it should ultimately be possible to assign modern individuals to the Chu tradition, even though they may not acknowledge their own indebtedness to the master.

Some Premodern Examples

I will illustrate the approach by considering briefly the cases of some well-known heirs of Chu's doctrines in the imperial period. It is tempting to treat the tension between the Tao mind and the human mind as central to the legacy, and selfless obedience to role duties and frugality (reflecting conquest of desires) as core values.

This is because so many famous emperors and scholars who made Chu's doctrines orthodoxy focused on these issues, handing down a legacy that stresses objective authorities. In the case of the emperors, this approach was probably seen as supportive of imperial autocracy for all the reasons discussed in Chapter Five: everyone's mind needs a master, so when the ministers' or people's minds are cloudy, external masters step in legitimately to complete the nurturing process the people are themselves unable to finish. The sagelike ruler properly assumes this responsibility because, assuming that all clear minds reveal the same principles, what his mind reveals will be the same as what theirs would reveal were they clear. He in turn models his actions on those of the sage-kings of old who understood nature's principles. Some examples will help to illustrate this authoritarian choice. Mindful of the range of traits to highlight within the content of the mind, I will also try to round out the picture by noting those who departed from the authoritarian strand yet have legitimate links with Chu.

A number of scholars and emperors who concentrated heavily on the conquest of selfish desires also stressed intuitive knowledge of the basic role sets, selflessness, and disciplined obedience to the role duties. William Theodore de Bary has charted the course of Chu's ideas from the time of his immediate successors through the Yüan and the first part of the Ming. In particular, he has shown how those successors moved away from Chu's twin interest in the investigation of things and the rectification of the mind toward primary concern with the moral mind. Chen Te-hsiu treated self-cultivation as the basis of imperial leadership and rectification of the mind as a key to part of that process. His message was the severe "no desires" one of Chou Tun-i, whose essential teaching was "subdue the self." According to de Bary, Chen addressed this "rigorism" to those whose wealth and power led them to self-indulgence.[11] Some future rulers inverted this message and demanded frugality by ordinary people.

An admirer of Chen, Hsü Heng (1209–1281) served as a teacher to Mongol rulers.[12] In 1313 Chu's doctrine became orthodoxy for civil-service examination purposes under the Mongols. The Ch'eng-Chu teaching of the moral mind endured after the fall of the Mongols. The third Ming emperor, Ch'eng-tsu (r. 1402–1424), compiled a work modeled on one by Chen Te-hsiu. Entitled *Sheng-hsüeh hsin-fa* (The system of the mind in the learning of the sages), it deals with, among other things, the Tao mind-human mind tension. It continues Chen's emphasis on self-discipline, the need for serious moral purpose, and the need to guard against selfish desires. It also stresses the appropriateness of heavenly rank differences and the unity of the minister's mind with that of the emperor. These themes seem to take center stage, although, like any follower of Chu, Ch'eng-tsu also makes a place for conforming with principle, reverential concentration, and loving the people.

John Dardess has described the teachings of a small group of late Yüan Ch'eng-Chu Confucians in the Chekiang area. Its members had an impact on the man who was to found the Ming, Ming T'ai-tzu. One of them, Liu Chi (1311–1375), could write simultaneously about the people's possible possession of an innate conscience (*liang-chih*) and their need to be pushed in the right direction by a ruler-teacher:[13] "The Sage establishes moral doctrine in such a way that the people's latent goodness is drawn forth and extended. His sympathy moves people and fosters them. . . . Heaven, Earth and parents give birth to the people, and the ruler-teacher completes them. If the people do not respond, then though they are called men, they are indistinguishable from beasts."[14] Liu believed that the masses are ignorant—and not just the masses. Like others in his group, he regarded the Confucians (*ju*) and literati (*shih*) from whom the officials were recruited as hopelessly corrupted by their selfish desires.[15] A model Ming official of a later day, Hai Jui (d. 1587), described the peasants as impulsive, driven by animal instincts, unthinking, and ruthless.[16]

Ming T'ai-tzu, who regarded himself as a proponent of Chu's ideas, wrote:

What is given and constant in the inborn nature is the Three Bonds and Five Constants [benevolence, righteousness, decorum, wisdom, reliability]. The sages formulated human moral relations on the basis of their understanding of the human condition. They did not do this in contravention of human nature, but pursued what was good in it. Thus they set up the Bonds and Constants for a myriad generations. No one has ever become ruler of men by deviating from this principle.[17]

He also believed that the minds of the Chinese people are cloudy and their selfish desires dominate. In sum, the stress is on hierarchy, roles, and strict control by the sole figure of the emperor in order to repair the mental damage and return the people to their original mind.[18] Frugality comes into existence when people (including the educated elite)[19] successfully conquer their desires.[20]

The K'ang-hsi emperor (r. 1662–1722) was a great admirer of Chu Hsi. K'ang-hsi said that "all of our learning comes from reverential concentration and carefulness."[21] From this it would appear that he appreciated the introspective, self-examining side of Chu's formulation; however, the obligation to enforce social role-related rules is more pronounced in his published statements. No section of K'ang-hsi's sixteen-part "Sheng-yü" (Sacred edict) of 1670 (a list of prescriptions summing up Neo-Confucian values) deals with self-discovery. Yet many sections deal with obeying the rules: "Esteem filial piety and brotherly submission," the opening section proclaims, "in order to emphasize the importance of the human relationships." And he writes later, "Clearly display propriety and yielding, in order to make customs genuine."[22] As for frugality, the fifth section admonishes, "Prize thriftiness in order carefully to use your property." By 1736 there was a requirement that periodic lectures be given in all villages in China on the *Sheng-yü kuang-hsün* (Amplified expositions on the "Sacred Edict"), written by K'ang-hsi's son, the Yung-cheng emperor.[23]

Both K'ang-hsi and his son treated uniformity of mind imposed by the emperor as a solution to the selfishness that can fragment society. Though not an advocate of imperial autocracy, Chu also valued the whole society's being "of one mind," as did most subsequent Confucians, and believed that the emperor could play a role in promoting uniformity.[24] From classical times Confucians maintained that a person derives legitimacy for acts by emulating the mind of a model ancestor, if he is a ruler; that of the emperor, if he is an official; or that of both emperor and officials, if he is a commoner. This is the way to realize "one mind" uniformity in the country. As the Yung-cheng emperor wrote in the preface to his exposition of the "Sheng-yü," "I take the late Emperor Sheng-tzu's mind [i.e., K'ang-hsi's mind] as my mind, and his government as my government."[25] Elsewhere, he says that people should take his mind as their mind, because his interest is always vastly impartial (*ta kung*), the same sagelike quality that Chu Hsi ascribed to successful self-cultivation. Yung-cheng's own preferences flesh out the rules of conduct, designed by the sages, that he also enforces. In his essay "P'eng tang lun" (On factions), he warns his ministers: "When one is a minister he should know only that he has a ruler. Then his sentiments will be firm and incapable of unraveling, and he can love and hate the same as a ruler does. This is called being one in virtue and mind, and the high and low in inseparable communication."[26] And in a proclamation to *chü-jen* degree-holders assembled for the capital examination, Yung-cheng explained, "I look upon the whole population as one body. Above all, this applies to those scholars and *chü-jen* degree-holders who can someday become my arms and legs and eyes and ears. This is why in my heart I really treat them as a single connected body."[27]

The authoritarian strands described above are not the only ones in Chu's legacy. The analyst should also be alert for heirs of Chu's teachings who tilted in other directions. Irene Bloom has introduced one such thinker, a Ming defender of the Ch'eng-Chu school, named Lo Ch'in-shun (1465–1547). Unlike many of the supporters of imperial Chu Hsi orthodoxy, Lo attempted to unify the innate heavenly principles and the human desires. In his view, desires do not cause evil; thus, the primary task confronting the individual is not the conquest of desires but the preservation and nurturing of the original nature, namely, the heavenly principles.[28]

During the Yüan dynasty, many literati did not become officials, yet still believed that they were acting as responsible Confucians. Among the prominent Confucians of the fifteenth and sixteenth centuries, a number resisted government service. Such action enhanced their attraction as alternatives to the emperor in the area of moral authority. They sought to live a rigorous moral life as scholars, such as that exemplified by Chu Hsi when he was out of office. There is nothing in the previous descriptions in this book of Chu's views on selfishness that is incompatible with their agendas. But they leaned in the direction of treating the mind more as a repository of the integrated patterns in the universe than as something hopelessly clouded over by desires. Uncovering the principles was considered an arduous task, so difficult that official service would interfere with it. Yet these men were sufficiently optimistic about the possibility of success to forego service and devote themselves to principles. The example of Wu Yü-pi (1391–1469) is instructive here. From the age of nineteen Wu refused to take the civil-service examinations. He studied the *Five Classics* and the writings of the Sung masters instead. He worked his own land and required the same of his students. Though the son of a Hanlin official, he refused the emperor's offer of appointment to office.[29]

A number of other early Ming Confucians emphasized investigating the principles in the mind more than in books. So reverential concentration (ᵇ*ching*) takes precedence in their list of priorities over the consultation of objective sources of authority. Using the image of the mirror that Chu had also favored, one of them (Hsüeh Hsüan, 1392–1464) wrote: "The mind is like a mirror and seriousness [ᵇ*ching*] is like polishing. When the mirror is polished, the dust will be removed and brightness will grow. When the mind becomes serious, human selfish desires will disappear and the Principle of Nature will become brilliant."[30] This passage places greater stress on the mind's capability for totalistic knowledge than on its being covered with a veil of unalterably selfish desires.

Others have argued that Wang Yang-ming thought he was being faithful to a number of Chu's themes.[31] I would add that even some of the doctrines supposed to be most characteristic of Wang, such as the unity of knowledge and action, owe much to the Ch'eng-Chu school.[32] In addition, Wang inherited a considerable amount of the structural imagery crucial to Chu's explanations. There are grounds, then, for seeking alternatives or supplements to the heavy stress on the Tao mind-human mind tension in Wang's writings and for treating them as additional threads of the Chu legacy that also are worth noting. It is true that Wang made a place for the selfishness that is supposed to obscure the heavenly principles, and he even explained the matter using Chu's images:

It [the mind] is like a bright mirror. It is entirely clear, without a speck of dust attached to it. Only when all such selfish desires as the love for sex, wealth, fame, and so forth in one's daily life are completely wiped out and cleaned up so that not the least bit is retained, and the mind becomes broad in its total substance and becomes identified with the Principle of nature, can it be said to have achieved equilibrium before the feelings are aroused and to have acquired the great foundation of virtue.[33]

When Wang introspected, he found more than selfish desires. He found the moral mind as the intuitive sense of right and wrong that all people possess and also familial sentiments for his father and grandmother. Like Chu, Wang employed the plant image to link development of the moral sense with cosmic processes of change. Expanding stages of growth in compassion, then, were described as corresponding to stages in plant growth:

Take a tree, for example. When in the beginning it puts forth a shoot, there is the starting point of the tree's spirit of life. After the root appears, the trunk grows. After the trunk grows, branches and leaves come, and then the process of unceasing production and reproduction has begun. . . . The love between father and son and between elder and younger brothers is the starting point of the human mind's spirit of life, just like the sprout of the tree. From here it is extended to humaneness to all people and love to all things. It is just like the growth of the trunk, branches and leaves.[34]

Within the mind, the individual can discover the root of family love and the possibility of altruism.

Not everyone was a follower of Chu. Even prior to the fall of the Ming, individual Confucian scholars repudiated Chu Hsi. In particular, the prominent seventeenth-century figures Huang Tsung-hsi (1610–1695), Fang I-chih (1611–1671), and Ku Yen-wu (1613–1682) showed little interest in the content of the mind and did not consider themselves continuators of the teachings of any prior master.[35] They were partisans of Evidential Research, a movement that had begun in the previous century. Some scholars associated with this movement used philology to try to undercut one of Chu's principal teachings, arguing that the Old Text chapter of the *Book of History* containing the Tao mind-human mind distinction is a forgery. They moved away from any split between the desires and a higher self, expanded the number of authoritative texts to include classics beyond the *Four Books*, and focused their energies less on self-cultivation than on such technical fields as astronomy, hydraulics (for flood control), and cartography.[36] The sages, they believed, were interested less in transcendental principles than in how to organize society efficiently and properly. Another issue on which some of these individuals took a stand was the kind of imperial autocracy that some emperors tried to justify in the name of Chu Hsi orthodoxy. Huang Tsung-hsi wrote that in the time of the sage-kings, "the emperor did not dare to determine right and wrong for himself, so he left to the schools the determination of right and wrong."[37]

It is especially interesting that many men in this school and their eighteenth-century successors chose not to seek government posts for a variety of historical reasons. For example, even though Ku's tao was the Confucian tao, in the 1670s he wrote that if one has a son one should not allow him to study for the official examinations, but should let him be a merchant, craftsman, or laborer instead.[38] Family ties were of paramount importance in his view. Fang I-chih decided that writing books that incorporated lessons drawn from history to serve as models for the emperor and others could have greater social benefit than official public service.[39] In any case, one important point is that these men differed in outlook from the followers of Chu Hsi to whom I have referred. Unlike the fifteenth- and sixteenth-century Neo-Confucians who stayed out of office to practice self-cultivation and thereby ultimately to gain the totalistic knowledge of the sage, these individuals stayed out of office to satisfy themselves with the incremental results of Evidential Research on empirical topics. The most famous eighteenth-century philosopher to carry on the Evidential Research spirit was the Han Learning specialist Tai Chen. He attacked Chu's use of a famous *Analects* phrase to explain "self" as synonymous with selfish desires that must be conquered. Confucians, Tai argued, did not advocate the absence of desires.[40]

Among the historical factors that help to explain these shifts were inquisitions into the activities of literati; they constituted an incentive to avoid the limelight and undertake instead textual scholarship of the kind to which some Han Learning scholars turned. Loyalty to the Ming could turn men away from the introspective topics popular when the Ming dynasty was weakening politically and toward new, supposedly practical themes from which the direct social benefits to a dynasty were more obvious.

Chu's defenders never died out. As China moved through the first half of the nineteenth century, Fang Tung-shu (1772–1851) mounted a counterattack against the attempt by Tai Chen and others to substitute the new philology for Sung Neo-Confucianism. Fang defended Chu Hsi and what he regarded as Chu's core teaching: honoring the moral nature (*tsun te-hsing*) takes precedence over following the path of study and inquiry.[41] Fang said that Mencius was correct that *jen* cannot be understood simply as the practice of humaneness but must also be "the virtue of the mind." According to Fang, the Evidential Research scholars did not comprehend that people need purpose in life and that purpose comes from a knowledge of the moral sense. In many cases, he argued, the philologists themselves, without acknowledging it, relied on some standard in choosing between competing interpretations of words. Although they denied the existence of innate principles in the mind, there was nowhere else for them to find such a standard.[42] And the heroes of the imperial government's successful effort to put down the T'ai-p'ing Rebellion were strong supporters of Chu's orthodoxy. The Chu school, therefore, was not moribund in the mid-nineteenth century.

THE MORAL SENSE IN THE MODERN PERIOD

The thesis of this section is that the idea of an innate moral sense (or of the sentiment that is part of its content) is alive in twentieth-century China and will continue to be a competitor for the attention of thoughtful persons. There is at least one influential study that might be used to oppose this thesis.[43] It states that Chinese now find in the objective political and technological world the tools for tapping a problem-solving power that they had previously sought in the mind, traditionally supposed to derive its power from links with a cosmic force of good. Given the existence of the newly found scientific tools and methods of political participation, the argument would run, people need no longer be concerned with an innate moral mind.

My response to this line of reasoning would be that my own study of Chu's concept of the mind reveals it to be a complex mix of different traits. It is more than a source of power for moral effort. It includes, among other things, a sense of right and wrong and of social role duties, as well as humanitarian sentiments that can be extended to a broad range of people. Some of these claims are as plausible in the twentieth century as they were in the twelfth, and this may give added vitality to Chu's idea of the mind. In fact, there are recent Chinese writers who work these ideas into their own doctrines. In addition, I would argue that the notion of attending to a moral sense is a defensible one. Just because people can control nature does not mean that they can dispense with setting priority standards for problems, determining appropriate methods for solving them, and deciding when they have been solved. There is a basis for arguing that intuition or the emotions may play a legitimate role in the discovery of the standards used in these judgments. Without admitting it, some Marxist-Leninists in China appeal to such sources to derive their first principles (the laws of historical change, the inevitability of socialism, the need for party rule). And the possession by citizens of a cultivated conscience built on moral intuitions may be of fundamental importance in ensuring harmony in any society.

Assertions about what constitutes Chu's legacy are easier to make about the imperial period because scholars and emperors identified themselves as heirs to the tradition. Within the modern period, to which I now turn, there are often only unlabeled threads of doctrine. But the broad strokes of continuity are there, with or without a label. Continuity is a plausible hypothesis. There were many types of Confucian doctrine in premodern China, and Chu does not represent them all. Still, the impact of his ideas was pervasive. Therefore, it is reasonable to focus on him and to try to note his legacy, while granting the existence of other strands in the modern period.

Selflessness as Uniform Discipline

I am about to uncover movements that stress uniform obedience to authority and those that emphasize intuitive self-discovery of truths, and both have antecedents in Chu's writings. Western readers may be reminded of a thinker whose writings contain the same philosophical tension between objective authority and introspection, namely, Jean-Jacques Rousseau. Rousseau based his ethics on the existence of an innate "conscience" equally present in all men.[44] *Émile or Education* opens with the observation that "God makes all things good; man meddles with them, and they become evil."[45] These words set the theme that society corrupts man by leading him away from the natural condition in which he can harmonize his competing desires and find harmony with other people. In short, society alienates him. The tutor in *Émile* is the source of an education that deflects the corruption and permits the natural potential to evolve. Education thus provides an antidote to socially induced alienation.

Certain European socialists, influenced by Rousseau's idea of alienation, developed doctrines that shifted away from his interest in the inner moral conscience. They emphasized instead the need to change society in order to end the estrangement of man from his true self. They implied that such social changes should be forced on people who oppose them, in the name of doing what is in the interest of their true selves, from which they are alienated.[46] Karl Marx is the most famous of the socialists who plucked this potentially authoritarian aspect from Rousseau and made thoroughgoing use of it, leaving behind the inner moral sense. When considering the modern legacy in China of the polarity between objective authority and self-discovery, Westerners should be mindful of Chu's Western counterpart; Rousseau incorporated both of these poles in his own doctrines, and his successors magnify one.

The Chu Hsi of imperial orthodoxy was often the Chu Hsi of Chen Te-hsiu, who focused on "conquering the self." While some individual Confucian thinkers may have praised the virtue of frugality through reduction of desires, it is a value that during the Ch'ing period was especially important in imperial Confucianism, whose adherents had the power to enforce orthodoxy. Frugality is a value that includes prizing self-sufficiency and denying the worth of commerce. The latter can serve only to increase people's selfish desires for goods that are unnecessary. And those who engage in commerce are motivated by personal profit rather than selfless impartiality. This perspective, in contrast with the European view of commerce, was the official position of many followers of Ch'eng-Chu Confucianism, among whom were leaders of the T'ung-chih Restoration (1862–1874).[47] Some individuals were more tolerant of merchants than others, thereby perpetuating a tradition dating from the eighteenth century in which the state facilitated the grain trade, promoting both self-sufficiency *and* commercial specialization.[48] The value of frugality cropped up again as an official part of the Kuomintang (KMT) New Life Movement in the 1930s.

In view of their persistence well into the twentieth century, one may ask whether those elements in Chu Hsi's Neo-Confucianism that seem to advocate the selfless overcoming of desires through discipline have endured even into the Communist period today as an unconscious part of the legacy of the past. An answer may be found in the consideration of the valuation of self-sufficiency over commercial specialization. In *The Last Stand of Chinese Conservatism*, Mary Wright argues that Kuomintang rule failed in the early twentieth century because it copied the T'ung-chih model, which was unsuitable for modernization.[49] The T'ung-chih leaders advocated two key values. One is that moral character is more important than technical or specialized skill in the success of those responsible for any enterprise. This means a downgrading of the need for the division of labor required by industrial modernization. The other value is frugality, possible in a self-sufficient agricultural community and the enemy of profit and trade. Both of these values were central also to Maoism. If the Wright thesis is applicable to the KMT, then it may be applicable to Maoist China as well. A difference is that while the KMT leaders consciously drew from the T'ung-chih Confucians, the Maoists may have simply inherited aspects of their culture, the roots of which they may have been unwilling or unable to acknowledge.

If any aspect of imperial Confucian ethics filtered into Chinese

Marxism during the Maoist period, it was the value of selflessness, the personality trait rendered verbally as "greatly impartial, nothing for the self" (*ta kung, wu ssu*).[50] During this period it was defined in terms of discipline, as it was in the Confucian ethical position associated with the family image and in contrast with its meaning of impartial love of all, linked with the water and embodiment images. As discipline, selflessness required the subordination of personal desires to uniformly accepted work place, class, or national goals. It was also intimately related to rural campaigns for frugality and against activities that would have increased personal or family wealth there. In the spirit of the Yung-cheng emperor, the Maoist message was that the center (i.e., the party element in any organization, including the state) always has the interest of the largest number in mind, and so the way to avoid selfishness is for all to accept totally its judgments and rules.

Booklets describing the qualifications necessary for party membership were likely to list selflessness defined in these terms.[51] Among all citizens, Lei Feng, the People's Liberation Army model, was most extensively lauded as an example to the people at large of selfless ability to heed the regulations. In 1963, when he was first put forward as a model, the press told the story of his AWOL experience as a young recruit. The lesson that he learned was to obey the rules, because "organizational rules represent the collective interest."[52] This message was directed particularly at rural areas. The government was campaigning to stop private-plot farming from interfering with collective production and to get communes to meet their responsibility to sell produce cheaply to the government.[53] One of the teachings of the Socialist Education Movement, in which Lei Feng's story played a role, was that commune members show their selflessness by obeying the rules pertaining to the sale of sideline agricultural products.[54]

In a manner consistent with the use of the plant image by Chu Hsi and the Confucians to describe the ceaseless cultivation required of the gardener (teacher) in tending seedlings (young minds), the Maoist educators told the public that their minds needed the help of external authorities. Their virtues should be "nurtured by the sunshine, rains, and dews of Mao Tse-tung's thought" (*tsai Mao Tse-tung ssu-hsiang te yang-kuang yü-lu p'u-yü hsia*). The reason for such nurturance is that "saplings can only grow and become timber if they are constantly under the care of the forester."[55] Continual campaigns of struggle against bad thoughts were required to prevent any protracted backsliding and to promote the growth of lush, healthy branches and leaves.

In his philosophical and educational writings, Chu emphasized the need for people to copy the minds of exemplars. The emperor models himself on the sage-kings and the ministers and people model themselves on the emperor. Even though modern models have replaced Confucian sage-kings, sagelike emperors, and scholar-officials, the assumption endures that the way to teach is through the presentation of models. This system has been applied to methods of social control and general educational practices in the Maoist and post-Maoist periods. Chinese teaching techniques should be subjected to close scrutiny by anyone concerned with China's modernization problems. In brief, the attempt to teach the creative and independent thinking required for technically advanced and entrepreneurial work may conflict with the authoritarian learning by rote and modeling practices that are part of everyone's learning experience.

Although Maoism has similarities to some aspects of imperial Chu Hsi Confucianism, such as the value of selflessness expressed as discipline and frugality, it rejected the essence of the Mencian ethic. This had been adopted and reworked by Chu Hsi and refers to the innateness and universality of certain moral traits. In Mencius' formulation, the principal trait was humaneness (*jen*), the jewel in the heart of human nature (*hsing*).

In order to understand the nature of the shift from the classical Confucian or Mencian conception of human nature to the Maoist idea, the analyst must be mindful of the difference between the ideas of perfectibility and malleability. The key point here is that the Maoists moved away from accepting the existence of any innate traits, whereas for Mencian Confucians, the existence of an innate evaluating mind and an innate moral sentiment of humaneness were fundamental. Both the Maoists and the Confucians believed strongly in the perfectibility (the ability to change for the good) of man through education. They differed, however, in their views of what it is that becomes transformed. For Mencius, achiev-

ing perfectibility was a matter of removing environmental obstacles to the discovery of the innate moral sense and sentiments.
What is changed through education and self-cultivation is the individual's understanding or awareness of traits he already possesses, his "original nature." He also develops the attitude that it
is possible to extend the application of the innate sentiment of
compassion to a wide range of things. This much of Mencius runs
through Chu Hsi and Wang Yang-ming. For the Maoists, it was
not a matter of uncovering anything innate but rather of molding
the individual by means of education and social experience into
the form deemed desirable by the rulers. The entire person is
changed so that he acquires previously nonexistent traits. Both the
traditional and the Maoist positions stress perfectibility through education, but only the Maoists believed in the total malleability of a
personality that is blank at birth.

To speak of the similarity of Confucians and Mao on the issue of
perfectibility is not the same as demonstrating that Mao derived
that claim from his Confucian predecessors. Similarity suggests
only the softer hypothesis that a familiar view of humans would
be favorably received. In actuality, the language that Mao used to
discuss malleability indicates that he viewed the idea as deriving
from Marx, for whom human nature is the sum total of the changing social relations with which individuals are involved over time.

The reason for the Maoist attack on Confucianism was Mao's
desire to transform the people rapidly into selfless Communists.
Discussions of innate characteristics were suspect because they
suggest that man possesses certain unchangeable characteristics.
In contrast, belief in malleability acts as a self-fulfilling prophecy;
filling people with optimism about the future, it encourages them
to reorganize their goals so as to accomplish noble ends rapidly.
The theoretical basis for the attack was that in a class-ordered society, there are no class-transcending, or universal, traits. It is assumed that the universal is the innate, although the nature of
members of one class differs from the nature of members of another. "Is there such a thing as human nature? Of course there is.
But there is only one human nature in the concrete, no human
nature in the abstract. In a class society there is only human nature
that bears the stamp of a class; human nature that transcends

classes does not exist."[56] No universal nature, no innate traits: "There has not been any such all-embracing love of mankind since the division of mankind into classes."[57]

Young Karl Marx, in the *Economic and Philosophical Manuscripts*, made a place for universal, innate human needs, such as the need to create in the manner of an original artist. None of this universalism is present in the writings of Mao. The classical Chinese Marxist justification for rejecting innate moral traits is contained in an essay entitled "Man's Class Nature," written by Liu Shao-ch'i in 1949:

> Man has two essences: one is man's natural essence, including his physical constitution, cleverness, state of health, instinctive capabilities, and so forth (for example, in medical science there are various types of physical constitution); the other is man's social essence, including his psychological state, thoughts, consciousness, viewpoints, habits, demands, and so forth.[58]

The social essence is the important part of man, and it is considered completely malleable. It comprises psychological phenomena, especially motives, emotions, and knowledge. It includes moral standards, and it is distinct from the biological nature, the realm of universal, often instinctive, characteristics. This was a device intended to trivialize the universal and innate, including such self-regarding traits as self-preservation (a natural right in some liberal democratic thought).

Concretely, the Maoist position had significant implications for literature and psychology. Writers could not assume in their works that there are things that all persons like, such as the fragrance of flowers or the song of a bird. In psychology, rather than focus on universal physiological characteristics, psychologists affirmed the plasticity of the nervous system. And many Chinese psychologists shifted away from physiology altogether, with its suggestions of what is common to all members of the human species. They preferred instead to speak entirely of thought (personality), which is socially malleable, and of how best to change it.[59]

In practice, the Maoist theory of the malleable class nature was not consistently implemented during the height of Mao's power.

Chou En-lai repeatedly stated, in a manner compatible with the Maoist view, that class traits are not passed on genetically from one generation to the next. Given the malleability of the self, a person's class label should depend entirely on his current attitude and conduct (*piao-hsien*, lit., his "manifestation"). In actuality, in rural areas negative class labels were often handed down the bloodline as far as paternal grandchildren, making them targets of abuse during campaigns.

In terms of the Chu Hsi legacy, Maoism perpetuates the ideals of selflessness as disciplined obedience, control of personal desires, and frugality. At the same time, it fails the principal test, which is acceptance of the centrality of the moral mind. But this is revealing. Maoism's very vehemence in attacking the moral sense and its universal values discloses something about the strength of the moral mind's endurance as an idea in Chinese ethics.

Other Heirs, Other Aspects

There are other twentieth-century thinkers who do not shirk from affirming the existence of a moral mind. Remembering the range of ideas revealed by Chu's structural images, one can look to a different set of thinkers for the inheritance of the more central components of Chu's concept of human nature. In this connection, Hsiung Shih-li (1885–1968) is an appropriate first example.

Like that of Chu Hsi, Hsiung's metaphysics was inspired by the ideas of change and of nature as permeated by life found in the *Book of Changes*.[60] He identifies the essence of the person in a manner consistent with his metaphysics, using Chu Hsi-style notions of the principles of life (*sheng-i*) and humaneness (*jen*) to describe it.[61] The focus is on the idea of the life force, associated originally with the seed image. But of primary concern is the way he focuses on the individual in identifying the unique contribution of Eastern philosophy (whether Confucian, Buddhist, or Taoist) to human beings. That contribution is prizing the inner life or the "original mind" in all people and nourishing it in daily activity so that it remains the master of all that people do and are.[62] Nourishment is a gradual matter, an idea consistent with the old value of ceaseless growth and nurturance; there is no sudden enlightenment, as some Buddhists maintained could occur. Although Hsiung rejects the Bergsonian idea of intuition as too close to raw instinct, his own idea of how the original mind within each individual manifests itself is in line with what a Westerner would normally call intuition. Hsiung's description of the manner in which it should be nurtured resonates with Chu Hsi's position: reverential concentration (ᵇching), combined with studying objective authorities such as texts and practicing their dictates by being reverential in managing affairs, being faithful with friends, and so forth.[63]

Hsiung believed that Western-style science (or objective standards for verification) and reason (presumably, belief in deductive rules of thinking) have utility. But these can be properly used only under the guidance of a nurtured intuitive moral sense (the manifestation of the original nature) that provides the ethical standards for the application of scientific methodology.[64] The cynic, of course, could claim that by the twentieth century the metaphysics, theory of history, and ritual rules of Neo-Confucianism had become so discredited that the only thing left untainted in them was the stress on the inner life.

The young Liang Sou[Shu]-ming (1893–) constructed a metaphysics resembling that of Hsiung Shih-li: a holistic universe in constant change that reveals the influence of Consciousness Only Buddhism and Bergsonian vitalism.[65] Other roots of his formulations can be found in the thought of Wang Yang-ming, who incorporated a vitalistic universe into his philosophy, the Neo-Confucian origins of which were first comprehensively laid out by Chu Hsi, who used the plant image to explain the universe.

According to Liang, humaneness is the way to abide in harmony with natural things, and intuition is the means of grasping their essence. By the late 1920s, he had shifted his attention away from the metaphysics of Bergsonian vitalism. He retained the centrality of moral intuition, however, in a manner similar to Hsiung, identifying it as China's special contribution to world civilization. While li-hsing, the name by which he referred to moral intuition, is "actually the distinguishing characteristic of humanity, it is also at the same time the special feature of Chinese culture."[66] Li-hsing refers to the discovery of the innate standards and rules that may be used to direct action. It is the aspect of the moral sense that reveals right and wrong, and it is different from knowledge of how to do something. Consistent with the Mencian tradition, Liang uses the term *jen* (humaneness) to refer to *li-hsing*, and he claims that its presence is universal.[67] In short, all persons who appeal to it will discover the same values.

There is no claim here that the quantity of thinkers philosophically akin to Hsiung and Liang is great. The stature and influence of such individuals, however, is considerable.

Perhaps it is not surprising to find that twentieth-century thinkers who have sought to modernize Confucianism drew on a conception of an innate moral sense that was once part of the plant organicism of Chu Hsi and Wang Yang-ming. But it should certainly startle even the most jaded to discover grounds for claiming that arch anti-Confucians of the first half of the century were influenced in varying degrees by the same idea.

Hu Shih is generally considered to be the quintessential Westernizer of modern China, casting away his Chinese heritage to assume the roles of pragmatist and individualist. He satirized Confucian self-cultivation and misunderstood the Ch'eng-Chu idea that what begins in solitude can be completed only through the fulfillment of duties in a social setting.[68] Taking into account the cultural influences to which he was subject but did not credit, however, the picture changes. Part of this unconscious legacy of the Neo-Confucian past was his faith in the possibility of a consensus on values.

Pragmatism requires a consensus on moral first principles because it can justify itself only as a method. As a result, a standard by which to judge the consequences implied by hypotheses (are the consequences good or bad? do the hypotheses work?) is needed. Philosophical pragmatists do not like to articulate first principles. They assume them.

It is true that the pragmatists in America during the early decades of this century had to fight against conservative educators and philosophical idealists; in fact, there has not been a universal value consensus in America. But among a large number of intellectuals in the first part of this century who saw themselves as progressive and were willing to act politically on their values, there was a *t'i* (cultural essence). The most famous of these intellectuals were John Dewey, Teddy Roosevelt, Walter Lippmann, and

Thorstein Veblen. The *t'i* provided the consensus for this broadly based and active group. It included the values of progress through an increase in scientific knowledge and industrialization, the Protestant work ethic, and the values of individualism (rights, privacy, autonomy, and so forth).

No such agreement existed in China among the intellectual and political elite. There were many deep and abiding social fissures. The splits between the rural gentry and the urban commercial class and between the Western-educated and the Chinese-educated elites are but two of the prominent ones. Hu Shih's belief that similar consensus was possible in China simply blinded him to the significance of the crucial difference between China and America. He assumed that all rational Chinese, meaning those who were educated in modern schools or in democratic settings, would agree on matters of value. The educated individual would discover the standard for evaluating the consequences of actions. As far as he could judge, therefore, attaining one mind democratically in his country was not a major problem; pragmatism could succeed. His faith in the miracles that modernizing Chinese minds through education would bring diminished his recognition of other problems, such as the necessity of modernizing the economy and the military. Jerome Grieder has described Hu's belief (which endured into the 1930s) in a "supraparty politics" that would draw strength from a "qualified electorate."[69] In fact, the electorate was uninformed or divided in opinion on most national concerns. Hu Shih even believed in an easily attainable value consensus among nations, hoping to rely on it rather than force to resolve China's problems with Japan.[70]

There were surely personality factors at work in Hu's preference for libraries and schools rather than party meetings that led him to espouse "supraparty politics." But there is an additional plausible explanation for his reasoning: the enduring legacy of the Neo-Confucian claim that through education a nation of one mind can be attained, because all thoughtful persons will agree on the basic principles. In other words, Hu's faith in a consensus originated in the belief that all educated persons instinctively will agree on matters of value. And this idea originates in a belief in a universal moral sense. Moreover, twentieth-century political parties fit right into the traditional characterization of parties as selfish factions or cliques that fragment the one-mindedness that education can achieve. Perhaps there is, on this point of attaining consensus through education, an echo of imperial Confucian autocracy in the positions of the liberal democrat Hu Shih.

In a manner inconceivable in the writings of Mao Tse-tung, the Chinese Marxist Li Ta-chao as a young man described the moral sense as an innate human trait: "Because the ethics of men has been a powerful social ability since the most ancient period of human life, there has developed in the human heart a voice of authority that down to the present day still echoes in our own hearts. It has a mysterious quality that is not due to the stimulus of the outside world, nor is it a matter of advantage or disadvantage."[71] This is an astonishing position for a Marxist-Leninist, although not inconsistent with the ethical assumptions of the early Marx. Maurice Meisner explains the content of the moral sense so eloquently described by Li as self-sacrifice and the willingness to substitute public for private interest. In short, he suggests that it may be coextensive with socialist consciousness.[72] But regardless of content, the notion of a universal moral sense is surprising in an early proponent of the class theory of social organization.

Family

There is a famous message in Chang Tsai's "Hsi ming" (Western inscription): "That which extends throughout the universe I regard as my body. . . . All things are my brothers and sisters, and all things are my companions."[73] Chu Hsi was not necessarily partial to the image of all things forming one body, but his ethics carries essentially the same message as the "Western Inscription": people should expand compassion as widely as possible. And there is a basis in nature for doing so. Nature is permeated by the life force *jen* (lit., humaneness), and so it is not indifferent to human compassion and suffering. To the extent that people are compassionate, they are in accord with nature. The reader of the complaints of many leading nineteenth- and twentieth-century figures to whom I refer below may wonder where the essence of this ethic has gone. And yet the very act of bemoaning its absence illustrates the strength of the longing for an expansive compassion or altruism as a value. The complaints point to precisely the gap identified in Chapter Four, that between family and public love. I argued there that Chu's attempts in his own philosophy to close the gap were not successful, in spite of his own exemplary life as a compassionate Confucian. If other aspects of the content of the moral mind have endured, the impetus to altruism has done so only weakly.

Influential writers associated with the May Fourth Period (1919 to the early 1920s), such as Ch'en Tu-hsiu (1879–1942), accused the Confucians of oppressing the individual by confining him within the bounds of strictly defined family roles. The individual's choices, went the charge, are limited by the duties and expectations traditionally associated with his roles. He has no rights that transcend them. The present study has pointed to the need for a corrective to this line of attack. Beginning with the water image's suggestion of potentially equal worth and culminating in the discussions of empathic projection (involving the images of the light source and the body), there are additional values in Chu's doctrines that are publicly altruistic in spirit. These are realized when the individual expands his range of concern beyond his immediate role duties. Chu was far ahead of most of his scholar-official class in prizing altruism. And his educational actions on behalf of a large population are exemplary.

The modern criticisms of Neo-Confucianism nevertheless reveal something significant, even when their evaluations are unfair. The critics most likely are responding to the fact that Chu Hsi's ethics failed to generate the kind of public-spirited response sought by the author.

Doubtless, there are historical factors, in addition to internal doctrinal ones, that contributed to the eventual disregard by some Confucians of Chu Hsi's formulation of the ideal of impartiality, or being "one with heaven." There are reasons to suspect that his goal of sagehood (inseparable from a holistic theory of heaven) had failed in the eyes of many thinkers of the seventeenth century and later.[74] Some, perhaps, viewed it as unattainable; others viewed it as unintelligible. The actual goal of thinkers like Yen Yüan (1635–1704) was to become proficient in practical matters, such as military science, agriculture, the administration of justice, and public finance. These men did not refer much to an all-embracing mind. They said that the distinguishing feature of the sagelike emperors and Confucians was their active attempt to solve practical social and political problems, not the possession of a mind that integrates all principles or empathizes with all persons. The historical circumstance that provided a note of urgency to the contest between talk of "one mind" and practical action was the Manchu conquest (1644) and its causes.

There were therefore both doctrinal and historical reasons why Chu Hsi's ideal of sagehood had faded as a realistic goal by the early Ch'ing period. This explains why Chu's remaining message was seen by some late Ch'ing figures as centering around role fulfillment within the limited, standard social positions, especially those within the family. Another historical consideration was the desire of China's modern thinkers to generate nationalistic loyalty to China as a country so that patriots would come to its defense against the foreigners.

Liang Ch'i-ch'ao (1873–1929) said, "In China there are duties of individuals to individuals. There are not duties of individuals to society."[75] He was influenced by Yen Fu's claim that public spirit in the West, unlike that in China, was a positive force, resulting in the collective pursuit of common state goals. And there is no lack of supporting citations for this view from prominent contemporaries, for example, Sun Yat-sen: "But the Chinese people have only family and clan solidarity, they do not have national spirit."[76] Chiang T'ing-fu said, "Chinese citizens are generally loyal to individuals, families, or localities rather than to the state."[77] Given Chu Hsi's claim (and that of so many other Confucians) that nature is not indifferent to human suffering, it is amazing that the young Yen Fu turned to Herbert Spencer's concept of nature to find something worth emulating. Spencer's nature is the realm of survival of the fittest. There is ample room for the bloodthirsty group to be the morally good group in this model (because of its socially teleological function). To cast his ethics into a more palatable form, Yen Fu had to supplement Spencer with a European altruistic strain of public-spiritedness. How curious this is, when Chu Hsi's humanity-permeated nature was there as a model all along.

The elderly Yen Fu rediscovered the Neo-Confucian value of impartiality. It is reasonably clear that the memory of it had not died, although many were simply ignoring it. That ideal does help to inform K'ang Yu-wei's vision of the utopian "Great Union." Describing himself, he said, "Being that I was born on the earth, then mankind in the ten thousand countries of the earth are all my brothers [lit., 'of the same womb'] of different bodily types."[78] When the Great Union exists, vegetarian man, having exterminated most animals dangerous to himself, will love all creatures. Humaneness will prevail.[79] K'ang identified also the chief barrier to utopia: the legacy of the family image used to explain humanity, the natural hierarchical positions surrounded by barriers that are not to be transgressed. These "nine boundaries" for K'ang include nation, class, race, gender, family, and so forth. On the family barrier within China, K'ang had this to say: "Thus, [China] has persons who are wealthy and good as well; they give offerings to the ancestors, contribute to public fields, succor the poor, found schools; [but in these acts], likewise, they only protect clansmen, and other clans cannot benefit [from them], much less their fellow-countrymen."[80]

By the end of the May Fourth Period, there was no agreement in China that the Western model provided a viable substitute. Many shared Liang Sou-ming's view that the Western doctrine of individual rights established a different barrier between individual and individual:

> But a result of the [doctrine of naturally endowed rights] is that the lines of demarcation between individuals must be very clearly drawn. As soon as you open your mouth, you must speak in terms of rights and obligation, legal relationships, through which everyone holds everyone else to account, even to the point of affecting the relationship between father and son or man and wife.[81]

But lack of enthusiasm about Western alternatives did not blind commentators to the failure of Chu Hsi's utopian vision of impartiality and the roots of that failure in the family ethic. The pervasive nature of the complaint about the limited range of concern or affection for fellow humans suggests the strength of longing for the lost ideal of "Western Inscription" expansive love.

There are serious negative social and economic consequences to limiting the individual's range of concern to those with whom he has defined role relations. These consequences inevitably have an impact on modernization policies. For example, they may affect hiring practices in large and small organizations. This has been noted by Chinese, many of whom have described their inability to do very much about it. Long ago, Yen Fu described it thusly: "While China favors relatives, Westerners esteem the capable."[82] Today they call it "back-doorism." Another practical consequence derives from the tendency to construct any leader-follower relation in familiar family-role terms. The result is the prizing of harmony as the chief value of an organization, often to the detriment of competing values. Chang Chih-tung put it this way: "I humbly state that ministers serving the sovereign are like sons serving the parents. The chief minister is like the household manager, and the other ministers are like the remaining sons. . . . If the family is harmonious, it will prosper; if the court is in agreement, the empire will be regulated."[83]

The family patriarch's principal duty is to maintain harmony by ensuring, through proper moral instruction, that each member observes his role. As applied to organizations as small as a shop and as large as a state agency, the value of group harmony thus transcends those of product quality, efficiency, or any other value. So long as a manager, in accordance with family role practices, remains the ultimate arbiter of harmony, there are strong inhibitions to independent initiative or criticism that might result in disharmony. While advice may be solicited, there is a premium on stability. Management as science has aims that can be incompatible with harmony. In commenting on the official viewpoint of leaders of the T'ung-chih period, Mary Wright said, "The Confucian official himself was assumed to be a competent judge of policy on all matters, however complex, because government was conceived as the art of ordering human relations, not as the science of legal administration."[84]

It was not uncommon to run an army battalion like a family, with the same stress on roles, moral education, and harmony. The value of family-style harmony in work places may not itself be sufficient to inhibit changes in management practices and skill acquisition by workers, especially if there are other variables present, such as material incentives. But paired with state control over the economic life of an organization, a stress on such harmony can produce apathy toward innovation.

Perhaps the most striking manifestation of the continual influence of the structural image of the family is the tendency of modern Chinese thinkers to describe all ethically significant objects relationally. This certainly applies to the identity of persons. Coupled with this tendency is a belief in fundamental, timeless social roles that transcend the lives of the individuals who fill them generation after generation. During the Maoist period, the official content of the relationships changed from Confucian roles to social class roles defined in terms of each other. For example, the landlord was defined in terms of his relation to the peasant, and the peasant in terms of his relation to the commune (though this is not to say that the traditional social relations evaporated altogether). The educational system aimed at creating uniform attitudes toward class duties and expectations, just as Confucian training did with respect to its standardized social positions. Individuality had a place, under the slogan "Teach according to the man" (*yin jen shih chiao*), a variation on the Confucian phrase, "Teach according to the individual's abilities." But this was a means, not a goal. It meant that teachers should be sensitive to the varying personalities of their students in order to make teaching the uniform attitudes to class relations or values efficacious.

Judith Stacey has argued that by the early decades of the twentieth century the economic base of the patriarchal family system had eroded in North China. The symptoms were landlessness, decrease in farm size to the point where a farm could not support a family, decrease in family size, and men doomed to bachelorhood by their lack of land (a terrible fate in a clan society, because there will be no descendants to perpetuate sacrifices, and so the bloodline will disappear). By offering peasants in North China the possibility of a traditional family life and, through land reform, the economic base to make it possible, the Communist party gained the political support of the peasants in the 1940s. She says,

The Party's appreciation of family sentiment was evident throughout the revolutionary period. It scrupulously tried to avoid making demands that would confront peasants with direct conflicts between loyalty to the family and loyalty to the revolution. Indeed, land reform policy demonstrated the CCP's ability to turn familial sentiment and loyalties to its own advantage. Because that sentiment was so profoundly patriarchal, concessions to patriarchal morality came to facilitate and shape CCP mass-line politics.[85]

Great Leap Forward (1958–1960) policies that were antipatriarchal included eliminating family plots, socializing housework through collective dining halls and sewing centers, and leveling family grave mounds for cultivation. These practices were deeply resented and soon abandoned, and the spirit of the earlier policies reemerged. If anything, the leaders of post-Mao China have encouraged even tighter family ties, in part as a way of combating juvenile delinquency. So the argument is that during the Communist period, the old roles have endured along with the new.

In spite of all that has just been said about the weakness of altruism in the modern legacy of the moral sense, it is still alive. Knowing what to look for from studies of Chu, the analyst can find it in the value of humanitarianism.

Public Love

The Maoist theoretical position on the absence of universal, innate traits is not the only one to have endured in the People's Republic of China. The Mencian legacy has lived on to create renewed tensions. The philosophical history of China under and after Mao has been dominated by debates on the issue of whether or not there are class-transcending, or universal, human traits and on the related issue of humanism as an ethical standard.

Before proceeding any further, one should distinguish four senses of humanism as the term has been used in recent decades. The first two are, respectively, that a person should be compassionate or benevolent to other people, and that the government (or ruler) should be compassionate to its subjects. These two constitute the Mencian ethical position. The third sense applies to a form of Marxist humanism that has been prevalent in Eastern European countries. It draws on Marx's discussions of universal, basic human needs in the *Economic and Philosophical Manuscripts* of 1848. One such need is individual control over work, both the production process and the disposal of the product produced, rather than their control by an "alien" agent. Humanism requires that governments permit the basic needs to be satisfied. The fourth meaning emerged in the debates beginning around 1980 and focuses on the individual human rights that are basic to Western democracies. Humanism requires that individuals and governments respect and protect those rights. Mindful of these distinctions, it is interesting to note that some but not all of the advocates of humanism in the debates have been perpetuating the Mencian legacy (the first two senses of humanism).

In the debates, all sides claim to be taking a Marxist perspective. Foreign commentators usually have explained the debates as between critics and supporters of the Communist party's "proletarian dictatorship." As the external commentators see it, the critics draw on the early Marxist idea that there are basic human needs possessed by all persons. These include the need to control one's work freely. The measure of a government's merit, critics of the party say, is its progress in satisfying these needs. The party's failure in this area is due to arrogant bureaucrats and similar impediments; it has produced alienation in the people and shown its antihumanistic disinterest in individual self-realization. Meanwhile, some defenders of the dictatorship of the proletariat have interpreted humanism as a bourgeois value (sometimes the protection of universally possessed natural rights) that once had a progressive function. In socialist societies, they say, it is used by naive Marxists and counterrevolutionaries to avoid legitimate class struggle (in the case of the latter) or to attack socialism itself in hopes of replacing it with capitalism.

On one level the debates have involved critics and defenders of party control over people's lives and work, so the common interpretation of the debate is accurate. What is missing from the foreign interpretations, however, is recognition that Confucian values, tied to a Confucian view of man, have been powerfully active in the categories of the debates. All Confucians in the Mencian tradition describe the core trait that is universal to persons and discoverable by introspection as feelings, especially humaneness (*jen*, love of fellow humans that begins in the family). This may be either the sentiment or both the sentiment and the insight that a person should act on the sentiment so as to extend it to other people, in accordance with their relationships to him. This is why contemporary Chinese theoreticians so often explain the idea of humanism (*jen-tao chu-i*) as love of fellow humans, or *humanitarianism*, manifested in acts of compassion, such as aiding the handicapped, rather than in terms of the early Marxist idea of developing the individual's "basic human needs." The continuation of the debates decade after decade reveals the endurance of the Mencian belief in a universal, innate moral sentiment and the principle of acting on it that provide the innate moral sense with its content.[86] At the official level, of course, such innateness would be repudiated as contrary to man's malleable class nature. In any case, for purposes of formulating a modern ethics, innateness is not the crucial matter; what is crucial is belief in the universality of the sentiment and the principle that one should act on it.

The presence of this belief in a moral sense or in the value of humaneness, seen in the continuing echo of a humanistic voice in the debates, is just as important as any criticism of party dictatorship in determining the significance of the controversy. Essentially, it means that there are many who regard the primary question in analyzing a society as an ethical one—does it conform with the dictates of man's universal trait, which is to be humane?—rather than the "scientific" question, actually drawn from Marxist metaphysics: how do the society's political structure and economic policies fit in with the society's developmental stage as described by the laws of historical materialism? The scientific question asks only if a governmental action or institution is congruent with the historical stage. The dictatorship of the proletariat passes this test. Those asking the scientific question demote humanism from a central issue to merely the principle of kindness, one of many tenets in Communist ethics.

Chinese writers say that those who regard the primary question as the ethical one "take humanism as a world view and as a historical view" and find inspiration and reinforcement for their position in Western philosophy, including European Marxist thought. The advocates of the scientific position, who treat humanism as merely one among many ethical principles, have their roots in China's modern revolutionary experiences. Both sides may acknowledge premodern sources of the idea of humanism as it exists in their country today.

The new ingredient in the debates that was introduced in the 1980s was the claim that individual human rights exist and that their protection is the primary moral responsibility of persons and governments.[87] Humanism as this kind of obligation overlaps somewhat with and reinforces the universal love or humanitarian requirements of the Mencian thread. But it basically injects the new idea of rights into the discussion.

To the degree that Confucian tenets float freely in future ethical debates, one may expect to encounter Chu Hsi's Mencian cornerstone again. The ideas of a universal sentiment of humaneness and of a principle to act upon it, which, like living things, require endless nurturance, cannot avoid the serious attention of the formulators of new doctrine. Those formulators, in turn, will be vulnerable to criticism from some heirs to the Maoist legacy, who deny the existence of any "abstract, class-transcending human nature."

CONCLUSION

A number of the ideas in modern China that have been most competitive are similar to the two polarized aspects of Chu Hsi Confucianism. One of these is the authoritarian aspect that focuses on model emulation and extols the virtues of selfless discipline, manifest in the repression of many desires and in frugality. Its modern advocates have abandoned the moral sense. The other is that aspect which encourages self-discovery of an innate moral sense, universally possessed. The significant thing is that this moral sense is chiefly manifest as the sentiment of altruistic humaneness or compassion (hence, "humanism" in Chinese dress). This aspect generates some fundamental modern ethical tenets: that the origin of ethical knowledge and the ultimate test of ethical claims is a moral sense, perhaps intuitive; that part of the content of that moral sense is principles of proper behavior within standardized, universally found relationships; and that part of its original and still justifiable content is a sentiment of sympathy that can extend to all people and creatures.

It may not be surprising to learn that, in part, the authoritarian practices of China's modern governments echo Chu Hsi's legacy. It is less well known, however, that the other aspect has a strong, enduring presence. As a result there has always been, and presumably will continue to be, a ready-made, lively, not archaic, and distinctively Chinese, not foreign, perspective for opposing coercive and austere government practices: the moral sense that any person may nurture and the humanitarian sentiments that accompany it. Obviously, the traditional content of the innate moral sense includes among its imperatives disciplined obedience to the social role duties described in Chapter Two. These include absolute loyalty to one's ruler. The moral mind itself, however, is separable from such content. It is neutral and requires no particular obedience to anything. Europeans of differing political views respectively filled the "innate ideas" that were their counterpart of Chu's moral sense with the notions of the divine right of kings and then of the equal rights of man ("We hold these truths to be self-evident"). So the moral sense can retain the duties accompanying certain basic human relationships, such as those concerning family, teacher, and friend, while rejecting others. The door therefore remains open for it to adopt a variety of new moral imperatives.

I noted that one aspect of the Confucian legacy that endures in China today is an attitude that favors the individual's family and his work organization, modeled on the family, over other people. Yet an antidote to this limited range of concern lies in the revitalization of the equally Confucian idea of a moral sense; specifically, it lies in accentuating the humanitarian impulses that so many Confucians have claimed are also part of the content of that sense. An altruism that widens the range of compassion outside the family has an authentically Chinese, not simply Western, basis. At the same time, it has the added advantage of being intelligible and plausible to Westerners because it has modern Western counterparts.[88] Such altruism is compatible with the value of close family ties. Chu Hsi's real error lay in addressing his message of empathy

231

and nurturance only to the potential *chün-tzu* and in providing insufficient detail concerning how to implement it, not in suggesting that love of family and compassion for others can coexist. What remains is for China's modern thinkers and leaders to cultivate the idea that a moral sense colored by such compassionate aversion to suffering exists, and to begin to think through the incremental steps by which to harness it for the common good.

In thinking through these incremental steps, among the first priorities is figuring out organizational and legal innovations that turn pious sentiment into reality. For a thousand years, the ability of emperors and Confucian officials to probe adequately how their society does and could work has been limited. What has limited it has been the family model that supposedly describes its ideal structure and the belief that cultivating various family-rooted values uniformly latent or present in the minds of rulers and ruled can sustain it. As a consequence, the source of all problems disturbing social harmony has often been traced to flawed moral standards in minds and solutions said to rest in tampering with those moral ideas through improved control of schools and examinations. The administrative and judicial aspects of the problems have been ignored. A commitment to the moral sense combined with dedication to new structural changes form the twin pillars of an effective consensus on China's future.

NOTES

One

1. Among his many invaluable contributions to our knowledge of Confucianism, Wing–tsit Chan has given us studies of key terms. See especially "The Evolution of the Confucian Concept of *Jen,*" *Philosophy East and West* 4 (1955), 295–319, and "The Evolution of the Neo-Confucian Concept of *Li* as Principle," *Tsing-hua Journal of Chinese Studies* 4 (February 1964), 123–49. For historical sociology, see Thomas A. Metzger's *Escape from Predicament* (New York: Columbia University Press, 1977). Metzger treats Chu Hsi's Neo-Confucianism as the world view of a certain social class and finds in its doctrines evidence of a psychological tension that he discovered in late imperial and modern China. In contrast, for purposes of this book, I treat the Neo-Confucianism of Chu Hsi in terms of the twelfth-century texts alone and as I understand the structure of the ideas in them. My agenda and Metzger's are simply different, not in conflict. Among William Theodore de Bary's many contributions to the understanding of Neo-Confucianism, I have learned most from his *Neo-Confucian Orthodoxy and the Learning of the Mind-and-Heart* (New York: Columbia University Press, 1981). Among the favored approaches of Chinese scholars past and present is to attempt to identify the authentic teaching of the Chou sages and then to determine which later Confucians came closest to capturing their insights. This method was applied by Chu Hsi in the Sung and was used by scholars of Han Learning in the Ch'ing. The latter, who began to flourish in the Soochow area in the early eighteenth century, returned to the Han writers as the ones most likely to have comprehended the earlier teachings. Typical of this approach today is the monumental study by Mou Tsung-san, *Hsin-t'i yü hsing-t'i* (Mind and human nature), 3 vols. (Taipei: Cheng-chung shu-chü, 1968–1969). His methodology includes philology and intellectual biography. He concludes that Chu Hsi represents a departure from the more authentic inheritors of the Mencian core teaching, which in fact was more faithfully

carried on by two other schools. See the review by Tu Wei-ming in *Journal of Asian Studies* 30 (May 1971), 642–47.

2. John W. Haeger, "The Intellectual Context of Neo-Confucian Syncretism," *Journal of Asian Studies* 31 (May 1972), 512.

3. Ibid., 511.

4. Linda Ann Walton-Vargo, "Education, Social Change, and Neo-Confucianism in Sung-Yuan China: Academies and the Local Elite in Ming Prefecture (Ningpo)" (Ph.D. diss., University of Pennsylvania, 1978), 187.

5. In the T'ang dynasty, Han Yü (768–824) described an orthodox transmission of the tao. Ch'eng I did the same, stressing the role of his brother Ch'eng Hao. Chu Hsi discusses the transmission of the tao in the preface of his commentary on the *Doctrine of the Mean*, and he refers to Chou Tun-i as first recovering it in the Sung. According to de Bary, all were at pains to underscore the fragility of the tradition and the difficult task of retrieving it. See de Bary, *Neo-Confucian Orthodoxy*, 2–7. On Chu's role, see Wing-tsit Chan, "Chu Hsi's Completion of Neo-Confucianism," in *Études Song: Sung Studies in Memoriam Étienne Balazs*, ed. Françoise Aubin, 2d ser., no. 1 (1973), 59–90.

6. Hoyt C. Tillman, *Utilitarian Confucianism: Ch'en Liang's Challenge to Chu Hsi* (Cambridge, Mass.: Harvard University Press, 1982), 200.

7. De Bary, *Neo-Confucian Orthodoxy*, pp. xv–xvi.

8. George C. Hatch, "The Thought of Su Hsün (1009–1066): An Essay in the Social Meaning of Intellectual Pluralism in the Northern Sung" (Ph.D. diss., University of Washington, 1972), 5–6. Hatch notes that he draws from the hypothesis of Naitō Torajirō, which was first presented in lectures in Kyoto in the 1920s and then posthumously published in 1947. There is a summary of the Naitō position in H. Hiyakawa, "An Outline of the Naitō Hypothesis and its Effects on Japanese Studies on China," *Far Eastern Quarterly* 14 (1954–1955), 533–52. Naitō believed that a shift in power away from the old medieval aristocracy to the new gentry society occurred between mid-T'ang and the beginning of the Sung. Some American historians have tried to demonstrate that the old aristocratic families retained power into the first few reigns of the Northern Sung. With the shift came increased power for the

emperor, who was no longer dependent on the northern clans for support.

9. Hatch, "Thought of Su Hsün," p. 7.

10. Arthur Waley, trans., *The Analects of Confucius* (New York: Modern Library, 1938), bk. 13, chap. 18, pp. 175-76. The parenthetical book and chapter numbers are in James Legge, trans., *The Chinese Classics*, 5 vols. (Hong Kong: Hong Kong University Press, 1960), vol. 1. Hereafter, unless otherwise indicated, all references to the *Analects* give book and chapter numbers in the Legge edition. Unless otherwise specified, translations are mine.

11. *Analects* 12.22.

12. Chu accuses the Mohists of having no idea of rank distinctions (*wu fen*).

13. See Wang Hsien-ch'ien, ed., *Hsün-tzu chi-chieh* (*Hsün-tzu* with collected annotations) (Taipei: Shih-chieh shu-chü, 1957), "Wang chih p'ien" (The regulations of a king), 104 (5.9a).

14. Walton-Vargo, "Education, Social Change, and Neo-Confucianism," 134.

15. Suzuki Chūsei, "Sōdai Bukkyō kessha no kenkyū" (A study of Buddhist societies in the Sung period), *Shigaku zasshi* (Journal of historical studies) 52 (1941), 94.

16. Ibid., 93.

17. Ibid., 92 (free food) and 94 (street paving).

18. Chu Hsi, *Hui-an hsien-sheng Chu Wen-kung wen-chi* (Collection of literary works of Master Chu), *Ssu-pu ts'ung-k'an* (SPTK) ed., vol. 5, 11.16a; hereafter cited as *Wen-chi*. The passage accurately describes the organizational principles of society, with one amusing exception. Chu offers a Confucian's romanticized view of how the premiership *should* operate (sharing decision making with the emperor) rather than how it actually operated.

19. Some small prefectures (*chou*) were called *chün*. The prefecture to which I refer is Nan k'ang *chün*, to which Chu was appointed in A.D. 1178 (T'o-t'o, *Sung shih* [History of the Sung] [Beijing: Chung-hua shu-chü, 1977], 7:2188).

20. *Wen-chi*, vol. 5, 11.15a–b.

21. Ibid., vol. 12, 25.7b.

22. Robert P. Hymes, "Prominence and Power in Sung China: The Local Elite of Fu-chou, Chiang-hsi" (Ph.D. diss., University of

Pennsylvania, 1979), 262–69. Chu's innovation included charging 20 percent interest until the original amount of borrowed rice was repaid. According to Hymes, in supporting local academies, the community compact, community granaries, and altars honoring local persons or Neo-Confucian heros, Chu Hsi wanted to introduce some structure into the local community as an entity apart from the central state and its local organs. He tried to accomplish through volunteerism in the community what Wang An-shih had tried to do through the state political apparatus. Hymes contrasts Chu's approach with that of Lu Chiu-yüan (1139–1192), for whom charity stops with the extended family, which itself operates as a community. For Lu, there was no intermediate level between the family and the state (Robert P. Hymes, "On Academies, Community Institutions, and Lu Chiu-yüan," unpublished paper prepared for the "Conference on Neo-Confucian Education: The Formative Stage," Princeton, New Jersey, 1984. Cited by permission of the author.) For the memorial advocating that the community granaries be set up throughout the empire, see *Wen-chi*, vol. 6, 13.17b–18a.

23. *Wen-chi*, vol. 12, 15.7a.

24. Ibid., vol. 5, 11.16b.

25. Ibid., vol. 6, 13.2a.

26. Ibid., vol. 5, 11.8a.

27. Ibid., vol. 5, 11.39a, and vol. 6, 12.4a.

28. Ibid., vol. 6, 13.1b.

29. Ibid., vol. 8, 18.22a.

30. On peasants, see ibid., vol. 5, 11.12a; on soldiers, ibid., vol. 5, 11.23b; on merchants, ibid., vol. 8, 17.30a.

31. Chu Hsi, *Chu Tzu ch'üan-shu* (Complete works of Master Chu), facsimile reprint of the 1885 reprint of the 1715 ed., 2 vols. (Taipei: Kuang-hsüeh she, 1977), 44.4b (2:989); hereafter cited as *CTCS*. References are to *chüan* and page in the original, followed in parentheses by volume and page in the modern edition cited here.

32. Brought to my attention by Lionel Jensen.

33. Hatch, "Thought of Su Hsün," 16.

34. John W. Chaffee, "Education and Examinations in Sung Society (960–1279)" (Ph.D. diss., University of Chicago, 1979), 61.

The dissertation was published as *The Thorny Gates of Learning in Sung China: A Social History of Examinations* (Cambridge: Cambridge University Press, 1985), 35–37.

35. Chaffee, "Education and Examinations," 162.

36. Tillman, *Utilitarian Confucianism*, 170.

37. Haeger, "Neo-Confucian Syncretism," 507.

38. In a community of one mind the people model themselves on a sagelike ruler and the ruler in turn models himself on the views of the early sages, who themselves took the natural order as their model in formulating rules of conduct (ªli). This is discussed in Chapter Five. There are readily accessible references in English to Ch'eng I's discussion of the idea of "one mind": see Wing-tsit Chan, *Reflections on Things at Hand* (New York: Columbia University Press, 1967), 206–207.

39. Translated by John Chaffee in "Education and Examinations," 138. See also his *Thorny Gates*, 79.

40. Hatch, "Thought of Su Hsün," 8.

41. Chaffee, "Education and Examinations," 219.

42. Ibid., 141. See Chaffee, *Thorny Gates*, 74–76.

43. These are the *Book[s] of Changes, Odes, History, Rites* and *Music*, and the *Spring and Autumn Annals*.

44. Walton-Vargo, "Education, Social Change, and Neo-Confucianism," 196.

45. Patricia B. Ebrey, *Family and Property in Sung China* (Princeton: Princeton University Press, 1983), 158–62.

46. For example, George Berkeley. See his "Three Dialogues," in *Essays, Principles, Dialogues*, ed. Mary W. Calkins (New York: Charles Scribner's Sons, 1929), 251–52. His attack on abstract ideas and on the idea of substance assumes an imagistic way of thinking.

47. S. M. Ulam, *Adventures of a Mathematician* (New York: Charles Scribner's Sons, 1976), 183.

48. Freeman Dyson, "Disturbing the Universe," *New Yorker*, 13 August 1979, 69.

49. George Lakoff and Mark Johnson, "Conceptual Metaphor in Everyday Language," *Journal of Philosophy* 77 (August 1980), 455.

50. For a discussion of the emotive function of metaphor, see

James Fernandez, "The Mission of Metaphor in Expressive Culture," *Current Anthropology* 15 (June 1974), 123–24.

51. In the academic debates, one approach popular among anthropologists is to presume that utterances in another culture that the ethnographer cannot understand or finds irrational are metaphorical. The opposing position is that sufficient awareness of context can often render seemingly strange "metaphorical" statements intelligible. In his study of Nuer religion, Edward Evans-Pritchard notes that the Nuer may say, of rain or of a crocodile, "it is Spirit." Evans-Pritchard opposes treating this as a metaphor for the idea of mystical identity. He argues that the Nuer are perfectly capable of explaining that they mean that rain is not really Spirit but an instrument that a spirit uses to manifest itself. As he interprets the anthropological controversy, "anthropological explanations display two main errors. The first, best exemplified in the writings of Lévy-Bruhl, is that when a people say that something is something else which is different they are contravening the Law of Contradiction and substituting for it a law of their own mystical participation. I hope at least to have shown that Nuer do not assert identity between the two things" (Edward E. Evans-Pritchard, *Nuer Religion* [Oxford: Oxford University Press, 1956], 140). (Bruce Mannheim, of the Department of Anthropology at the University of Michigan, clarified for me the nature of the controversy and recommended a number of sources, including the Evans-Pritchard work.) In other words, if in translating the statements of a person in another culture the ethnographer does not completely grasp something, he tries to work around it by classifying it as "metaphor." What is lost is situational or cultural context. The ethnographer implicitly assumes a Platonic-like universe that transcends the differences between the world implicit in his culture and that in the other (Jacques Derrida, "White Mythology: Metaphor in the Text of Philosophy," in *Jacques Derrida: Margins of Philosophy*, trans. Alan Bass [Chicago: University of Chicago Press, 1982], 207–71). If the ethnographer and someone belonging to the culture under study differ on the interpretation of a commonplace natural object, the latter's account often becomes explained as metaphor. Here again the critic of this approach would say that the researcher who assumes such a universe misses something in his translated ac-

count, namely, the culture-specific ontology presumed to exist in that other culture. His account will obscure differences between the two worlds that are a function of how members of each respectively envision their universe.

Philosophical, literary, and anthropological analyses often have claimed that metaphors have hidden meanings in addition to literal ones and that the reader must interpret, not simply comprehend, the words in order to grasp these submerged ideas. This seems to be the position in Max Black's "interaction view" of metaphor, in which one's ideas of a subject and the entity used metaphorically to describe it interact and together produce a new meaning that is a result of the interaction (Max Black, *Models and Metaphors: Studies in Language and Philosophy* [Ithaca, N.Y.: Cornell University Press, 1962], 38). In challenging this position, Donald Davidson has written, "The theorist who tries to explain a metaphor by appealing to a hidden message, like the critic who attempts to state the message, is then fundamentally confused. No such explanation or statement can be forthcoming because no such message exists" (Donald Davidson, *Inquiries into Truth and Interpretation* [Oxford: Clarendon Press, 1984], 263–64). Davidson also says, "We must give up the idea that a metaphor carries a message, that it has a content or meaning (except, of course, its literal meaning). The various theories we have been considering mistake their goal. Where they think they provide a method for deciphering an encoded content, they actually tell us (or try to tell us) something about the *effects* metaphors have on us" (ibid., 261).

To apply the idea of a hidden message to Chu's material means mainly to claim that even in his own day the meaning and/or function of the images was not clear to much of his audience. So today's interpreter who believes in the hidden messages supposedly has privileged access to those in Chu's writings. My own position with respect to Chu Hsi is different. It is that the set of images that he used are in some ways different from, and certainly interrelated differently from, those used in today's Western culture. But their role in explaining theories and promoting values was not entirely hidden to his disciples. My task is to clarify to someone living today what they were and how they functioned. In the process I hope to show something about how one of history's important thinkers formulated and used his theories. This approach uncovers more about how people think than about hidden messages. I focus on something straightforward, namely, the salient points of the organizational relationships among parts of a whole suggested by a particular structural image. In addition, I am concerned with the emotional responses that Chu Hsi's images seem designed to elicit from his readers.

52. Ch'eng Hao and Ch'eng I, *I-shu* (Written legacy), 22A.14b, in *Erh Ch'eng ch'üan-shu* (Complete works of the two Ch'engs) ed. Ssu-pu pei-yao; hereafter cited as *I-shu*. See also *Chu Tzu yü-lei ta-ch'üan* (Complete edition of the *Classified Conversations of Master Chu Hsi*), ed. Li Ching-te, 1207; ed. Yamagataya Shoshi, Kyoto, 1668 (reprint, 8 vols., Kyoto: Chūbun Shoten, 1973), 95.5b–6a, sec. 17 (6:5010–11) [95.4b; 6:3898]; hereafter cited as *CTYLTC*. All references to this work have the following format: the first set of numbers refers to the *chüan* and page(s), followed by the section within the *chüan* (counting from the beginning of each *chüan*) and, in parentheses, by the volume and consecutive page number(s) of the citation in *CTYLTC*. For purposes of cross-reference, the references in brackets following these numbers indicate the corresponding passages in the *Chu Tzu yü-lei* (Classified conversations of Master Chu Hsi) (1473; reprint, 8 vols., Taipei: Cheng-chung shu-chü, 1962); the first set of numbers indicates the *chüan* and page, and the second set gives the volume number and consecutive pagination.

53. In the first thirteen *chüan* of the *Classified Conversations*, the reader will encounter a host of other pictorial images that generally occur only once or at most a few times: bamboo basket, alchemy, cleaning a table, big stone, brewing wine, colors, hatching an egg, cutting a peach, stomach, climbing a mountain, wings of a bird, raining, catching a thief, collecting a tax, cleaning a house, accumulating wealth, boating, and a boat. In addition to these images that occur rarely and with no particular significance, three other images do occur in philosophically interesting contexts. One is breath, appearing about four times. I discuss it in Chapter Four in connection with the cyclical pattern of movement of the yin and yang. The second comprises various aspects of a house. The references to houses have no overlapping themes of any philosophi-

cal significance, except for three to house foundations, all to the effect that study needs a foundation in the same way that a house does. This image is not frequently used, however, nor does it spawn subsidiary ones. The third image, of which there are about three examples, is the knife, used to explain how the moral sense (ᵃ*i*) cuts right through to illuminate distinctions.

54. Rodney Needham, *Symbolic Classification* (Santa Monica, Calif.: Goodyear, 1979), 63–64. If one picks the right standpoint, any two things can be said to be similar. All things could be said to belong to the class of physical objects and share material properties.

55. *CTYLTC* 15.15b, sec. 67 (2:740) [15.12b; 1:534].

56. See Donald J. Munro, *The Concept of Man in Early China*, (Stanford: Stanford University Press, 1969), 51ff.

57. Wang Hsien-ch'ien, *Hsün-tzu chi-chieh*, "Li lun p'ien" (A discussion of rites), 236 (7:11a); this translation is a modified version of that by Homer H. Dubs, *The Works of Hsuntze* (London: Probsthain, 1928), 223–24.

58. Thomas Metzger describes totalistic understanding in *Escape from Predicament*, 66.

59. During the Chou period, the family image with its picture of social positions and their duties was a well-established explanation of society as a whole. The ruler was "the father and mother of the people," a phrase appearing in the *Book of Odes* and the *Mencius*. The corresponding value of role fulfillment accompanied the image, even when the topic was not the actual family, as in the statement, "Filial piety is that by which one serves his ruler" (*Great Learning* 9; here and throughout, unless otherwise indicated, references to *Great Learning* are to chapter numbers in Legge, and, unless otherwise specified, translations are mine). Han-dynasty texts treated nature as a model for humans. Things in nature have their appropriate positions and duties, the fulfillment of which is appropriate for all that nature encompasses. The *Book of Changes* commentaries treated the first two trigrams as father and mother and the other six as their children, with predictable obligations for all things classifiable under them. Within their respective geographical positions, the five elements have allotted duties that it is "proper" for them to carry out. (Much of this is discussed in Chap-

ter Two of this work; see, for example, Chapter Two, n. 14.) If planets move east, consistent with their positions, they are obedient; if west, they are disobedient (Steven Craig Davidson, "Tung Chung-shu and the Origins of Imperial Confucianism" Ph.D. diss., University of Wisconsin, 1982, 216).

The principal Taoist texts in which the water and mirror images appear in association with the values of purity and clarity are the *Chuang-tzu* and *Huai-nan-tzu* (The book of [the prince of] Huai); the latter was compiled during the reign of a prince who died in 122 B.C. Water must be free from mud and calm in order to reflect, just as a mind must be free of desires and prejudices to respond to things in a sagelike manner. Running water in a stream suggests that the impurities have already been agitated. Clarity exists in still water, a point also made in Hsün Tzu's "Chieh pi" (Dispelling obsessions) chapter. The Taoist works also introduce the mirror image to explain many of the same things that the water image does. Mirrors free of dust reflect properly. On the water and mirror images, see Paul Demiéville, "Le miroir spirituel," *Sinologica* (Basel) 1, no. 1 (1948), 117–21. *Tao-te ching* (chap. 10) suggests the need to polish one's mirror (mind) in order to get rid of the dust, that is, desires and prejudicial standards. Buddhist works make the same points with the mirror image; however, as Paul Demiéville showed ("Le miroir spirituel," 122), whether or not they advocated getting rid of the dust (exerting effort to purify the mind) was a function of whether they were gradualists on the question of enlightenment (yes, polish away), or believers in sudden enlightenment (no, even the dust is part of the Buddha). For the mirror as light source rather than as mere passive reflector of objects, one must look to post-Han sources. In Chapter Three I refer to post-Han Taoist references. There is a report that at the beginning of the eighth century one patriarch compared the purity of the great tao to the sparkle of a bronze mirror that is self-bright and to the light of the sun (ibid., 114). Though the mirror dominates the Buddhist imagery, other light sources, such as the sun, moon, and lamps, appear, especially in the Ch'an texts. Although there would be differences among the Ch'an schools in the meaning and desirability of special religious efforts to keep the light glowing, there is always the value of avoiding its obscuration: "self-nature is always pure, just as the sun and moon are always shining. It is only when they are obscured by clouds that there is brightness above but darkness below . . ." (Wing-tsit Chan, trans., *The Platform Scripture* [New York: St John's University Press, 1963], 59). The monk Shen Hsiu (605?–706) is identified with the maxim, "Do not allow it to become dusty" (ibid., 35), meaning that he advocated the value of special effort to cleanse the mind. In contrast, the sixth patriarch negated the subject-object distinction between "mirror and dust."

Mencius repeatedly used the plant image to explain the relation between man's innate traits and environmental nurturance. (*Mencius* 6A.7–8 are among the most famous passages. The value of inner nurturance is pervasive. See for example, ibid., 1A.2. Here and throughout, unless otherwise indicated, references to *Mencius* are to book, part [A or B], and chapter in Legge, and, unless otherwise specified, any translations are mine.)

Finally, on the matter of describing facets of the mind with the analogy of the ruler-ruled division in the world or in society, see Mencius' distinction between a heavenly "nobility," certain innate moral tendencies that should be valued above "human nobility," and the occupation of a position of rank (symbolizing the other human traits) (*Mencius* 6A.16 and 2A.7). Those persons who emerge from self-cultivation with a commitment to follow the inner ruler have established their wills (*li chih*) or they have unmoved minds (ibid., 2A.2 and 7B.15). Hsün Tzu spoke of the mind as the "heavenly ruler" (*t'ien-chün*) (Wang Hsien-ch'ien, *Hsün-tzu chi-chieh*, "T'ien lun" (A discussion of heaven), 206 [11.17b]). This label had been used exclusively to designate the reigning king during the Western Chou. On this topic, see Munro, *Concept of Man in Early China*, 58–65.

60. Margaret MacDonald, "The Language of Political Theory," in *Logic and Language*, ed. Antony Flew (Oxford: Basil Blackwell, 1955), 171–74. This was brought to my attention by James MacAdam of Trent University.

61. Commentators often cite *Analects* 9.16.

62. From Chu Hsi's commentary on sec. 2 of the *Great Learning*.

63. Discussion with Barbara Congelosi has helped clarify my thinking about this matter, especially as it applies to contemporary

Chinese society. The topic is addressed in more detail in Chapter Six.

64. *CTYLTC* 18.10b–11a, sec. 30 (2:952–53) [18.8b; 2:700].

65. In considering this matter, I have benefited from the papers entitled "The System of Chu Hsi's Philosophy," by Tomoeda Ryū-tarō, and "Chu Hsi's Doctrine of Principle," by Qiu Hansheng, both presented at the International Conference on Chu Hsi convened in Honolulu in 1982 and published in *Chu Hsi and Neo-Confucianism*, ed. Wing-tsit Chan (Honolulu: University of Hawaii Press, 1986), 158–68 and 116–37, respectively.

66. *CTYLTC* 13.4a, sec. 30 (1:593) [13.3b; 1:418].

67. See the discussion in Chang Li-wen, *Chu Hsi ssu-hsiang yen-chiu* (Study of Chu Hsi's thought) (Beijing: Chung-kuo she-hui k'o-hsüeh ch'u-pan she, 1981), 528–29.

Two

1. *CTCS* 42.8a (2:954). There is a discussion of Ch'eng I and Chu Hsi on the shared traits of all humans and the use of the seed image to describe the presence of ᵇ*li* in Olaf Graf, *Tao und Jen* (Tao and *jen*) (Wiesbaden: Otto Harrassowitz, 1970), 52.

2. Chan, *Reflections*, 15–16.

3. Ch'eng Hao and Ch'eng I, "Li hsü" (Preface on rites), 2.1b, in *He-nan Ch'eng shih i-wen* (Literary legacy of the two Ch'engs of He-nan), appended to the *Erh Ch'eng ch'üan-shu*.

4. *CTCS* 46.15a–b (2:1022).

5. *Book of Odes*, no. 172. See also *Mencius* 1B.7 and 4A.5.

6. Referring to the famous and contested phrase at the beginning of the *Great Learning*.

7. Ch'eng I, *I chuan* (Commentary on the *Book of Changes*), 1.2b, in *Erh Ch'eng ch'üan-shu*; hereafter cited as *I chuan*.

8. Quoted in Chan, *Reflections*, 202.

9. *Mencius* 3B.4, brought to my attention by Robert Eno.

10. Hsieh Yu-wei, "Filial Piety and Chinese Society," in *Philosophy and Culture East and West*, ed. Charles A. Moore (Honolulu: University of Hawaii Press, 1962), 424.

11. *Politics*, bk. 1, secs. 3–4 (l.125b).

12. Another example: Fustel de Coulanges, *The Ancient City* (1864), trans. Willard Small (Garden City, N.Y., 1956).

13. *Hsiao ching* (Classic of filial piety), Ssu-pu pei-yao SPPY ed., 3.1b.

14. The *Book of Documents* (*Shu ching*) contains the passages, "From Heaven are the social arrangements with their several duties" (*t'ien-hsü yu tien*) and "From Heaven are the social distinctions with their several ceremonies" (*t'ien-chih yu li*). See James Legge, trans., *The Chinese Classics*, vol. 3, *The Shoo King, or The Book of Historical Documents*, "The Counsels of Kaou-Yaou," p. 73 (2.3.3.6). Chu Hsi quotes from the passage. The *Tso chuan* lists four ranks of rulers (king, duke, minister, and knight) and six of ruled, in an apparent attempt to pair ten social positions with the ten time divisions of the day (*Tso chuan*, Chao *kung* 7). *Analects* 2.1 refers to the pole star staying in its place (*so*) while the myriad stars pay respect to it, perhaps an early example of the application to nature of the idea of social place. Hsün Tzu analogized from the set of ritualized rules (ᵃ*li*) that order a hierarchical society according to the "rules" that account for orderly behavior by planets and rivers: "ᵃ*Li* is that whereby Heaven and Earth unite, whereby the sun and moon are bright, whereby the four seasons are ordered, whereby the stars move in the courses, whereby rivers flow" (Dubs, *Works of Hsuntze*, 223–24). By the Han period, the analogy of social space with inviolable boundaries (i.e., social duties and rights that are exclusive to a given group) applied to the cosmos began to appear regularly: "Each of the five elements circulates according to its sequence; each of them exercises its own capacities in the performance of its official duties. Thus wood occupies the eastern quarter where it rules over the forces of spring" (Fung Yu-lan, *History of Chinese Philosophy*, trans. Derk Bodde [Princeton: Princeton University Press, 1952], 2:21); and "The five fluids come forward in turn, each of them takes precedence once. When they do not keep to their proper sphere, there is disaster; when they do, everything is well ordered" (*Su wen*, quoted in Alfred Forke, *World Conception of the Chinese* [London: Probsthain, 1952], 252). The Taoist Hsi K'ang (A.D. 223–262) differentiated his proper cosmic place from any Confucian social place, from which we know that social and cosmic place were not always the same thing.

See Richard B. Mather, "The Controversy over Conformity and Naturalness During the Six Dynasties," *Journal of the History of Religions* 9, nos. 2–3 (1969–1970), 166, 168. Correspondences between man and nature in the Han period also derive from analogizing from the human organism, with its emotions and will, to heaven and nature.

15. Davidson, "Tung Chung-shu," 216.

16. *Hsiao ching*, SPPY ed., 7.1b.

17. See the *Hsi tz'u chüan* (Commentary on the appended judgments to the *Chou I*), SPPY ed., *hsia*, 8.3b. The point is discussed in Richard Wilhelm, trans., *The I Ching or Book of Changes*, English trans. from German by Cary F. Baynes (London: Routledge and Kegan Paul, 1960), 1:361. The light trigrams are the three sons and the dark ones are the three daughters.

18. See Chu Hsi's annotated and arranged version of Chou Tun-i's *T'ung shu* (Penetrating the *Book of Changes*), in *Chou Lien-hsi chi* (Collected works of Chou Lien-hsi), ed. Chang Po-hsing (1651–1725) (Shanghai: Shang-wu yin-shu-kuan, 1937), *chüan* 5, 105.

19. Fung Yu-lan, "The Philosophy at the Basis of Traditional Chinese Society," in *Ideological Differences and World Order*, ed. Filmer S. C. Northrop (New Haven: Yale University Press, 1949), 26.

20. *CTYLTC* 3.16b, sec. 56 (1:234) [3.13a; 1:135].

21. *Han Fei-tzu*, trans. Burton Watson (New York: Columbia University Press, 1964), 35.

22. Francis M. Cornford, *From Religion to Philosophy* (New York: Harper, 1957).

23. *The Li Ki*, trans. James Legge, in F. Max Muller ed., *Sacred Books of the East* (London: Oxford University Press, 1926), 27:379–80.

24. Legge, trans., *The Chinese Classics* 2:251–52 (*Mencius* 3A.4). The *Doctrine of the Mean* 20 reverses the order of the first two sets, placing prince-minister first. (Here and throughout, unless otherwise indicated, references to *Doctrine of the Mean* are to chapter numbers in Legge, and, unless otherwise specified, any translations are mine.)

25. Hsü Dau-lin, "The Myth of the 'Five Human Relations' of Confucius," *Monumenta Serica* 29 (1970–1971), 33. Chu also refers to the set of roles in *CTCS* 60.14a–b (3:1312).

26. Hsü Dau-lin, "Myth of the 'Five Human Relations,' " 30–32.

27. *I-shu* 1.2a.

28. The idea is important in Confucian and Legalist works, and Hsün Tzu developed a theory about it. The assumption is that terms simultaneously describe, carry moral judgments, and persuade. Confucians maintained that Confucius compiled the *Spring and Autumn Annals* (a terse record of the state of Lu, 722–481 B.C.) using this method. By calling an illegitimate ruler a brigand rather than a king, he conveyed his disapproval and tried to persuade other rulers to abide by kingly duties. Legalists sought such clarity in the wording of their laws that the people would be led to do their duties correctly.

29. *I-shu* 14.2a.

30. Ibid., 18.1b. Ch'eng I interpreted in this manner. Chu followed him, as is seen in his commentary on *Analects* 1.2.

31. Kingsley Davis and Wilbert E. Moore, "Some Principles of Stratification," *American Sociological Review* 10 (April 1945), 242. The authors argue that institutionalized inequality is necessary. Rewards and their distribution foster the stratification. These rewards include things that contribute to "sustenance and comfort" and things that contribute to "self-respect and ego expansion" (ibid., 243).

32. Ch'eng Hao and Ch'eng I, *Ts'ui-yen* (Pure words), 1.9a, in *Erh Ch'eng ch'üan-shu*; hereafter cited as *Ts'ui-yen*.

33. *I chuan* 4.20b.

34. *CTYLTC* 78.44b, sec. 238 (5:4210) [78.35a; 5:3269].

35. Wilhelm, trans., *The I Ching*, *Ken* hexagram, 2:303. The quotation has been altered slightly here.

36. *Ts'ui-yen* 1.29a.

37. *I-shu* 6.3a.

38. *I chuan* 4.21a.

39. Quoted in Fung Yu-lan, *History of Chinese Philosophy*, 2:503. The reference is to a *Book of Odes* passage cited in *Mencius* 6A.6. Mencius used the poem to argue that man's distinctive law (or nature, *hsing*) is his disposition to approve of and emulate goodness. Ch'eng I is reinterpreting *wu*, which the *Book of Odes* and Mencius treated as "species of thing," to mean ᵇ*shih*, or "role-defined af-

fair." Roles rather than things have thus become the vessels for heavenly norms. Robert Eno suggested this point to me.

40. *CTCS* 19.8b (1:413) and 53.59a (2:1195). The first passage is also in *CTYLTC* 47.3b, sec. 11 (4:2520) [47.2b–3a; 3:193]. See also *I chuan*, preface, 1a.

41. *CTYLTC* 52.31a, sec. 135 (4:2675) [52.24b; 3:2058]. On ᵇ*li* as ruler, see *CTCS* 43.34b–35a (2:985).

42. See note 1, this chapter.

43. *I-shu* 11.11b.

44. See the discussion and citations in Hou Wai-lu, *Chung-kuo ssu-hsiang t'ung-shih* (General history of Chinese thought), 5 vols. (Beijing: Jen-min ch'u-pan she, 1963), 4 (*hsia*):607, 622.

45. *CTCS* 46.13a (2:1021); also in *CTYLTC* 6.14b–15a, sec. 138 (1:390–391) [6.19b; 1:256].

46. *Ts'ui-yen* 1.2a.

47. *CTCS* 48.3b (2:1047).

48. *I-shu* 18.2a. Chan Sin-yee suggested to me that the social virtues have the form of attitudes.

49. Ibid., 11.2a.

50. Ch'eng Hao and Ch'eng I, *Wai-shu* (Additional works), 7.1a, in *Erh Ch'eng ch'üan-shu*; hereafter cited as *Wai-shu*.

51. Ibid.

52. *CTYLTC* 94.22b, sec. 195 (6:4986) [94.33b; 6:3878].

53. Ibid., 78.44b, sec. 239 (5:4210) [78.35a; 5:3269].

54. *I-shu* 5.16.

55. Ibid., 2A.4b. See also *Ts'ui-yen* 1.21b.

56. *I-shu* 15.1b.

57. Ibid., 2A.16a.

58. Ibid., 17.2b.

59. *CTCS* 7.29a–b (1:169).

60. *I-shu* 2A.13a.

61. Ibid., 14.2a.

62. *CTCS* 43.25b–26a (2:980–81).

63. T'an Po-fu and Wen Kung-wen, *The Kuan-tzu* (Carbondale, Ill.: Lewis Maverick, 1954), essay no. 39, pp. 86–87.

64. *CTYLTC* 8.1a, sec. 1 (1:405) [8.1a; 1:267].

65. Ibid., 3.4b–5a, sec. 19 (1:210–11) [3.3b–4a; 1:16–17].

66. *CTCS* 44.12b (2:993).

67. Ibid., 44.7b (2:990), gives a typical description of a cyclical pattern.

68. Ibid., 47.17a (2:1034).

69. Ibid., 45.4a (2:1007); also in *CTYLTC* 5.12a–b, sec. 72 (1:332–333) [5.10a–b; 1:211–212].

70. *CTYLTC* 4.19a, sec. 67 (1:289) [4.15a; 1:177]. See also *CTCS* 48.15b (2:1053).

71. Fung Yu-lan, *History of Chinese Philosophy*, 2:384.

72. John Blofeld, *The Zen Teaching of Huang Po* (New York: Grove Press, 1980), 41–42.

73. Chan, "The Evolution of the Neo-Confucian Concept of *Li* as Principle," *Tsing Hua Journal of Chinese Studies* 4 (February 1964), 134.

74. *Philebus* 15b, in *The Collected Dialogues of Plato*, ed. Huntington Cairns and Edith Hamilton (New York: Bollingen, 1961), 1091.

75. The picture of the moon is not entirely convincing, because only the moon's reflection is present in the many rivers.

76. *CTCS* 52.37b (2:1154) and 49.10b (2:1066). The former is also in *CTYLTC* 54.45a, sec. 205 (6:4991) [94.35b; 6:2882].

77. Étienne Lamotte, *La Somme du Grand Véhicule d'Asanga (Mahāyānasamgraha)* (Louvain: Institut Orientaliste Louvain-la-Neuve, 1973), 124. I am indebted to Luis Gómez of the University of Michigan for references to the Buddhist sources.

78. Edward Conze, ed., *Buddhist Texts through the Ages* (New York: Philosophical Library, 1954), 214.

79. One of the fragments collected in Tao-yüan's eleventh-century repository, *Ching-te ch'uan teng lu* (The transmission of the lamp of the Ching-te era [1004–1007]); Takakusu Junjirō and Watanabe Kaikyoku, eds., *Taishō shinshū daizōkyō* (The Taishō edition of the Chinese Buddhist canon), (Tokyo: Taishō shinshū daizōkyō kankōkai, 1927; reprint, 1968), work no. 2076, vol. 51, p. 460c. Luis Gómez assisted me with this translation. For a similar T'ien-t'ai reference, see work no. 1509, vol. 25, pp. 101b, 102b.

80. In the Mahāyāna Buddhist Yogācāra school, the water image suggests the passage of time. The *ālaya*, or storehouse consciousness (remotely evocative of what today would be called the subconscious), flows onward like a fast stream. This is a single homogeneous consciousness, not the private or discrete possession

of each individual. In this school and in T'ien-t'ai, the clarity of water suggests the degree of clarity of individual minds. The relationship between the ocean and waves suggests the relationship between the Absolute Mind, or Buddha, and the transitory phenomena of the empirical world. See Daisetz T. Suzuki, trans., *The Laṅkāvatāra-sūtra* (London: Routledge and Kegan Paul, 1973), 190; and Alex Wayman, "The Mirror as a Pan-Buddhist Metaphor-Simile," *History of Religions* 13 (May 1974), 255. Chu Hsi refers to the Buddhist use of the water image; see *CTCS* 44.9a (2:991). Buddhists also use water to suggest pure consciousness, or the Buddha nature; ice, or the reflections sometimes visible in it, suggests illusion, or conceptual thought (see Hou Wai-lu, *Chung-kuo ssu-hsiang t'ung-shih* 4 [*shang*]:558). The point is that Chu Hsi was structuring the cosmological underpinning of his ethics by using an explanatory image already familiar to his opponents.

81. *CTYLTC* 18.10b–11a, sec. 29 (2:952–53) [18.8b; 2:700]. Chu Hsi regularly speaks of the *tao-li* (natural principles) flowing forth everywhere.

82. *CTCS* 52.25a (2:1148); also in *CTYLTC* 94.16a–b, sec. 122 (6:4953–4954) [94.21a; 6:3853].

83. *CTYLTC* 4.12b, sec. 44 (1:276) [4.10a; 1:167]. See also *CTCS* 44.14a (2:994).

84. *CTYLTC* 5.8a, sec. 59 (1:323) [5.7a; 1:205]. Chu seems to be claiming that if a person sees clear water flowing, he can infer that the spring must be the source, in some way, of the clarity.

85. *CTCS* 52.25a (2:1148). The quote is from a commentary to the *Book of Changes*. Chu innovates by connecting the idea with his structural image. Also in *CTYLTC* 94.16a–b, sec. 122 (6:4953–4954) [94.21a; 6:3853].

86. *CTYLTC* 41.1a, sec. 4 (3:2251) [41.1a; 3:1721].

87. On the flow of the material force through man, see *CTYLTC* 4.22b, sec. 79 (1:296) [4.17b; 1:182].

88. *CTCS* 48.15b (2:1053).

89. Legge, trans., *The Chinese Classics* 1:222 (*Analects* 9.16).

90. *I-shu* 25.5a.

91. Takakusu and Watanabe, *Taishō shinshū daizōkyō*, work no. 1877, vol. 45, p. 647.

92. Ibid., p. 644. The quotation is from Fa Tsang (643–712), *Hua-*

yen yu-hsin fa-chieh chi (Record of the Avataṁsaka sutra's [teaching on] letting the mind roam free in the Absolute).

93. Chan, trans., *The Platform Scripture* sec. 18, p. 55.

94. *CTCS* 47.2a (2:1026); also in *CTYLTC* 6.14a, sec. 77 (1:369) [6.11a; 1:239].

95. *CTCS* 47.9a (2:1030).

96. I discuss this in Chapter Four. The inspiration for the progression from nourishing family to other people to all creatures comes from *Mencius* 7A.45 and *Doctrine of the Mean* 22.

97. Chan, *Reflections*, 14, 74.

98. For an early precedent, see J. K. Shryock, *The Study of Human Abilities: The Jen Wu Chih of Liu Shao* (New Haven: American Oriental Society, 1937), 39.

99. My own position would be that for Hsün Tzu there were also universal positive features of *hsing*. I have discussed the matter in *Concept of Man in Early China*, 77–81.

100. *CTCS* 43.6a–b (2:971); also in *CTYLTC* 4.16b, sec. 64 (1:284) [4.12b–13a; 1:172–173].

101. *CTCS* 43.4b (2:970); also in *CTYLTC* 4.15a, sec. 59 (1:201) [4.11b; 1:170].

102. *CTCS* 43.6b (2:971); also in *CTYLTC* 4.16b–17a, sec. 64 (1:284–285) [4.13a; 1:173].

103. *CTCS* 43.13a (2:974).

104. *CTYLTC* 4.3b, sec. 14 (1:258) [4.2a; 1:151].

105. Ibid.

THREE

1. *CTCS* 60.12b (2:1311); also in *CTYLTC* 126.6b–7a, sec. 12 (8:6266–6267) [126.5b; 8:4884].

2. *CTCS* 60.27b (2:1318).

3. *I-shu* 18.10b. For some examples of Chu Hsi making similar points, see *CTCS* 60.14a–15b (2:1312). Also in *CTYLTC* 126.11a–12b, secs. 40–42 (8:6275–6278) [126.8b–10a; 8:4890–4893].

4. *CTCS* 60.15b (2:4312); *I-shu* 2A.9a.

5. *CTCS* 48.15b (2:1053).

6. *Wen-chi*, vol. 32, 67.20a–b.

7. Wing-tsit Chan, *Instructions for Practical Living and Other Neo-*

Confucian Writings by Wang Yang-ming (New York: Columbia University Press, 1963), 94.

8. An idea associated with Hui Neng (638–713), one of the patriarchs of the Ch'an school.

9. The pure mind is the one that is referred to in the Buddhist phrase *kuan hsin*, "to observe the mind" (*Wen-chi*, vol. 32, 67.20a–21b).

10. Chu Hsi understands by *ke* (as in the phrase *ke wu*, "the investigation of things") "to come in contact with" or "to arrive at." For a comparison of his interpretation with that of Wang Yang-ming, see Tu Wei-ming, *Neo-Confucian Thought in Action: Wang Yang-ming's Youth (1472–1509)* (Berkeley: University of California Press, 1976), 163–64. For a reference by Chu Hsi to the four basic fonts or sentiments "touching" (*ch'u*) phenomena, see *CTYLTC* 14.15a, sec. 82 (2:669) [14.12a; 1:479]. In other places (such as his study of the *Great Learning*), he uses the phrase *chi wu* (touch or approach things) to explain the way in which one increases knowledge to the utmost (used in the passage cited in n. 26, this chapter). One touches things and thereby exhausts their principles. See also my discussion of the clustering of knowing and feeling in *The Concept of Man in Contemporary China* (Ann Arbor: University of Michigan Press, 1977), chap. 2.

11. *CTYLTC* 26.3b, sec. 13 (2:1452) [26.3a; 2:1093].

12. *CTCS* 44.23b (2:998).

13. The image of light ties in with Chapter Two's discussion of the image of water's light-conducting properties as an explanation of the pure principle found in everyone. Light is a characteristic of pure water. People must use that light, as it brightens their minds, to comprehend the principle that already links them together. The image of the mind projecting outward is consistent with the broader portrait of the mind found in the writings of Chu Hsi and the Ch'eng brothers. Chu Hsi literally describes the mind as having within it hollow places, something humans can infer empirically from observing the hearts (mind is located in the heart) of chickens and pigs. See *CTYLTC* 98.9b, sec. 43 (7:5206) [98.7b; 6:4052]. The spatial picture is significant, because Chu Hsi repeatedly uses terminology meaning thrusting out or projecting from the mind, which the Ch'engs call the "door" from which morality

proceeds (Ch'eng I, *Ching shuo* [Explanation of the classics], 1.2b, in *Erh Ch'eng ch'üan-shu*; hereafter cited as *Ching shuo*). The sentiments (ª*ch'ing*) constitute the location from which yang ª*ch'i* issues forth (*CTYLTC* 5.14a, sec. 79 (1:335) [5.11a; 1:213], quoting Master Ch'eng). Ch'eng Hao says that when a person has a humane and righteous mind, "the ª*ch'i* of his humaneness and righteousness glides easily outward into the external realm" (*I-shu* 4.2a). In the case of those with sagelike wisdom, the mind's principle "flows forth" (*liu-hsing*), pervading everything (*CTYLTC* 98.13b, sec. 63 (7:5214) [98.11a; 6:4059]). Members of the Chu Hsi school love to quote the *Book of Changes* passage that says that when affected by things, the mind then penetrates all things in the universe (*CTCS* 44.24a [2:998]). Among the popular terms for "to understand" are ª*t'ung* and *t'ou*, both of which literally mean "to penetrate." There is a pejorative reference to the mind's "going out," in which the phrase is a metaphor for the self's being seduced into undue preoccupation with material things (ibid., 44.23b [2:999]). That usage, however, is different from the description of the mind's affective and cognitive reaction to things as an outward projection that serves to connect the self and the external object.

14. *CTYLTC* 57.3b, sec. 10 (4:2836) [57.3a; 4:2187]; see also 5.3b, sec. 24 (1:314) [5.3a; 1:197] for use of the light metaphor.

15. Ibid., 31.9b, sec. 30 (3:1746) [31.7b–8a; 2:1322–23]. This interpretation of *tzu-ming* is justified by the discussion in ibid., 31.3a, sec. 8 (3:1733) [31.2b; 2:1312].

16. Wang P'i-chiang, ed., *T'ang jen ch'üan-ch'i hsiao-shuo* (T'ang romances) (Taipei: Shih-chieh shu-chü, 1969), 7. This reference was brought to my attention by James Crump. Mirror light was considered to be yin rather than yang. Such light had the capacity to reveal demons, find water, and penetrate walls. It is quite reasonable to assume that Chu Hsi learned such popular beliefs about mirrors from childhood stories. There are earlier references than these T'ang ones to the ability of at least some minds to project light. *Jen-wu chih*, written in the mid-third century A.D. by Liu Shao (translated by Shryock as *The Study of Human Abilities*), contains the following description of certain types of people: "A man of clear vision may understand the secret of action, yet be unable to think profoundly. A man of profound intellect may know the

source of meditation, and yet be distressed when he is forced to act quickly. The former is like fire and the sun, shining without, but invisible within. The latter is like metal and water, bright within, but unable to radiate light. The significance of these two is the difference between *Yin* and *Yang*" (pp. 96–97).

17. Richard H. Robinson, *Early Mādhyamika in India and China* (Madison: University of Wisconsin Press, 1967), 216. See also p. 128. The original is in Takakusu and Watanabe, *Taishō shinshū dai-zōkyō*, work no. 1858, vol. 45, p. 153. I am grateful to Livia Kohn for alerting me to the importance of Seng Chao in this connection, and for other references to the Six Dynasties and T'ang writers' explanations of cognition in terms of projecting light.

18. Chan, *Platform Scripture*, sec. 6, p. 35.

19. An early eighth-century text speaks of a fifth-century patriarch who compared the purity of the "great tao" to the sparkle of a bronze mirror that is seen to be self-bright once one rubs the dust off it, or to the light of the sun that is self-projecting. Subsequent Buddhist texts use the lamp and the sun as well as the mirror to describe wisdom or the Buddha nature. See Demiéville, "Le miroir spirituel," 114, 124.

20. Isabel Robinet, "The Taoist Immortal: Jesters of Light and Shadow, Heaven and Earth," *Journal of Chinese Religions* 13–14 (1985–1986), 91–92. The inner light is associated with water. See Isabelle Robinet, *Méditation Taoiste* (Paris: Dervy Livres, 1979), 252. For meditation practices by which the adept can cause divinities to appear in his magical mirror, see Max Kaltenmark, "Miroirs magiques," in *Mélanges sinologiques offerts à M. Demiéville* (Paris, 1974), 2:151–166.

21. Livia Kohn, "Taoist Insight Meditation—The Tang Practice of *Neiquan*" (Ann Arbor: Center for Chinese Studies, University of Michigan, forthcoming). The translation is from the early T'ang Taoist meditation text, the *Canon on Introspective Observation* (*Nei-kuan ching*).

22. Livia Kohn, *Seven Steps to the Tao: Sima Chengzhen's "Zuowanglun," Monumenta Serica* Monographs, no. 20 (St. Augustin/Nettetal, 1987), 37, 55–56.

23. *CTYLTC* 55.2b, sec. 8 (4:2774) [55.2a; 4:2137]. This refers to the sun.

24. Ibid., 11.2a, sec. 11 (1:497) [11.2a; 1:341] and 96.11a–b, sec. 47 (6:5115–16) [96.9a; 6:3981].

25. Ibid., 14.15a, sec. 82 (2:669) [14.12a; 1:479].

26. Ibid., 12.7a, sec. 56 (1:555) [12.5b; 1:386–87].

27. Ibid., 15.2a, sec. 4 (2:713) [15.1b; 1:512].

28. *Hsi-shan hsien-sheng Chen Wen-chung kung wen-chi* (Collected works of Chen Te-hsiu), SPTK ed., vol. 15, 30.11a–12b.

29. *CTYLTC* 16.33a, sec. 146 (2:843) [16.26a; 1:613]. See also 16.30b, sec. 141 (2:838–839) [16.24b; 1:610].

30. Ibid., 15.15b, sec. 67 (2:740) [15.12b; 1:534].

31. Ibid., 15.11a, sec. 47 (2:731) [15.9a; 1:527]. I read "that" as external and "this" as internal. There is direct evidence for the fact that the "investigation of things" (or study, which is Chu Hsi's typical example of it) illuminates the mind by removing the material obstructions that obscure the self-bright principles. See ibid., 17.8a, sec. 28 (2:908) [17.7a; 1:665], and 12.10b–11a, sec. 78 (1:562–63) [12.8b–9a; 1:392–93]. Investigating is "like polishing a mirror" so that it illuminates and is illuminated. See ibid., 14.19b, sec. 92 (2:678) [14.15b; 1:486] and 5.11b, sec. 69 (1:330) [5.9b; 1:210]. Personal effort to brighten the mind in turn enhances the ability to know and respond properly to objective things and their principles (ibid., 130.24b, sec. 93 (8:6485) [130.19a; 8:5055]).

32. From his commentary on the passage, "The extension of knowledge lies in the investigation of things," quoted in Ch'en P'an, *Ta-hsüeh Chung-yung chin shih* (Modern explanation of the *Great Learning* and *Doctrine of the Mean*) (Taipei: Kuo-li pien-i kuan, 1966), 27.

33. *CTYLTC* 15.21b, sec. 101 (2:752) [15.17a; 1:543].

34. Ibid., 15.10a, sec. 44 (2:729) [15.8a; 1:525].

35. Ibid., 18.12a, sec. 37 (2:955) [18.9b; 2:702]. Chu says that merely studying the principles of externals without making the round trip to oneself is like the progress of a wandering horse with no home stall where it can rest. For Chu Hsi's meaning of [b]*li* as mainly moral principles in this connection, see ibid., 6.3b, sec. 23 (1:348) [6.3a; 1:223]. See also Chu's commentary on *Analects* 12.1. He says that the rules of conduct ([a]*li*) are the specific details of the heavenly principles. For other examples, see Chang Li-wen, *Chu Hsi ssu-hsiang yen-chiu*, 522, 549.

36. *CTCS* 44.19a (2:996). Once the sentiments are aroused, what we know are the *i-li* (moral principles); see *CTYLTC* 62.39a, sec. 137 (4:3187) [62.30a; 4:2465]. The social role sentiment or duty aspect of ᵇ*li* continued to be stressed by later scholars influenced by Chu Hsi. In his inscription for a school near Hangchow in 1345, a Hanlin academician wrote: "This principle [ᵇ*li*] is prepared in the heart of men and is expressed in the relations between ruler and minister, father and son, husband and wife, and between friends" (see Walton-Vargo, "Education, Social Change, and Neo-Confucianism," 210).

37. *CTYLTC* 15.11a, sec. 47 (2:731) [15.8b–9a; 1:526–27].

38. *CTCS* 9.16a (1:199); also in *CTYLTC* 18.10a, sec. 28 (2:951) [18.8a; 2:699].

39. *CTYLTC* 6.20a, sec. 107 (1:381) [6.15b; 1:248].

40. Ibid., 15.11a, sec. 47 (2:731) [15.9a; 1:527]. See also sec. 46.

41. Ibid., 15.15b, sec. 67 (2:740) [15.12b; 1:543].

42. Ibid., 130.24b, sec. 93 (8:6486) [130.19a; 8:5055] and 14.12b–14b, secs. 65–81 (2:664–69) [14.10b–12a; 1:476–79]. The phrase *ming ming-te* is from the *Great Learning*.

43. See, for example, *CTYLTC* 18.19a, sec. 96 (2:989) [18.13a; 2:729]. There is a discussion of some of these terms in Chang Li-wen, "Lun Chu Hsi che-hsüeh te luo-chi chieh-kou" (A discussion of the logical structure of Chu Hsi's philosophy), *Che-hsüeh yen-chiu* (Philosophical investigations), no. 4 (1981), 49–50.

44. *CTYLTC* 115.2b, sec. 5 (7:5744) [115.2a; 7:4471] and 96.11a–b, sec. 47 (6:5115–16) [96.9a; 6:3981]. There is mental illumination of the structure of the object or situation and of how to act toward it.

45. *CTCS* 44.33a (2:1003).

46. Ibid., 42.26a (2:963); also in *CTYLTC* 4.2a–b, sec. 9 (1:255–256) [4.1b–2a; 1:150–151].

47. *Wen-chi*, vol. 14, 32.28b–29a. See also *CTYLTC* 101.30b, sec. 166 (7:5350) [101.24b; 7:4166]. The second reference concerns Ch'eng I's correction of an earlier position in which he polarized mind (*hsin*) and nature (*hsing*), the one as already manifest and the other as not yet manifest. Instead, they are phases of a linked process.

48. *CTCS* 45.7b (2:1008).

49. There is a discussion of this matter in Chang Li-wen, *Chu Hsi ssu-hsiang yen-chiu*, 470.

50. *I-shu* 2A.3a.

51. Wing-tsit Chan, "Patterns for Neo-Confucianism: Why Chu Hsi Differed from Ch'eng I," *Journal of Chinese Philosophy* 5 (June 1978), 112.

52. Brought to my attention by Conrad Schirokauer, "Chu Hsi and Hu Hung," in *Chu Hsi and Neo-Confucianism*, ed. W. T. Chan (Honolulu: University of Hawaii Press, 1986).

53. Tai Chen, *Meng-tzu tzu-i su-cheng* (Evidential explanation of the meaning of terms in the *Mencius*) (Beijing: Hsin-hua shu-tien, 1982), *shang*, 5.

54. *Chung-kuo che-hsüeh shih* (History of Chinese philosophy), (Beijing: Chung-hua shu-chü, 1980), 2:239.

55. *CTYLTC* 6.3b, sec. 23 (1:348) [6.3a; 1:223].

56. Ibid., 19.8b, sec. 50 (2:1030) [19.7a; 2:761].

57. Chan, *Reflections*, 194.

58. *CTYLTC* 68.25a, sec. 118 (5:3583) [68.20a; 5:3775].

59. Ibid.

60. Ibid., 11.1a, sec. 1 (1:495) [11.1a; 1:339].

61. Ibid., 8.16a, sec. 139 (1:435) [8.13a; 1:291].

62. Ibid., 20.8a, sec. 41 (2:1067) [20.6a–b; 2:789–90].

63. Ibid., 10.7a, sec. 50 (1:477) [10.6a; 1:325].

64. Ibid., 9.4b, sec. 26 (1:448) [9.3b; 1:300].

65. *CTCS* 44.12b (2:993); also in *CTYLTC* 98.13b, sec. 63 (7:5214) [98.11b; 6:4059].

66. *CTCS* 44.13a (2:993). For a similar example, see *CTYLTC* 98.13b, sec. 63 (7:5214) [98.11b; 6:4059].

67. *CTCS* 44.12b (2:993); also in *CTYLTC* 98.13b, sec. 63 (7:5214) [98.11b; 6:4059].

68. *CTYLTC* 98.14a, sec. 64 (7:5215) [98.11a; 6:4059].

69. *I-shu* 2A.3a–b.

70. *Analects* 15.23; also in 6.28 and 12.2.

71. This point is made in Philip C. Mercer, *Sympathy and Ethics* (Oxford: Oxford University Press, 1972), 9.

72. Max Scheler, *The Nature of Sympathy*, trans. Peter Heath (New Haven: Yale University Press, 1954), 78–79.

73. Mercer, *Sympathy and Ethics*, 82.

74. Quoted in Chan, *Reflections*, 23. Yeh Ts'ai (?–1248) was an imperial librarian who wrote the earliest existing commentary on Chu Hsi's *Chin-ssu lu*.

75. Chan, *Reflections*, 75. The passage is from *CTYLTC* 98.13a, sec. 63 (7:5214) [98.11a; 6:4059].

76. *I-shu* 15.1b.

77. *Ts'ui-yen* 1.2b.

78. Ibid., 1.7b.

79. Chan, *Reflections*, 45.

80. Chu Hsi and Lü Tsu-ch'ien, *Chin-ssu lu* (Reflections on things at hand), ed. Chang Po-hsing (1651–1725) (Taipei: Shih-chieh shu-chü, 1967), 2.71.

81. *Ts'ui-yen* 1.38a.

82. *Phaedo* 67a, in *Plato's Phaedo*, trans. R. S. Bluck (New York: Library of Liberal Arts, n.d.), 51.

83. *Republic* 500c, in Hamilton and Cairns, *Collected Dialogues of Plato*, 735.

84. *De Anima* 3.5.430a, in *The Basic Works of Aristotle*, ed. Richard McKeon (New York: Random House, 1941), 592.

85. *Nichomachean Ethics* 6.6.1141a, in *Basic Works*, 1027. Nicholas White helped clarify Aristotle's position for me.

86. Ibid., 10.7.1177a, in *Basic Works*, 1104.

87. See especially the first three chapters of Book 1.

88. Cited in Ronald H. Nash, *The Light of the Mind: St. Augustine's Theory of Knowledge* (Lexington: University Press of Kentucky, 1969), 91.

89. Ibid., 48.

90. From a letter dated 27 May 1630, cited in Norman Kemp Smith, *New Studies in the Philosophy of Descartes* (New York: Russell and Russell, 1963), 181.

91. From a letter to Chanut, 1 February 1647, in *Descartes' Philosophical Letters*, trans. and ed. Anthony Kenny (Oxford: Oxford University Press, 1970), 212–13.

92. D. J. McCracken, *Thinking and Valuing* (London: Macmillan, 1950), 88–89.

93. *Ethics* 4.28, in *Chief Works of Benedict de Spinoza*, trans. R. H. Elwes (New York: Dover, 1955), 205.

94. On this theme, see Richard Rorty, *Philosophy and the Mirror*

of Nature (Princeton: Princeton University Press, 1979), 12, 39–51. Louis Loeb helped greatly to clarify for me the relations in Descartes's theory of perception among the ideas, brain, brain patterns, and external things.

95. Meyer H. Abrams, *The Mirror and the Lamp* (New York: Oxford University Press, 1953), 59.

96. Ibid., 64–65.

97. Tu Wei-ming suggested this difference to me.

98. *Doctrine of the Mean* 27.

FOUR

1. Joseph Needham, *Science and Civilisation in China*, 6 vols. to date (Cambridge: Cambridge University Press, 1956–), 2:474.

2. Yung Sik Kim, "The World-View of Chu Hsi (1130–1200): Knowledge about the Natural World in *Chu-tzu ch'üan-shu*" (Ph.D. diss., Princeton University, 1980), 122–123, includes a good discussion on ancestral spirits.

3. I have modified the translation found in Legge, trans., *The Chinese Classics* 1:384, 391 (*Doctrine of the Mean* 1, 12).

4. D. C. Lau, trans., *Lao Tzu Tao Te Ching* (Baltimore: Penguin, 1963), sec. 64, p. 125.

5. *CTYLTC* 6.1a, sec. 1 (1:343) [6.1a; 1:219].

6. Ibid., 74.15a, sec. 128 (5:3967) [74.19b; 5:3078].

7. Ibid.

8. *I-shu* 15.8a.

9. *CTYLTC* 20.18a, sec. 79 (2:1087) [20.14b; 2:806].

10. Ibid., 75.20b, sec. 95 (5:4032–33) [75.16b; 5:3130].

11. Translation of these terms is by Derk Bodde, in Fung Yu-lan's *History of Chinese Philosophy* 2:636. Edward L. Shaughnessy has questioned this traditional interpretation of these terms in "The Composition of the 'Zhouyi' " (Ph.D. diss., Stanford University, 1983).

12. *CTCS* 45.4b (2:1007).

13. *Doctrine of the Mean* 25.

14. Ibid.

15. Ibid., 22.

16. Ibid., 26.

17. *CTCS* 52.25a (2:1148).

18. *CTYLTC* 64.20b, sec. 89 (4:3318) [64.16a; 4:2567].

19. Ibid., 64.18a, sec. 79 (4:3313) [64.14a; 4:2563].

20. *CTCS* 45.4b (2:1007). For the growth stages caused by the mind of heaven and earth, and present in all living things, see 44.7b (2:990).

21. Ibid., 44.10b (2:992).

22. Ibid., 45.4b (2:1007).

23. *CTYLTC* 74.15a, sec. 128 (5:3967) [74.19b; 5:3078].

24. The association of *yüan* (originating growth) with spring occurs in the *Kung-yang* commentary (*Kung-yang chuan*) to the *Spring and Autumn Annals*.

25. *Mencius* 6A.7.

26. Ibid., 2A.2.

27. *CTCS* 44.21a–b (2:997).

28. Metzger, *Escape from Predicament*, 97–98.

29. *CTCS* 45.2a–b (2:1006); also in *CTYLTC* 5.8a, sec. 56 (1:323) [5.6b; 1:204]. See also Chan, *Reflections*, 29.

30. See Munro, *Concept of Man in Early China*, 74–76.

31. Liu Shao's *Jen-wu chih* of the mid-third century A.D. contains an explicit distinction between the "within," or inner aspect of human traits, and the "without," or the performance aspect of the same traits. See Shryock, *Study of Human Abilities*, 61.

32. *I-shu* 18.15a. This is Ch'eng I's position. See *Wen-chi*, vol. 14, 32.28b.

33. *CTYLTC* 62.38a, sec. 137 (4:3187) [62.30a; 4:2465]. See also *Wen-chi*, vol. 14, 32.28a–b.

34. *CTYLTC* 9.4a, sec. 26 (1:447) [9.3b; 1:300].

35. *Wen-chi*, vol. 32, 67.20a–b. In T'ang Buddhism, there was a distinction between the Buddha nature (which accounts for the fact that a person is alive) and the seed in which it exists (which accounts for the person's karma). One type of mind (the original nature, comparable to the Buddha nature) can observe the other (karma).

36. My thanks to Peter Bol for suggesting this translation. For a comprehensive discussion of the meaning of the maxim, see Mou Tsung-san, *Hsin-t'i yü hsing-t'i*, 3:475ff. Chu borrowed it from Chang Tsai.

37. *Wen-chi*, vol. 14, 32.28b.

38. Ibid., vol. 31, 64.30b–31a. See also *CTYLTC* 101.20b, sec. 166 (7:5350) [101.24b; 7:4166].

39. *CTYLTC* 12.18b, sec. 137 (1:578) [12.15a; 1:405].

40. *Wen-chi*, vol. 13, 30.21b.

41. Ibid., vol. 14, 32.28a–b.

42. Ibid., 32.27a–b. See also *CTYLTC* 62.32a–b, sec. 118 (4:3175–76) [62.25b; 4:2456].

43. *Wen-chi*, vol. 14, 32.27a. See also 32.28a–b.

44. *CTYLTC* 9.5a, secs. 29, 31 (1:449) [9.4a; 1:301].

45. Ibid., 62.32b, sec. 118 (4:3176) [62.25b; 4:2456], and 12.14b, sec. 116 (1:570) [12.11b–12a; 1:398–400].

46. Ibid., 12.18b–19a, sec. 140 (1:578–79) [12.15a; 1:405], and the next few pages.

47. *Wen-chi*, vol. 14, 32.28b.

48. Ibid., 32.27b–28a. Cf. *Analects* 19.12 as an early reference to such activities as sweeping and watering.

49. *CTYLTC* 12.13a, sec. 97 (1:567) [12.10b; 1:396].

50. The idea that piety as an attitude should be extended to all acts is implicit in *Analects* 12.1.

51. *CTYLTC* 12.16a, sec. 123 (1:573) [12.13a; 1:401].

52. Ch'ien Mu, *Chu Tzu hsüeh t'i-kang* (Selected studies on Master Chu) (Taipei: San-min shu-chü, 1971), 114. Livia Kohn's work on an eighth-century Taoist meditation manual reveals that Taoists referred to the need to weed out desires and passions in order to attain concentration, so the imagery predates Chu.

53. Benjamin A. Elman, "Criticism as Philosophy: Conceptual Change in Ch'ing Dynasty Evidential Research," *Tsing-hua Journal of Chinese Studies* 17, nos. 1–2 (December 1985; publ. 1987), 165–98.

54. *Mencius* 7B.24. See the original discussion in Chan, *Reflections*, 154–55. A similar comment about the universality of physical desires is made in *CTYLTC* 62.10b, sec. 41 (4:3132) [62.8a; 4:2422]. There is a discussion of the passage cited in Chan's translation in Chang Li-wen, *Chu Hsi ssu-hsiang yen-chiu*, 528–29.

55. Francis M. Cornford, *Plato's Timaeus* (New York: Library of Liberal Arts, 1959), pp.20, 30a. Plato refers to the Form that contains all intelligible beings (especially gods, birds, fish, and mam-

mals) as the "Living Creature." The physical universe is an actual living creature created in its image.

56. David G. Hale, *The Body Politic* (The Hague: Mouton, 1971), 39.

57. J. O. de la Mettrie (1709–1751) wrote *L'Homme machine*, probably the most famous work along this line.

58. Francis W. Coker, *Organismic Theories of the State* (New York: Columbia University Press, 1910).

59. *Physics* 2.1.119b, in *Basic Works*, trans. McKeon, 251.

60. *Physics* 2.1.192b, ibid., 236.

61. In discussing the difference between natural and manufactured objects, Aristotle focuses on the fact that the former initiate motion from within. He is able to defend this thesis so long as he is talking about animals, but not when he is talking about inanimate things. For a brief account of the influence of the analogy of living animals on Aristotle's physics, see Bertrand Russell, *A History of Western Philosophy* (New York: Simon and Schuster, 1945), chap. 23.

62. *Analects* 9.16.

63. Chan, *Reflections*, 146.

64. Early modern European political positions influenced by the Aristotelian view, such as Catholic natural law theories, were inherently conservative in focusing on fixed and static ends, on limits to allowable development. The more liberal doctrines of people like Condorcet and Herder could incorporate stages perfectly well. But their openness came from lopping off the idea of a fixed *telos* to which every process develops (I owe this point to Steven Tonsor). This made growth protean. If Chu Hsi's position has conservative political implications, they lie in the idea of cycles, in which change occurs in fixed, repeated patterns and is not progressive. This cosmological view bolsters the conservatism inherent in his view of natural hierarchies and fixed social roles. Tu Wei-ming argues that in Chinese organicisms, many aspects of the future remain indeterminate. Cyclical repetition does not account for all future possibilities. See Tu Wei-ming, "The Continuity of Being: Chinese Visions of Nature," in Tu Wei-ming, *Confucian Thought: Selfhood as Creative Transformation* (Albany: State University of New York Press, 1985), 39.

65. *CTYLTC* 20.29a, sec. 118 (2:1109) [20.23a; 2:823]. Filiality is the root of practicing humaneness. It cannot be treated as the root of humaneness itself, because humaneness is principle (*bli*), which is the hidden root of all virtue. I discussed in Chapter Two the origins in the *Mencius* and the *Mean* of the idea of love that expands beyond the family to other people and creatures or things.

66. Legge, trans., *The Chinese Classics*, 1:416 (*Doctrine of the Mean* 22).

67. *CTCS* 44.9b (2:991).

68. *CTYLTC* 20.17a, sec. 75 (2:1085) [20.13b; 2:804].

69. Ch'eng I, *I ch'üan wen-chi* (Collection of literary works of Ch'eng I), 5.12b, in *Erh Ch'eng ch'üan-shu*.

70. *CTYLTC* 7.4a, sec. 18 (1:401) [7.3b; 1:264].

71. In his article "The Concept of *PAO* as a Basis for Social Relations in China," Lien-sheng Yang cites this famous passage from the *Book of Rites*: "In the highest antiquity they prized (simply conferring) good; in the time next to this, giving and repaying was the thing attended to. And what the rules of propriety value is that reciprocity. If I give a gift and nothing comes in return, that is contrary to propriety; if the thing comes to me, and I am given nothing in return, that also is contrary to propriety." The article appeared in *Chinese Thought and Institutions*, ed. John K. Fairbank (Chicago: University of Chicago Press, 1957), 291. See ibid., 296–97, for a discussion of the idea of the "return of grace" (*pao en*) in connection with the Five Relations and as a principle of nature.

72. Chu Hsi, *Hsiao hsüeh chi-chu* (Collected commentaries on the *Elementary Learning*), SPPY ed., 2.15b, 5b.

73. Ibid., 6.3b–4a. In his commentary on *Analects* 6.3, Chu says that people living in the same neighborhood should help each other.

74. On the vagueness of the idea of "group," see Ambrose Y. C. King, "The Individual and Group in Confucianism: A Relational Perspective," in *Individualism and Holism: Studies in Confucian and Taoist Values*, ed. Donald J. Munro (Ann Arbor: Center for Chinese Studies, University of Michigan, 1985), 57–70.

75. *Wen-chi*, vol. 12, 25.12a.

76. Ibid., vol. 6, 13.18a.

77. For his commitment to the government's obligation to set up

and maintain school officials throughout the country, see *CTCS* 64.16b (2:1401–2). For a brief summary of his curriculum proposals, see Mao Li-jui, *Chung-kuo ku-tai chiao-yü shih* (History of China's premodern education) (Beijing: Jen-min chiao-yü ch'u-pan she, 1982), 388ff.

78. Hymes, "On Academies, Community Institutions."

79. *Wen-chi*, vol. 15, 33.29a, includes a reference to the community contract.

80. Hymes, "Prominence and Power in Sung China," 279.

81. Ebrey, *Family and Property in Sung China*, 158, 166.

82. Hsiao Kung-chuan, *Rural China: Imperial Control in the Nineteenth Century* (Seattle: University of Washington Press, 1967), 356. Within clan villages, the rich or powerful families dominated the judicial system (292). As for the philanthropy of local gentry and scholars in setting up granaries for famine relief, Hsiao accepts self-interest as a leading motive, specifically, to prevent uprisings by a starving population: "Without denying the presence of humanitarian sentiments on the part of some of the gentry and scholars, one can safely assume that 'the feelings of self-preservation' to which Sir Henry Gray referred were normally at work when they devoted their energies to promoting local grain reserves" (178). Gray's report is cited on p. 177.

83. For example, David Herlihy's *Medieval Households* (Cambridge, Mass.: Harvard University Press, 1985), and David Herlihy and Christiane Klapisch-Zuber, *Tuscans and Their Families: A Study of the Florentine Catasto of 1427* (New Haven: Yale University Press, 1985).

84. T'ang Chün-i, "The Development of the Concept of Moral Mind from Wang Yang-ming to Wang Chi," in *Self and Society in Ming Thought*, ed. William Theodore de Bary et al. (New York: Columbia University Press, 1970), 104–105. T'ang also traces Wang's doctrine to Lu Hsiang-shan (1139–1193).

85. Ibid., 102, 107.

FIVE

1. Mou Tsung–san, *Hsin-t'i yü hsing-t'i*.

2. Okada Takehiko says that exercising reverential concentration

and extending knowledge are both crucial, but that the latter is somewhat more important. Tomoeda Ryūtarō says that, like wings of a bird or wheels of a car, both are equally important. See Okada Takehiko, "Sō min no Shushigaku" (Chu Hsi studies of the Sung and Ming), in *Shushigaku taikei* (System of Chu Hsi studies), ed. T. Murohashi and M. Yasuoka (Tokyo: Meitoku shuppansha, 1974), 92–93; and Tomoeda Ryūtarō, "Shushi no gakumon ron" (On some questions concerning Chu Hsi), in *Shushigaku taikei*, 1:333, 337. There is no discussion of external authorities other than books in these works or in Tomoeda Ryūtarō, *Shushi no shisō keisei* (The form of Chu Hsi's thought) (Tokyo: Shunjūsha, 1969) or in Shimada Kenji, *Shushigaku to Yōmeigaku* (Chu Hsi studies and Yangming studies) (Tokyo: Iwanami shoten, 1967).

3. This is the "Naitō thesis." See Chapter One, note 8, above.

4. F. W. Mote, "The Growth of Chinese Despotism," *Oriens Extremus* 8 (August 1961), 19.

5. Lionel M. Jensen, "Wang Yang-ming and the Quest for Authenticity: An Essay on the Chinese Hermeneutic Tradition and the Individual" (M.A. thesis, Washington University, 1980), 20–21, deals with the problem of the weakened integrity of the examinations. Discussions with Jensen have helped me understand better the historical background to matters discussed in this chapter.

6. Chaffee, "Education and Examinations," 22, 61, 67.

7. Hymes, "Prominence and Power in Sung China," 186–87.

8. *CTCS* 44.20a (2:997); also *CTYLTC* 78.35a, sec. 194 (5:4191) [78.27b; 5:3254].

9. *CTYLTC* 78.34b–35a, sec. 193 (5:4190–91) [78.26a–b; 5:3253–54].

10. *CTCS* 49.25a (2:1073).

11. Ibid., 78.36a, sec. 196 (5:4193) [78.28a; 5:3257].

12. Ibid., 78.37a, sec. 206 (5:4195) [78.29a; 5:3257].

13. I owe this point to Lionel Jensen.

14. The political image is in the first two phrases: *jen-hsin wei wei tao-hsin wei wei*. (*Shu ching*, "The Counsel of the Great Yü," 2.2.2.15 [in Legge, vol. 3, p. 61]). The authenticity of this Old Text passage has been in dispute since at least the Sung dynasty. Some, claiming the Old Text version of the *Book of History* is a forgery, say that

the forgers lifted the passage from the *Hsün-tzu* and pasted it together with some characters from the *Analects*. The philological case against the passage's being part of the authentic *Book of History* was most forcefully reopened in the early sixteenth century, though those arguments did not cause much of a stir until the end of the Ming. See Benjamin A. Elman, "Philosophy (*i-li*) versus Philology (*k'ao-cheng*): The *Jen-hsin tao-hsin* Debate," *T'oung Pao* 69, nos. 4–5 (1983), 192–211. Although perplexed by the differences between the Old Text and New Text chapters of the *Book of History*, Chu Hsi did not say that the former were forgeries. Today many believe that the passage dates from the Eastern Chin (265–419) period.

15. *CTYLTC* 23.19a, sec. 72 (2:1271) [23.15a; 2:949]. Linguistically speaking, *chih* can be modified to refer to a negative characteristic (as in "narrow in his goals") but, appearing unmodified, it is generally positive (ibid., 29.23a, sec. 99 (3:1667) [29.18a; 2:1261]). A person makes a commitment to a goal (*li chih*) and then regularly nurtures or reconfirms it (lit., "preserves it") (ibid., 18.33a, sec. 114 (2:997) [18.25b; 2:734]). Chu Hsi would evaluate a person's goal in terms of the impartiality-selfishness categories described in Chapter Three. Unselfish goal commitment can run the gamut from broadly impartial to somewhat narrow, with Confucius and his disciples Yen Hui and Tzu Lu among the early Confucians spanning the spectrum in that order (ibid., 29.23a, sec. 99 (3:1667) [29.18a; 2:1261]). Chu's favorite example of the committed individual, from roughly his own era, is Ch'eng I, who at a young age set his goal of study. Chu Hsi would have people start by "committing themselves to recovering the basis of life [original nature] and then attaining the heights of the sages" (ibid., 118.12a, sec. 34 (7:5907) [118.9b; 7:4600]).

16. Chu Hsi, *Chung-yung chang-chü ta-ch'üan* (Great collection on the sections and paragraphs of the *Doctrine of the Mean*) in *Chung-kuo tzu-hsüeh ming-chu chi-ch'eng* (Collected compilations of famous authors on Chinese philosophical studies), ed. Hu Kuang et al. (Taiwan: Chung-kuo tzu-hsüeh ming-chu chi-ch'eng pien yin chi chin hui, 1977), 17:5. See also *Wen-chi*, vol. 31, 65.21b. For an example of Chu's extracting the passage on being single-minded (*wei*

ching wei i) and using it to denote single-mindedness, see *Wen-chi*, vol. 31, 11.3b–4a.

17. *CTYLTC* 62.9b–10a, sec. 41 (4:3130–31) [62.8a; 4:2421].

18. *Wen-chi*, vol. 5, 11.3b.

19. *CTCS* 44.22a (2:998).

20. *Wen-chi*, vol. 6, 12.6a. See *CTCS* 44.9b (2:991) for a discussion of the mind's having a master or ruler (*chu*). Reverential concentration helps keep the master in control.

21. Munro, *Concept of Man in Early China*, 58–65. See also T'ang Chün-i, "Hsien-Ch'in ssu-hsiang chung chih t'ien-ming kuan" (The concept of *t'ien-ming* in pre-Ch'in thought), *Hsin-ya hsüeh-pao* (Journal of New Asia College) 3, no. 2 (1957), 1–33.

22. Mou Tsung-san discusses the special place of the *Great Learning* in *Hsin-t'i yü hsing-t'i*, vol. 3.

23. *CTCS* 6.2a (1:117).

24. See *Doctrine of the Mean* 27. Cited in Chan, *Reflections*, 82.

25. *Wen-chi*, vol. 18, 39.7b. See also vol. 20, 43.3a.

26. Curiously, in one categorization scheme, the ruler's mind fits on the inner or subjective side of a set polarizing the ruler's mind with "outer" or political institutions as competing tools for transforming the people.

27. *Wen-chi*, vol. 33, 70.24a.

28. For modeling on ancestral and sagelike minds in the Chou period, see Munro, *Concept of Man in Early China*, 99–116. Since then, my understanding of the significance of modeling on ancestors has been enriched by William Savage. The citation referring to the king as model of the world is from Ch'eng I. See Chan, *Reflections*, 207. See also p. 206.

29. *Wen-chi*, vol. 31, 65.20b–21a.

30. Ibid., vol. 7, 15.7b.

31. Ibid., vol. 34, 72.14a–b.

32. De Bary describes the Ming emperor Ch'eng-tsu (r. 1402–1424) writing, among other things, that the minister cannot properly serve unless his heart is one with that of his prince. Ch'eng-tsu is a good example of a powerful figure who adopted Chu Hsi's doctrines for his own purposes. He wrote and spoke as if he himself were a sage. For this he was criticized by the editors of the

Ssu-ku ch'üan-shu ts'ung-mu t'i-yao (Catalogue of the imperial manuscript library). See de Bary, *Neo-Confucian Orthodoxy*, 163–64.

33. *Wen-chi*, vol. 7, 15.7b, and vol. 6, 14.11a.

34. Ibid., vol. 32, 66.2b, and Chan, *Reflections*, 207.

35. *Wen-chi*, vol. 5, 11.16a.

36. Ibid., vol. 6, 13.8a.

37. Ibid., vol. 5, 11.3a.

38. This theme runs through many memorials.

39. *CTCS* 38.1a (2:854); also in *CTYLTC* 84.9a, sec. 22 (6:4534) [84.7b; 6:3526].

40. *CTCS* 1.9a (1:24). Also in *CTYLTC* 8.5a, sec. 27 (1:413) [8.4a; 1:273].

41. *Wen-chi*, vol. 6, 12.8b.

42. Isaiah Berlin identified a similar problem in the history of Western philosophy. See "Two Concepts of Liberty" in his *Four Essays on Liberty* (Oxford: Oxford University Press, 1969), 132–139.

43. Tillman, *Utilitarian Confucianism*, 101, 113, 148. Those considering highly practical utility often took as models Han and T'ang rulers who were good at dealing with barbarians. Chu denied that any rulers after the Three Dynasties (Hsia, Shang, and Chou) were entirely suitable models, although his educational materials contain worthy statements from post-Han figures. One of Chu's targets in this connection was Ch'en Liang (1143–1194), who encouraged expedient governmental policies aimed at driving the Jurchen Chin dynasty out of North China.

44. *Wen-chi*, vol. 6, 14.22 a–b.

45. Ibid., vol. 5, 11.8a.

46. Ibid., vol. 31, 65.20b–21a.

47. Ibid., vol. 5, 11.31a.

48. Ibid., vol. 6, 12.6a and 13.1b.

49. Ibid., 14.13b.

50. Ibid., 13.2a.

51. Ibid., vol. 8, 8.22a.

52. Ibid., vol. 16, 35.19b.

53. Ibid., vol. 6, 14.1a.

54. Ibid., 65.20a.

55. Thomas C. Bartlett, "Ku Yen-wu's Response to 'The Demise

of Human Society,' " (Ph.D. diss., Princeton University, 1985), 19, and Elman, "Philosophy (*i-li*) versus Philology (*k'ao-cheng*)," 202.

56. The central issue is not whether Confucians ever talked of choice making or of the cluster choice-responsibility-blame, but it is interesting to note Herbert Fingarette's comment: "To be specific, Confucius does not elaborate the language of choice and responsibility as these are intimately intertwined with the idea of the ontologically ultimate power of the individual to select from genuine alternatives to create his own spiritual destiny, and with the related ideas of spiritual guilt, and repentance or retribution for such guilt" (Herbert Fingarette, *Confucius—The Secular as Sacred* [New York: Harper and Row, 1972], 18). This is a controversial claim, criticized by some on the grounds that Confucius does describe people as coming to a crossroads in the sense of moments when they can act so as to go off the straight and narrow path. It is more difficult to find notions of responsibility and blame in the *Analects*. As the present chapter indicates, Chu Hsi certainly talks about choice making in a very direct manner.

The main problem with some Western accounts is that they attribute to Confucians a doctrine of free will, and this has the potential of confusing Western understanding of Confucian thought. Thomas Metzger says, "Although the word 'free' did not exist, the idea of free will was entirely plain and heavily emphasized. There could be no moral efforts unless one were *k'en* (willing) to exert them. Therefore Chu Hsi said that 'the capacity to choose a goal is the deep part of the mind,' enabling a person 'not to go down another road but rather go down this road.' The basic term here is *li-chih* (determine one's goal)" (Metzger, *Escape from Predicament*, 115). Elsewhere he says that one of the three factors on which Neo-Confucians blamed the existence of evil was "the individual's bad choice freely arrived at" (ibid., 111). In discussing the will, Metzger refers to the term *kung-fu* (ibid., 133), which Western sinologists like to translate as "moral effort." Metzger is aware of Chu's murky position on the efficacy of moral effort, which may be reduced by one's natural endowment (ibid., 130). He says that most important in the Confucian tradition (as T'ang Chün-i pointed out) is "the ability of the self to act autonomously by rejecting group pressures" (ibid., 45).

I would point out, however, that the notion of free will as it has existed for many centuries in the West refers to a specific inner faculty; the idea often has assumed a certain theory of causation and that some events (choices) are uncaused; and it is intimately bound up with the ideas of responsibility, the possibility of moral blame, and, especially, belief in God. I would not advise muddying the Neo-Confucian position by attributing free will to it. Moreover, it is possible to speak of exerting effort without referring to choice or freedom. And *li-chih* has to do with determining on a long-term goal or aspiration, or on life's priorities (such as to be a sage), not on routine choices of moral action. The term *^ci* (intention, volition) refers to the outthrust of the mind, not to a separate faculty as is the case with the Western "will." See *CTYLTC* 15.26a, sec. 127 (2:761) [15.20b; 1:550]. One avoids confusing Chu Hsi's position with Western ideas of causation, responsibility, and blame in the eyes of God if one steers clear of the terminology of free will. It is difficult to speak clearly about Confucian counterparts of blame, an idea that refers to abuse of a God-given power to will and thus an affront to God, along with its other traits.

57. *CTCS* 46.4a (2:1017).

58. If one were to compare Chu Hsi's account with an influential Western view on the cause of evil (such as that of Augustine), one would consider both the will and God's grace. The will, the instrument of choices, is good, but in following a desire for the bad, man of his own choice turns away from its injunction to obey God's law. There is a place for individual effort in removing the immediate causes of evil, which are the desires or lusts for the bad. If an individual succumbs, each sin will blind him more. Augustine's ultimate solution to achieving goodness is not the removal of that which blinds but reliance on something that is external to all humans, namely, God's grace. See Gillian R. Evans, *Augustine on Evil* (Cambridge: Cambridge University Press, 1982), 115–121. Many pre-Christian Platonists, in contrast with Augustine's view, had located the source of evil in ignorance and the solution in knowledge. Proper teaching overcomes the ignorance that causes people to heed physical desires rather than reason.

59. *Doctrine of the Mean* 20. See Chan, *Reflections*, 38.

60. *Analects* 2.4.

61. Chan, *Reflections*, 70.

62. A. A. Long focuses on Zeno as the source of the problems of materialistic determinism and of dealing with an omniscient God. See his *Hellenistic Philosophy* (New York: Charles Scribner's Sons, 1974), 61. But the Stoics held that Providence is not to blame for human evil because humans can acquiesce or not to the deterministic series of events for which Providence is responsible.

63. R. E. Latham, trans., *Lucretius: On the Nature of the Universe* (Baltimore: Penguin, 1951), 67 (bk. 2, l. 264).

64. Irene Bloom quite accurately has stressed the importance of the Augustinian view of the will in any contrast between Neo-Confucian and European views of the self. In clarifying my own views about the European idea of freedom of choice, including the Augustinian influence, I owe a debt to several discussions with her, and to her paper, "On the Matter of the Mind: The Metaphysical Basis of the Expanded Self," in *Individualism and Holism*, ed. Munro, 293–327. We differ in that I believe in the importance of the antideterminist, Epicurean source; we also identify different aspects of Augustine's doctrine as significant. In my case, it is protecting an omnipotent and omniscient God from blame for human evil. In her case, it is the interior life of the individual that is a seat of anguished battles between mind and body and reason and desire. In terms of political images used to explain the mind, there is a considerable overlap of Chu Hsi with Augustine. Augustine inherits the apostle Paul's reference to two "laws" to which the individual listens. One, "the voice of a master demanding obedience," is the law of the mind or of God; the other is the law of the body. Human beings have a spiritual and a carnal will. This composite will is still explained as an executive organ, commander of the body. See Hannah Arendt, *The Life of the Mind: Willing* (New York: Harcourt Brace Jovanovich, 1978), 87, 95. Purely in terms of the influence of a political image that describes how people think, one might expect similar ethical positions from Chu Hsi, with his Tao mind as ruler, and from a Christian like Augustine, with his spiritual will dominant. In other words, one might expect Augustine to emphasize nondeliberative or automatic obedience. There is, however, another factor at work in Augustine's theory, extraneous to the explanatory images for the mind, that alters the entire

picture. That factor is God, both good and omniscient, and separable from his creation.

65. See *De Libero Arbitrio Voluntatis*, bk. 3, chaps. 1 ("Why God's foreknowledge does not take free will away from sinners, a question that troubles very many men"), 2 ("God's foreknowledge does not so act that we do not sin by free will"), and 3 ("A foreknowing God does not compel men to sin, and therefore punishes sins justly"), in *St. Augustine on Free Will*, trans. Carroll M. Sparrow (Charlottesville: University of Virginia Press, 1947).

66. Evans, *Augustine on Evil*, 113. Long before this, however, the skeptic Sextus Empiricus (ca. A.D. 200) had identified this problem: "Those who positively affirm God's existence are probably compelled to be guilty of impiety; for if they say that he forethinks all beings they will be declaring that God is the cause of evil, while if they say that he forethinks some things or nothing they will be forced to say that God is either malignant or weak, and obviously this is to use impious language" (*Sextus Empiricus*, trans. R. G. Bury, [Cambridge, Mass.: Harvard University Press, 1955], 333 [bk. 3, chap. 3, l. 12]). Aristotle did not have any conception of free will. He had no idea of a thing called a "will" and no idea of events that are uncaused (for many indeterminists some events, such as some choices, are uncaused). But if one is concerned about origins, his discussion of the voluntary and involuntary in the *Nichomachean Ethics* (3.1.1111a) is certainly relevant. W.F.R. Hardie points out that the Greek terms have a vaguer meaning than the English terms in that lower animals are capable of voluntary action, which requires only an intention to act. Aristotle gave two reasons for discussing the voluntary and involuntary. Society awards praise and blame for them, and legislators assign honors and punishments in accordance with them. The voluntary is "that of which the moving principle [*arche*] is in the agent himself, he being aware of the particular circumstances of the action" (W.F.R. Hardie, *Aristotle's Ethical Theory* [Oxford: Oxford University Press, 1968], 152–59). This notion still lacks the idea of a faculty of will, the idea that choice is uncaused, the relation to God, and the idea of praiseworthy and blameworthy in the eyes of God.

67. René Descartes, *Meditations on First Philosophy*, trans. Laurence J. Lafleur (Indianapolis: Library of Liberal Arts, 1976).

68. The Epicurean assertion of free will is opposed to the physical determinism of Stoics like Zeno and materialists like Democritus. For the Epicurean, the existence of free will represents man's mastery over his own destiny, thereby fostering his zeal for the good life and contributing to its realization through pursuit of his own personal interests (attaining pleasure, avoiding pain). The doctrine of free will stemming from Augustine is intended to oppose a different doctrine, namely, any thesis such as that of the Manichees that blames God for human evil.

There are probably a number of subordinate concerns here. One is purely aesthetic. The image of an omnibenevolent God is more pleasing than that of an evil or limited deity. Another has to do with the legitimacy such a thesis provides rulers, the self-proclaimed instruments of God's purpose, with respect to the meting out of rewards and punishments: it asserts the individual's control over his own fate. But the main concern lies in the assumption that blaming individuals not only absolves God but will also be an effective way of changing their behavior. It will work only if people believe they are responsible, a position they should accept because they have free will. In fact, as some writers have argued, determinists can make a better case for the efficacy of blaming an individual than can indeterminists. This is because in order for blaming an individual to succeed, it must change his behavior by causing a change in his choices of action. This means that an individual's choices cannot be uncaused, as the indeterminist would have it, but subject to future influence and causation by present blaming.

69. The American prerevolutionary pamphleteers and the authors of the *Federalist Papers* assumed that humans are self-regarding, motivated by the pursuit of self-interest, though many believed this to be a sign of degradation. See Cecelia M. Kenyon, "Conceptions of Human Nature in American Political Thought: 1630–1826" (Ph.D. diss., Radcliffe College, 1949).

70. On Plato's political analogy, see Thomas M. Robinson, *Plato's Psychology* (Toronto: University of Toronto Press, 1970), 44.

71. *CTCS* 7.7a (1:158); also in *CTYLTC* 14.13b, sec. 114 (2:686) [14.17b; 1:490].

72. *CTCS* 16.23b (1:356); also in *CTYLTC* 37.6b, sec. 32 (3:2142) [37.5a; 3:1633].

73. Chan, *Reflections*, 116.

74. *Mencius* 4A.17.

75. *Analects* 2.23, 3.9. These passages were brought to my attention by Robert Eno.

76. *CTCS* 21.7a (1:473); also in *CTYLTC* 56.8b, sec. 32 (4:2818) [56.7a; 4:2173]. Where the correct course is likely to be uncontroversial and a matter of general agreement, individual choice overrules obedience to ᵃ*ching*. It is fine for someone to ignore the taboo against touching the hand of a female not his wife or from his bloodline in order to save her from drowning, and it is fine to drink a summer liquid in winter if the weather turns unseasonably warm. Situational choice will still be consistent with some ultimate, unwritten moral principle (*tao-li*). See *CTYLTC* 37.9a, sec. 42 (3:2147) [37.7a; 3:1637]. That passage discusses *Mencius* 4A.17. See also *CTYLTC* 37.6b, sec. 29 (3:2142) [37.5a; 3:1633], and 37.13b, sec. 51 (3:2156) [37.10b; 3:1644].

77. *CTYLTC* 37.15a, sec. 54 (3:2159) [37.12a; 3:1647]. The expression is also used in sec. 27 of the same *chüan*.

78. Mencius approves of the sage-king Shun marrying before getting his parents' permission, and Chu approves too. See also *CTYLTC* 37.9b–10a, sec. 46 (3:2148–49) [37.7b–8a; 3:1638–39].

79. Ibid., 37.9b, sec. 45 (3:2148) [37.7b; 3:1638]. I did not become sensitive to how exclusively reserved for sages was this situational weighing (*ch'üan*) until I read "Chu Hsi on the Standard and the Expedient," prepared by Wei Cheng-t'ung for the International Conference on Chu Hsi. Among other citations, he referred to this passage. This paper has been published in *Chu Hsi and Neo-Confucianism*, ed. Chan, 255–72.

80. *Wen-chi*, vol. 6, 14.9a–b.

81. *CTCS* 16.23b (1:356); also in *CTYLTC* 37.6b, sec. 32 (3:2142) [37.5a; 3:1633].

82. *I-shu* 15.14b. On the exclusion of mind from the principle, see *CTCS* 44.1b (2:987); also in *CTYLTC* 5.3b, sec. 22 (1:314) [5.3a; 1:197].

83. *I-shu* 6.2b.

84. *Analects* 12.1.

85. *CTCS* 44.27b–28a (2:1000–1001). See *I-shu* 18.7a for Ch'eng I on transformation of the physical nature (cited in Chan, *Reflections*, 164).

86. *CTYLTC* 62.10b, sec. 41 (4:3132) [62.8b–9a; 4:2422–23]. Chu Hsi remains consistent with the Confucian stress on obedience to social role duties (rooted in principle) and also with Buddhist-inspired talk about purifying the mind. Yet he is able, simultaneously, to make a place for the legitimacy of satisfying certain routine desires, biological and otherwise. He thereby avoids the perceived suggestion of certain Buddhists and Confucians (such as Chou Tun-i) that the desires should be eliminated (*wu yü*, or "no desires").

There are traces of the Buddhist legacy of asceticism in Ch'eng-Chu writings. The Ch'eng brothers spoke of getting rid of human desires and preserving heavenly principle. And Chu Hsi himself says that "the heavenly principles and human desires should not coexist." See Chu Hsi's commentary on *Mencius* 3A.3. See also Chan, *Reflections*, 150, for a reference to Ch'eng I's asceticism. Ch'eng I was the extreme puritan, more so than Chu. And there is an aspect to Chu's position that indicates movement away from asceticism. The *Classified Conversations* says that people cannot get rid of desires for food and drink, so they should concentrate on eating and drinking in the right manner and with the right attitude. "Although one is a sage, he cannot be without the human mind, such as desiring to eat when hungry and drink when thirsty." See *CTYLTC* 78.35b–36a, secs. 195–96 (5:4192–93) [78.28a; 5:3255]. The heavenly principles in fact produce bodily desires. People pursue them properly or improperly. Some commentators find that Chu Hsi makes a distinction between human desires (*jen-yü*), which are evil, and ordinary desires (ᵃ*yü*), which refer to natural bodily needs and are morally neutral (Chang Li-wen, *Chu Hsi ssu-hsiang yen-chiu*, 528, 529, 532). This is another way of maneuvering away from the ascetic's denial of desires. The maneuvering is inevitable, given the doctrine's fundamental premise that principle must have some place to reside. Principle gives the proper patterns to some concrete object or event, termed "its resting place." In the case of humans, one of the resting places for principle is in the desires, which are one form of the mind's activity.

Chu says that where the heavenly principles are, there will also be human desires, because the former need a resting place (*an-tun ch'u*). The desires, then, may or may not remain true to the principles that can order them, depending on the mind's clarity, as discussed in Chapter Three.

87. Classical Platonism has a place for both conquest and transformation. The message of some dialogues is that the life of reason involves as much distance as possible from the emotions and bodily desires and requires the conquest by reason of bodily passions. The *Phaedo* says: "And purification—isn't it just what it has long been said to be, according to the old accounts, the separation (so far as is possible) of the soul from the body, and the attempt to habituate her to collecting herself up and gathering herself together, away from the body, into herself—and to living so far as possible, both now and in the future, alone by herself, freeing herself from the body as though from bonds?" (*Plato's Phaedo*, trans. Bluck, 52 [67c–d]).

In other dialogues, a place is provided for the bodily passions. Love of physical beauty is a necessary step on the ladder leading to love and knowledge of the Forms (*Symposium*); the energy is shifted in the philosopher from physical object to divine Ideas. The first of these Platonic psychic portraits was most influential throughout the early Middle Ages. Based on the mind-body split, it casts reason as the ruler charged with conquering the bodily passions. The consequence is the characterization of the inner life of man as a constant battle between polarized enemies. Seneca wrote of this inner struggle, "For we also must be soldiers and in a campaign where there is no intermission and no rest" (C. S. Lewis, *The Allegory of Love* [Oxford: Clarendon Press, 1958], 59).

The impact of the *Phaedo*-style ascetic ideal on the emotion of passionate love in medieval Europe was described by C. S. Lewis in the following manner: "But according to the medieval view, passionate love itself was wicked, and did not cease to be wicked if the object of it were your wife. If a man had once yielded to this emotion, he had no choice between 'guilt' and 'innocent' love before him: he had only the choice, either of repentance, or else of different forms of guilt" (Lewis, *Allegory of Love*, 14). In contrast with this picture of mental conflict, Chu Hsi's transformed psyche, under the rule of the Tao mind, would have no trouble making a place for passionate love, provided it was directed toward the proper objective.

88. *CTYLTC* 12.6a, sec. 45 (1:553) [12.5a; 1:385]. For another example, see 12.2b, sec. 24 (1:546) [12.2b; 1:380]. This is one of those places in which my interpretation of Chu Hsi differs from Thomas Metzger's. He says, "T'ang Chün-i shows that the 'inner' life of moral struggle, not cosmology, is the key to Neo-Confucian thought" (*Escape from Predicament*, 91). In his view, many Neo-Confucians see in the flow of human feelings an "almost irrepressible tendency toward evil" (ibid., 114). And he says that the mind's "functioning was a spasmatic, pain-ridden, contingent process" (ibid., 126). I do not find in Chu's writings anything like the magnitude of inner struggle that Metzger finds. The tone of his interpretation seems to me to obscure the spirit of man's redeemability that permeates Chu's works. It takes a lot of effort, but not a bitter struggle of the kind known to biblical figures and Augustine.

89. Reference is made to the morally acceptable ones in *CTYLTC* 53.9b, sec. 38 (4:2728) [53.7b; 4:2100]. Julia Ching refers to this division in the paper she prepared for the International Conference on Chu Hsi.

90. The built-in discrimination against the emotions and sensory appetites is attacked by certain Ming-dynasty Confucians who claim that they, too, are innate to man's nature. See William Theodore de Bary, "Individualism and Humanitarianism in Late Ming Thought," in *Self and Society in Ming Thought*, 182.

91. *CTYLTC* 78.35b–36a, sec. 196 (5:4192–93) [78.28a; 5:3255].

92. *CTCS* 60.12b (2:1311) contains the usual criticism of Buddhists for fearing death; also in *CTYLTC* 126.7a, sec. 13 (8:6267) [126.5b; 8:4884]. In compiling the *Chin-ssu lu*, Chu included Ch'eng I's infamous comment that talk about widows remarrying comes from the fact that people of later generations are afraid of starving to death. Starving to death is a minor irritation compared with losing one's integrity by remarrying (Chan, *Reflections*, 177).

93. Ch'ien Mu, *Chu Tzu hsüeh t'i-kang*, 88.

94. Legge, trans., *The Chinese Classics*, 1:147 (*Analects* 2.4).

95. Wang Hsien-ch'ien, ed., *Hsün-tzu chi-chieh*, "Li lun p'ien" (A discussion of rites), 233 (13.19b).

96. Shryock, *Study of Human Abilities*.

97. Ibid., 102.

98. *CTCS* 43.4b (2:970); also in *CTYLTC* 4.15a, sec. 59 (1:281) [4.12a; 1:171].

99. *Wen-chi*, vol. 32, 67.20b.

100. *I-shu* 15.1b.

101. See Chu Hsi's commentary on *Analects* 15.38.

102. *CTCS* 44.22a (2:998).

103. *Analects* 15.23, 6.39, 12.2, 6.28.

104. See Chu Hsi's commentary on *Doctrine of the Mean* 13.

105. One can infer quite a bit about Chu Hsi's views on the emperor's role in ensuring uniformity from his comments about political factions. A faction is like an interest group, the members of which may have unorthodox positions in somebody's eyes on some significant issue. This may in turn call into question their general goal orientation. One should also recall Chu Hsi's belief that, if the emperor only takes the trouble to rectify his mind, it will serve as the positive basis for renovating the world, bringing in line with principle the mixed motivations of all the people. His mind is their supreme model, as are the minds of all sages. One promotes uniformity by presenting a single type of model. In discussing Confucius' favorite pupil, one commentator wrote, "Yen Tzu never objected, as if he were stupid, to what Confucius told him. Thus he was completely identified with the character of the Sage" (Chan, *Reflections*, 290). Yen Tzu's apparent dullness in never objecting to anything Confucius said was, in fact, a reflection of his complete identification with the character of the Master.

Many of the memorials in which this topic arises are ones in which Chu Hsi attacks certain political factions for influencing the emperor (improperly, in his opinion) to appease the non-Chinese conquerors of North China rather than to counterattack and regain the lost land. The analyst must sift through the memorials to extract the general principles on which Chu bases his case.

Normally, the term *tang* has a mildly pejorative connotation, suggesting a group of people bound together for the pursuit of personal profit. The contrasting classical ideal, spelled out in the

Book of Documents, was "without deflection, without partiality" (*wu tang*) (Frederic Wakeman, "The Price of Autonomy: Intellectuals in Ming and Ch'ing Politics," *Daedalus*, September 1972, 41; this was brought to my attention by Sophia Lee). I have already discussed some traditional views about factions in "The Concept of 'Interest' in Chinese Thought," *Journal of the History of Ideas* 41 (April–June 1980), 179–87. Confucius said that the superior man "is sociable, but not a partisan" (*pu tang*) (*Analects* 15.21).

There were Sung-dynasty defenders of factions. The statesman Fan Chung-yen (989–1052) made a distinction between good and bad factions, or those of the *chün-tzu* and *hsiao-jen*: "The factions of the crooked and the straight . . . have always differed. If, through friendship, men should work together for the good of the state, what is the harm?" He also said, "Factions should not be banned, but it is up to Your Majesty to tell the difference" (James T. C. Liu, *Reform in Sung China* [Cambridge, Mass.: Harvard University Press, 1959], 126). The champion of Confucian orthodoxy, Ou-yang Hsiu (1007–1070), memorialized the throne in 1045 in an effort to rally support for reforms that he advocated and to bring supporters into the government. In this memorial, entitled "On Factions" (P'eng tang lun), he tried to justify the existence of some such groups by identifying their motives and aims and by distinguishing them from other, unsavory cliques. He said that people in legitimate factions band together because they share common principles (*t'ung tao*). In so doing, they improve each other; their lives are characterized by loyalty, fidelity, honor, and integrity; and the state is improved by the presence of such virtuous persons. They can succeed because they are like-minded (*t'ung hsin*) (*Ou-yang Hsiu ch'üan-chi* [Complete works of Ou-yang Hsiu] [Taipei: Shih-chieh shu-chü, 1961], 1:124–25).

The striking thing about Ou-yang Hsiu's defense of factions is that he characterizes legitimate ones by portraying them almost as miniatures of the Confucian ideal state, distinguished by uniformity of mind. There is no reference to a group's desires, intentions, or needs; instead, members are like-minded people bound together by their sharing of the goals and moral principles that any Confucian state would embody. Their job presumably is to overcome the bad factions and help the emperor bring about the desired uniformity throughout the realm.

Chu's view of factions is mixed. He explicitly praises the existence of political factions whose members are loyal and able men. They have impartial minds (*Wen-chi*, vol. 13, 28.21a–22a). He attacks other factions that are divisive and disloyal. He says that they are formed by small-minded persons who seek power. Their members' goals are selfish, each one's overall aim being personal profit. In contrast, with the proper self-cultivation, the emperor's mind will be completely impartial (*ta kung* or *chih kung*), and so he will not favor such factions that fragment the body politic (*Wen-chi*, vol. 6, 12.8b). "Your servant has heard that heaven covers all without selfishness, the earth supports all without selfishness, and the sun and moon illuminate without selfishness. Modeling himself on the unselfishness of these three, the king . . . embraces all, loves universally, is impartial" (ibid., 12.4b). All emphasis is thus on the emperor's improving himself to the point where his goals and moral standards become those of the country as a whole. He should not court factions, which generally have goals inconsistent with his own. If he does favor them, the emperor himself will become partial, biased, and selfish. The choice of language for describing the relation between the mind of the emperor and the mind of factions endured. Six hundred years later the Yung-cheng emperor of the Ch'ing (r. 1723–1736) wrote in an essay also entitled "P'eng tang lun," opposing Ou-yang Hsiu's position that the imperial interest is always for the highest public good, meaning it is impartial (*ta kung*). The goals of factions are biased and aimed at the greatest partiality or selfishness. Ordinary persons should take the ruler's goal as their own, making their sentiments of approval and disapproval tally with his (*Ta Ch'ing Shih-tsung hsien* [*Yung-cheng*] *huang-ti shih-lu* [Veritable records of the Yung-cheng emperor] [Taipei: Hua-lien ch'u-pan she, 1964], 343–44). Then the people of the entire realm will be "like-minded."

On specific issues, the people learn the policy of the emperor and, by his example, are persuaded of its correctness. On general principles, uniformity can be introduced into the people's characters through their exposure to a common curriculum in ritual training. As *Analects* 2.3 puts it, "Use the rituals to unify them."

106. Arthur Danto, "Postscript: Philosophical Individualism in Chinese and Western Thought," in *Individualism and Holism*, ed. Munro, 389.

107. See Richard B. Mather, "Individualist Expressions of the Outsiders during the Six Dynasties," ibid., 206.

Six

1. Quoted in Hou Wai-lu, *Chung-kuo ssu-hsiang t'ung-shih*, 4 *shang*:2720.

2. *I-shu* 22A.14b. In studying the overlapping meanings of the various explanatory terms, I learned much from Angus C. Graham, *Two Chinese Philosophers* (London: Lund Humphries, 1958). See also Mou Tsung-san, *Hsin-t'i yü hsing-t'i*, 2:275.

3. *CTYLTC* 95.5b–6a, sec. 17 (6:5010–11) [95.4b; 6:3898].

4. See Fung Yu-lan, *History of Chinese Philosophy* 2:537.

5. Carson Chang, *The Development of Neo-Confucian Thought* (New York: Bookman, 1962), 2:222.

6. Tai Chen, *Meng-tzu tzu-i su-cheng, shang*, 5, 7, 19; *chung*, 35–36.

7. Alison Black alerted me to the significance of this function.

8. Yen Fu made no use of the plant image, probably due to its emotional impact. Seeking to generate psychic dynamism in the Chinese people, Yen Fu turned not to the native plant idea with its conservative image of cyclical change but to its European organicist counterpart—Herbert Spencer's image of the human organism applied to society. As Benjamin Schwartz puts it: "To Yen Fu, groping toward the notion of China as a society-nation rather than as a culture, the concept of the social organism as almost the exact analogue of the biological organism (a concept worked out in incredibly exhaustive detail in the *Principles of Sociology*) provides the most vivid possible image of the nation. It is an organism among other organisms within a Darwinian environment struggling to survive, to grow, and to prevail" (*In Search of Wealth and Power: Yen Fu and the West* [Cambridge, Mass.: Harvard University Press, 1983], 56). This is the same explanatory image that, many decades later, others such as Chiang (Tsiang) T'ing-fu and Chiang Kai-shek continued to employ. "Considering the state as an organism as far as its life is concerned, we may say that the Three Principles con-

stitute the soul of our nation, because without these principles our national reconstruction would be deprived of its guiding spirit. And, considering the state as an organism as far as its functions are concerned, we may say that the Kuomintang is the life blood of our nation and the members of the San Min Chu I Youth Corps may be likened to new blood corpuscles" (Chiang Kai-shek, *China's Destiny* [1943], quoted in *Sources of Chinese Tradition*, ed. William Theodore de Bary [New York: Columbia University Press, 1964], 2:150).

As might be expected, traditional nineteenth-century Confucians such as Chang Chih-tung wrote of "giving full development to the creatures and things of earth," in part through teaching students to "nourish the roots" of learning, to be followed by the students' study of the classics "in order to strengthen the roots" (William Ayers, *Chang Chih-tung and Educational Reform in China* [Cambridge, Mass.: Harvard University Press, 1971], 43, 111, 157).

In addition, however, intellectuals like Hsiung Shih-li and Liang Sou-ming, who tried to modernize Confucianism in the twentieth century and, in the attempt, dropped the idea of a cycle, continued to stress that the special feature of Chinese thought is its regard for the inner life of man. They also inherited the prizing of life as a feature of nature, a principle originally associated with the explanatory device of the plant.

9. As discussed in Chapter Three, Chu took a firm stand on the importance of the study of principle in objective things, especially in books. He coedited the *Chin-ssu lu*, a collection of writings from earlier Sung Neo-Confucians. He placed the chapter on the investigation of things prior to the one on preserving one's mind, which deals with introspective issues. The sequence, as in other Chinese works, has symbolic importance. Wang Yang-ming is quoted as saying, "Hui-weng [Chu Hsi] said that Tzu-ching [Lu Hsiang-shan] had taught people about honoring the moral nature but that he himself emphasized more strongly following the path of study and inquiry" (Chan, *Instructions for Practical Living*, 253). To many subsequent Confucians, Chu's advocacy of this bookish pursuit was so strong that it seemed to overwhelm what they considered to be the more important concern, the mind itself. Perhaps it seemed to establish a gulf between the self and things.

Unfortunately for the analyst, there is again no shortage of textual support in Chu's writings for the seemingly contradictory priority of mind rectification. Chu stressed introspective care of the moral sense as a standard of judgment. The key term that symbolizes self-discovery and mind rectification is "reverential concentration" (ᵇ*ching*) on one's "original nature" (*pen-hsing*), which was discussed in Chapter Four. Chu was prone to statements to the effect that "ᵇ*ching* is the key of the sage's teaching" (*CTYLTC* 12.12b, sec. 86 (1:566) [12.10a; 1:395]). Or he says that ᵇ*ching* is the doorkeeper to the mind (which seems to give it some sort of priority) (*CTYLTC* 9.4a–b, sec. 26 (1:447–48) [9.3a; 1:300]). He also says that in cultivation the individual's first step is to refocus the mind that has wandered away from moral principles; the second step is to investigate principle thoroughly (*CTYLTC* 12.3b, sec. 31 (1:548–49) [12.3a; 1:381–82]).

10. W. T. Chan long ago identified the "four scholars" of the early Ming who considered themselves to be followers of Chu Hsi and yet also helped move Neo-Confucianism in a new direction, thereby contributing to the rise of Wang Yang-ming's School of Mind in the late Ming. Each of them emphasized a conception of reverential concentration on the mind (ᵇ*ching*) developed by Chu Hsi. See Wing-tsit Chan, "The Ch'eng-Chu School of Early Ming," in *Self and Society in Ming Thought*, ed. de Bary et al., 29–52. The other major contribution on this topic is de Bary's *Neo-Confucian Orthodoxy*.

11. De Bary, *Neo-Confucian Orthodoxy*, 78, 120, 128.

12. Ibid., 131–48.

13. John W. Dardess, *Confucianism and Autocracy: Professional Elites in the Founding of the Ming Dynasty* (Berkeley: University of California Press, 1983), 136–37.

14. Ibid., 139.

15. Ibid., 181, 205.

16. Ray Huang, *1587: A Year of No Significance: The Ming Dynasty in Decline* (New Haven: Yale University Press, 1981), 149.

17. Dardess, *Confucianism and Autocracy*, 198.

18. Ibid., 240.

19. Huang, *1587*, 88.

20. Dardess, *Confucianism and Autocracy*, 198.

21. Ch'ing Sheng-tsu, *Sheng-tsu jen huang-ti sheng-hsün* (Sacred edicts of the emperor K'ang-hsi), 5.6b (54th year), in *Shih Ch'ao sheng-hsün* (Sacred edicts of the Ten Reigns) (Shanghai, ca. 1900), vol. 4.

22. There is a list of the sixteen points in Ch'en Ching-chih, *Chung-kuo chiao-yü shih* (A history of Chinese education) (Taipei: Commercial Press, 1963), 471.

23. Victor H. Mair's "Language and Ideology in the Written Popularizations of the *Sacred Edict*," in *Popular Culture in Late Imperial China*, ed. David Johnson et al. (Berkeley: University of California Press, 1985), 325–59, is an excellent study of the popular impact of imperial Confucian ideas.

24. The notion, congenial to authority, of the entire population sharing "one mind" was an ideal. To achieve it the government promoted the uniformity of values. And indeed, most Confucians believed that the Confucian social role–based ethics, centered around the rules of conduct (ᵃ*li*) and the imperial political system and aided by a meritocratic bureaucracy, was suitable to all people everywhere.

This ideal does not seem to have been challenged even by late nineteenth-century Chinese Westernizers. As late as 1898, when the translator Yen Fu (1853–1921) was face to face with the individualistic value of uniqueness in Mill's *On Liberty* (which includes the idea that each person can select his own values), he ignored it. Rather than talk about freedom as individuality or eccentricity, he explained it in terms of releasing the individual's energies so as to strengthen the state. See Schwartz, *In Search of Wealth and Power*, 136, 138. Similarly, K'ang Yu-wei, in his commentary on the *Doctrine of the Mean*, wrote, "If each man follows the dictates of his own nature which he received in common with all men, his conduct will be compatible with that of every other man." Filiality and brotherly love are among the basic shared traits. See Hsiao Kung-chuan, *A Modern China and a New World: K'ang Yu-wei, Reformer and Utopian, 1858–1927* (Seattle: University of Washington Press, 1975), 89.

25. Ch'ing Shih-tsung, "Sheng-yü kuang-hsün hsü" (Preface to the "Sacred Edict" of Emperor K'ang-hsi), in *Sheng-yü kuang-hsün* (Amplified expositions on the "Sacred Edicts") (n.p., 1800), 3.

26. *Ta Ch'ing Shih-tsung hsien (Yung-cheng) huang-ti shih-lu*, 343–44.

27. Ch'ing Shih-tsung, *Hsien huang-ti sheng-hsün* (Sacred edicts of Emperor Yung-cheng), in *Shih Ch'ao sheng-hsün*, 10:3–4.

28. Irene Bloom, trans. and ed., *Knowledge Painfully Acquired: The K'un-chih chi by Lo Ch'in-shun* (New York: Columbia University Press, 1987).

29. Willard J. Peterson, *Bitter Gourd: Fang I-chih and the Impetus for Intellectual Change* (New Haven: Yale University Press, 1979), 4–6.

30. Chan, "Ch'eng-Chu School of Early Ming," 38.

31. For example, de Bary, *Neo-Confucian Orthodoxy*, 178.

32. Like Chu, Wang treats the mind in its responsive mode (willing; feeling, as in loving and hating) as belonging to the realm of action. See Chan, *Instructions for Practical Living*, 10, 53, 92, 101. He thereby divides the self differently from the Westerner, who is accustomed to treating overt behavior as action and feeling as private and different from action. When the moral sense knows something, that knowledge is likely to be accompanied by a feeling, which is the beginning of action. The important point is that the beginnings of Wang's doctrine of the unity of knowledge and action can be traced back even earlier than Chu Hsi to Ch'eng I, who held that deep knowledge becomes action, a point with which Chu concurred. As Ch'eng I wrote, "When knowing is deep, then action in accord with it will necessarily be perfect. There is no such thing as knowing what should be done and not being able to do it. Knowing and not being able to act is only a sign that the knowing does not go deep" (*I-shu* 15.16b and Munro, *Concept of Man in Contemporary China*, 35–36). For a similar statement by Chu Hsi, see *CTYLTC* 9.1a, sec. 2 (1:441) [9.1a; 1:295].

To identify Chu's images in Wang's theory is not to deny that Wang enriched the Neo-Confucian concept of the moral sense. In particular, he treated the human moral sense as simply one manifestation of something that cosmically can take other forms: "Now innate knowledge is one. In terms of its wonderful functioning, it is spirit; in terms of its universal operation, it is force; and in terms of its condensation and concentration, it is essence" (Chan, *Instructions for Practical Living*, 133).

33. Chan, *Instructions for Practical Living*, 52.

34. Ibid., 57.

35. Peterson, *Bitter Gourd*, 12.

36. Elman, "Philosophy (*i-li*) versus Philology (*k'ao-cheng*)," 192.

37. William Theodore de Bary, "Chinese Despotism and the Confucian Ideal: A Seventeenth-Century View," in *Chinese Thought and Institutions*, ed. J. K. Fairbank (Chicago: University of Chicago Press, 1957), 178. As de Bary points out, this is an anti-Legalist position, contrary to the teachings of Han Fei-tzu (d. 233 B.C.), for whom the ruler's judgment on all matters is always to be followed. Huang's proposal does not depart from Confucian authoritarianism. It shifts the burden of authority over matters other than ultimate values to the local level, especially in the absence of a virtuous ruler. Within the schools, scholars who properly grasped the teaching of the sage-kings on such matters as the best laws would still be obediently followed by students. Diversity of opinion is not intrinsically good. This is therefore a softening, but not an abandonment, of Chu Hsi's authoritarianism.

38. Thomas C. Bartlett, "Ku Yen-wu's Response to 'The Demise of Hunan Society' " (Ph.D. diss., Princeton University, 1986), 113.

39. Peterson, *Bitter Gourd*, 154–56.

40. For a discussion of the issue, see Elman, "Criticism as Philosophy," 14.

41. Ibid.

42. Chang, *Development of Neo-Confucian Thought*, 2:378–79.

43. I refer to Thomas Metzger's *Escape from Predicament*. He argues that the failure of Wang An-shih's reform efforts in the "outer" political and economic sphere was followed by an inward orientation among Confucians. They sought through reverential concentration (*ᵇching*) and moral effort (*kung-fu*) to draw on power subjectively located in the mind. Politically, they refocused attention on local affairs and away from nationwide reforms dictated by the center. Ultimately, for Chu Hsi, that inner power derives from the linkage (present but imperfect) that exists between the principles within the mind and the patterns to which they correspond in nature. For Wang Yang-ming it lies in the cosmic will present in the mind. Yet in turning within, Confucians faced a predicament. The evil in men's selfish desires (ibid., 173) and the evil willed by the cosmos undercut their best efforts; the evil wins because of the

imperfect linkage of the "metaphysical and experiential realms" (ibid., 214). In the modern period, the escape from the predicament becomes possible because Chinese can tap objective power latent in the tools of science and in new forms of political participation to solve their most pressing problems in the outer realm, and the nation can be the instrument for organizing that power. Those who participate in the physical life of the nation as it seeks to cope with these problems have within their reach a new power, disconnected from the cosmic power sought through mental discipline by the Confucians.

This is an important thesis. And yet with respect to the issues with which I have been concerned in the present book, it is flawed. First, words like "good cosmic force" and "bad cosmic force" (ibid., 81) suggest magical powers that are not mentioned in Chu's writings. To speak of evil as being "willed by the cosmos" (ibid., 113) introduces anthropomorphic features into nature that are also absent from Chu's work. But there are more crucial problems, primarily involving differences in tone. According to Metzger, "the mind, for all its godlike potentiality, was inherently fragile and vulnerable" (ibid., 125). True enough. But it is also capable of enlightenment. There is an optimism, an expectation of perfectibility possible for many people as a result of the cognitive capacity, which is lost if one focuses on the mind's fragility. The other difficulty is that Metzger overdoes the evil that undercuts man's best efforts. He says that Chu and Wang Yang-ming "both saw the world, especially the 'outer', historical world, as a moral wilderness dominated by 'human material desires' " (ibid., 138). There are many places where Chu speaks of the evils of human desires, but he also speaks of the naturalness of desires (even sages have them) and of the possibility of satisfying them in accordance with the ritual rules. The theme of ascetic self-conquest was picked up by Chen Te-hsiu and promoted by some emperors, who were not disinterested in having their subjects live on a subsistence level.

44. Albert Feuerwerker suggested this comparison to me. In interpreting this work, I owe a debt to John Plamenatz's explanations in *Man and Society: A Critical Examination of Some Important Social and Political Theories from Machiavelli to Marx* (New York: McGraw-Hill, 1963), vol. 1. For reference to the conscience, see

Barbara Foxley, trans., *Émile or Education*, by *J. J. Rousseau*, Everyman's Library (London: E. P. Dutton, 1933), bk. 1, p. 34.

This basic innate faculty, described in *Émile or Education*, is not reason but feeling, although the latter comes to make use of the former: "Reason alone teaches us to know good and evil. Therefore conscience, which makes us love the one and hate the other, though it is independent of reason, cannot develop without it" (bk. 1, p. 34). These feelings urge people to find tranquility within the self and act altruistically beyond the self. They will be tranquil in this condition because following the conscience is natural to them. In short, Rousseau assumes that man is naturally good because he is predisposed to seek and develop such tranquility and altruism. That predisposition is rooted in conscience, the introspectively moral sentiments.

45. Foxley, *Émile or Education*, bk. 1, p. 5.

46. There is a discussion relevant to this matter in Berlin, "Two Concepts of Liberty," 162–72.

47. Mary Wright, *The Last Stand of Chinese Conservatism* (Stanford: Stanford University Press, 1962), 149–55.

48. I owe this point to Ernest Young.

49. Wright, *Chinese Conservatism*, 305ff.

50. Ting Ta-nien, *Kung-ch'an chu-i jen-sheng kuan* (The Communist view of life) (Shanghai: Hua tung jen-min ch'u-pan she, 1953), 22, and *Jen-min jih-pao* (*JMJP*) (People's daily), 28 May 1963, 5. I first discussed the material concerning selflessness referred to in this and the next four notes in "The Concept of 'Interest' in Chinese Thought," *Journal of the History of Ideas* 41 (April–June 1980), 189–91.

51. Sun Wei-pen, *Kung-ch'an tang yüan ying-tang tsen-yang tui-tai ke-jen li-i he tang te li-i?* (How should a Communist party member treat individual interest and party interest?) (Shenyang: Liao-ning jen-min ch'u-pan she, 1956), 23, and Ting Ta-nien, *Kung-ch'an chu-i jen-sheng kuan*, 59.

52. *JMJP*, 3 July 1963, 5.

53. *JMJP*, 20 March 1963, 2; 28 April 1963, 5.

54. *JMJP*, 20 March 1963, 2.

55. *JMJP*, 31 May 1963, in *Survey of China Mainland Press*, no.

3000 (17 June 1963), quoted in Munro, *Concept of Man in Contemporary China*, 93.

56. Mao Tse-tung, *Talks at the Yenan Forum on Art and Literature* (Peking: Foreign Languages Press, 1960), 36–37.

57. Ibid., 37.

58. Liu Shao-ch'i, "Jen te chieh-chi hsing" (Man's class nature), in *Lun ssu-hsiang* (On thought) (Beijing: Ch'ün-chung shu-tien, 1949), 9.

59. See Munro, *Concept of Man in Contemporary China*, chap. 3.

60. Believing himself to be completing a portrait of the universe in regular flux initially outlined in the *Book of Changes*, Hsiung drew also on the Consciousness Only Buddhist school. And Bergsonian-type evolutionary theory provided a modernizing and progressive aura for the theory of change. (In a published letter to Hsieh Yu-wei he speaks of having read the Chinese translation of Bergson's *Creative Evolution*; see Hsiung Shih-li, *Hsin wei-shih lun* [New idealism] [Taipei: Kuang-wen shu-chü, 1962], app., p. 66b.) A principal feature of his metaphysics is the rejection of any separation between the creator and the myriad created things. What Westerners would call "the Absolute" (the self-sufficient cause of all that exists) is the very process of change and creativity, possessing progressively evolutionary attributes. All things participate in it. To describe the Absolute, Hsiung uses the terms "original substance" (*pen-t'i*, which echoes Wang Pi's Neo-Taoism) and "Tathāgata" from Buddhism, both of which refer to a nonempirical, transcendental entity. Yet he describes it as "constant transformation," something of this world and not transcendental. The stuff that undergoes change is life force, so Hsiung is presenting here a species of vitalism akin to that of Chu Hsi and Wang Yangming.

61. Ibid., *hsia*, pp. 64a–b, 79b, 85a.

62. Ibid., *hsia*, pp. 77a, 78a.

63. Ibid., *hsia*, pp. 77a, 83a, 84a.

64. Ibid., *hsia*, app., p. 64a.

65. For examples of his acceptance of Chu Hsi-type vitalism in his explanation of nature, see Liang Sou-ming, *Tung Hsi wen-hua chi ch'i che-hsüeh* (Eastern and Western cultures and their philoso-

phies) (Taipei: Tzu-yu hsüeh jen pien-chi pu, 1960), 212, 271, 273, 282.

66. Quoted in Guy Alitto, "The Conservative as Sage: Liang Shu-ming," in *The Limits of Change: Essays on Conservative Alternatives in Republican China*, ed. Charlotte Furth (Cambridge, Mass.: Harvard University Press, 1976), 228. This essay was brought to my attention by Chan Sin-yee, from whom I have learned much about Liang Sou-ming.

67. Ibid., 229.

68. Jerome B. Grieder, *Hu Shih and the Chinese Renaissance* (Cambridge, Mass.: Harvard University Press, 1970), 99.

69. Ibid., 267, 274.

70. Ibid., 229.

71. Maurice Meisner, *Li Ta-chao and the Origins of Chinese Marxism* (Cambridge, Mass.: Harvard University Press, 1967), 147.

72. Ibid., 145, 147.

73. The "Western Inscription," quoted in de Bary, *Sources of Chinese Tradition*, 1:469.

74. This was suggested to me by Benjamin Elman.

75. Quoted in Schwartz, *In Search of Wealth and Power*, 70.

76. Quoted in de Bary, *Sources of Chinese Tradition*, 2:107.

77. Ibid., 131.

78. Laurence G. Thompson, *Ta T'ung Shu: The One-World Philosophy of K'ang Yu-wei* (London: George Allen and Unwin, 1958), 65.

79. Ibid., 266.

80. Ibid., 172.

81. Quoted in Grieder, *Hu Shih and the Chinese Renaissance*, 141.

82. Quoted in Schwartz, *In Search of Wealth and Power*, 62.

83. Quoted in Ayers, *Chang Chih-tung and Educational Reform in China*, 76.

84. Wright, *Last Stand of Chinese Conservatism*, 92, 198.

85. Judith Stacey, *Patriarchy and Socialist Revolution in China* (Berkeley: University of California Press, 1983), 126. Ernest Young brought this book to my attention.

86. The frequent explanation of humanism by Chinese Marxists in traditional Mencian categories (universal feelings, love of mankind, humanitarianism) rather than in terms of the fulfillment of basic human needs, as required by classical German Marxism, or

in terms of natural rights, as advocated by other European humanists, can be found both in the works of its advocates and in the
examples cited by the critics of humanism. For example, writing in
1957, Kuan Feng (later to become a leader of the Cultural Revolution Group) criticized one Comrade Hsü Mao-jung, saying, "According to him, this 'human nature' is a good trait common to all
classes, and it is only less revealed by the reactionary class." Kuan
went on to attack Comrade Pa Jen, adding his own italics to the
following passage that he quoted from Pa Jen as an example of
Pa's errors. In order to liberate the spirit of the hostile class, Pa
said, the following is necessary: "We must take as the basis *a thing
common to all persons. And this basis is human sentiments, that is, humanitarianism that emerges from the basic nature of mankind*" (Kuan
Feng, "Lüeh lun jen-hsing he chieh-chi hsing" [A brief discussion
of human nature and class nature], *Hsüeh-hsi* [Studies], 3 September 1957, 15). In 1963, Chou Yang attacked those revisionists who
describe Marxism as humanism in these words: "Now the revisionists have tampered with the teachings of scientific commu-
nism, and reverted to the preaching of human nature in the abstract and of 'love of humanity,' which Marxism-Leninism
transcended long long ago, and to such slogans as 'man is to man
a brother.' " Class love is possible. Universal love of humanity is
not. See Chou Yang, *The Fighting Task Confronting Workers in Philosophy and the Social Sciences* (Peking: Foreign Languages Press, 1963),
35. For Chinese edition, see Chou Yang, *Che-hsüeh she-hui k'e-hsüeh
kung-tso-che te chan-tou jen-wu* (Beijing: Jen-nien ch'u-pan she,
1963), 32.

The conservative party historian and ideologue Hu Ch'iao-mu
wrote an authoritative article on "The Question of Humanism and
Alienation" in 1984, in which he said that according to bourgeois
humanists, the motive force behind human development is man's
benevolent nature. Hu accepted humanism (something like kindness) only as part of socialist ethics, not as part of its world view,
which denigrates its importance. See Hu Ch'iao-mu, "Kuan-yü
jen-tao chu-i he i-hua wen-t'i," *Hung-ch'i* (Red flag), 26 January
1984, 4. Joining the debate on humanism and alienation in 1984,
Deng Pufang, son of Deng Xiaoping, wrote: "The concept of love
for man can date back to the times of Confucius. However, it was

the bourgeoisie who developed the concept into an ideological system. As a world outlook and an ethical principle, humanitarianism has very extensive and profound influence among the masses of people in capitalist countries. Although our country has never fully developed the capitalists' relationship of production, nor been touched by the spiritual wealth of the Western bourgeoisie in a systematic way, the influence of bourgeois ideology does exist and cannot be ignored. However, another fact that cannot be ignored either is that the influence of feudalism is more extensive and profound in our country. As compared with capitalism feudalism is even crueler and more inhumane. Therefore, we have a more backward background in China regarding attitudes toward the handicapped. . . . We cannot but admit that the abnormal criticism against humanitarianism after liberation has hindered our efforts to spread the idea of humanitarianism" (*JMJP*, 7 December 1984, translated by the Foreign Broadcast Information Service in *China: Daily Report*, 14 December 1984, K10). Generally speaking, in the debates within the People's Republic of China, European humanism stands for the claim that all persons possess natural rights. Chinese humanism with its Mencian overtones has stood for the promotion of harmony among people. Both stand for the reduction of the coercive activities of government. In contrast, the emphasis on man's class nature and dialectical materialism has symbolized an advocacy of struggle between groups and a retention of the coercive practices of the dictatorship of the proletariat. The exact targets of attack change with the years. Often, the debate follows upon a high-level factional dispute. For example, Kuan Feng's article reflected the Maoist position favoring an antirightist campaign and struggles against members of the bourgeoisie. On 26 April 1957, Liu Shao-ch'i had challenged the need for such conflict, saying the capitalists had changed, and so class struggle could be minimized.

87. The principal spokesman for the new doctrine of humanism has been Wang Jo-shui. Two of his articles, one on alienation and another entitled "A Defense of Humanism" (Wei jen-tao chu-i pian-hu), were published in 1980 and were followed a few years later by his book of the same title. The book was a critique of Hu Ch'iao-mu's article referred to above. Wang became deputy editor-

in-chief of the *People's Daily* in 1978 and was fired in 1984. Wang is reputed to be the actual author of the section on humanism in Chou Yang's 1963 article. If so, he performed quite a switch.

88. Speaking of the sentiments at the basis of utilitarian morality, John Stuart Mill wrote, "This firm foundation is that of the social feelings of mankind; the desire to be in unity with our fellow creatures, which is already a powerful principle in human nature" (*Utilitarianism, Liberty, and Representative Government* [New York: E. P. Dutton, 1950], "Utilitarianism," chap. 3, p. 38). Mill's idea of justice contains a typically Western place for individual rights, although they are defended on the basis of utility. But the idea of justice is based on enlargeable fellow feeling: "And the sentiment of justice appears to me to be, the animal desire to repel or retaliate a hurt or damage to oneself, or to those with whom one sympathizes, widened so as to include all persons, by the human capacity of enlarged sympathy, and the human conception of intelligent self-interest" (ibid., chap. 5, p. 65). The notion of human sympathy is clustered with different ideas in different cultures—with, say, rights and utility in the case of Mill, and with special family concerns in the Confucian case. There are therefore some issues on which Chinese inheritors of the Mencius-Chu Hsi legacy and Western thinkers will be unlikely to concur. But to find a place for agreement on starting points in ethics by some influential modern figures is something in itself.

an-tun ch'u 安頓處

Chan-jan 湛然

Ch'an 禪

Chang Chih-tung 張之洞

Chang Nan-hsien 張南軒

Chang Tsai 張載

chao 照

chao wu 照物

ch'ao-ch'u shih-ku 超出世故

Chen-chüeh 眞覺

chen ju 眞儒

Chen Te-hsiu 眞德秀

chen ti 眞諦

ch'en ch'en 臣臣

Ch'en Liang 陳亮

Ch'en Tu-hsiu 陳獨秀

cheng 正

cheng-ming 正名

[a]*ch'eng* 誠

[b]*ch'eng* 成

Ch'eng Hao 程顥

Ch'eng I 程頤

Ch'eng-tsu 成祖

chi wu 即物

[a]*ch'i* 氣

[b]*ch'i* 器

Ch'i 齊

ch'i-chih chih hsing 氣質之性

ch'i-hsiang 氣象

Chiang (Tsiang) T'ing-fu 蔣廷黻

"Chieh pi" 解蔽

chien-min 賤民

ch'ien 乾

ch'ien-yin 潛隱

chih 志

chih chih 致知

chih-chüeh 知覺

chih kung 至公

chin-shih 進士

Chin-ssu lu 近思錄

ch'in-min 親民

[a]*ching* 經

[b]*ching* 敬

ching-shuang 精爽

Ching-te ch'uan teng lu 景德傳燈錄

[a]*ch'ing* 情

[b]*ch'ing* 清

cho 濁

chou 州

Chou Tun-i 周敦頤

Chou Yang 周揚

chu 主

Chu Hsi 朱熹

chu li 燭理

chu-tsai 主宰

Chu Tzu ch'üan-shu 朱子全書

Chu Tzu yü-lei ta-ch'üan 朱子語類大全

chü-jen 舉人

ch'u 觸

ch'u ch'i i erh fan ch'i t'ung 絀其異而反
　　其同

ch'u chia 出家

ch'u shih 出世

ch'ü 渠

chüan 卷

ch'uan hsin 傳心

ch'üan 權

Chuang-tzu 莊子

chün 軍

chün-tzu 君子

chung 忠

Erh Ch'eng ch'üan-shu 二程全書

Fa Tsang 法藏

Fan Chung-yen 范仲淹

Fang I-chih 方以智

Fang Tung-shu 方東樹

[a]*fei* 非

[b]*fei* 費

fen 分

fu li 復禮

fu-mu kuan 父母官

Hai Jui 海瑞

Han Fei-tzu 韓非子

han yang 涵養

Han Yü 韓愈

heng 亨

Hsi K'ang 嵇康

"Hsi ming" 西銘

hsiang 鄉

hsiang-hsü 相恤

hsiang-yüeh 鄉約

Hsiao ching 孝經

Hsiao hsüeh 小學

hsiao-min 小民

[a]*hsien* 縣

[b]*hsien* 顯

hsin 心

hsin-hsüeh 心學

hsin wei yu wai 心為有外

hsing 性

hsing-ch'a 省察

hsing erh shang 形而上

Hsiung Shih-li 熊十力

Hsü Heng 許衡

hsüeh-che 學者

Hsüeh Hsüan 薛瑄

Hsün Tzu 荀子

Hu Ch'iao-mu 胡乔木

Hu Shih 胡適

Hua-yen 華嚴

Hua-yen yu-hsin fa-chieh chi 華嚴遊心
法界記

Huai-nan-tzu 淮南子

huan-wang 幻妄

Huang Po 黃檗

Huang Tsung-hsi 黃宗羲

hui 慧

Hui Neng 慧能

Hui-weng 誨翁

[a]*i* 義

[b]*i* 一

[c]*i* 意

i fa 已發

i hsin 一心

i-li 義理

i-li tzu-ming 義理自明

jen 仁

jen-chüeh 人爵

jen-fen 人分

jen-hsin wei wei tao-hsin wei wei 人心惟
危道心惟微

jen-hsing pen ching 人性本淨

jen-lun 人倫

jen-shih 人事

jen-tao chu-i 人道主義

Jen-wu chih 人物志

jen-yü 人欲

ju 儒

kang 綱

K'ang-hsi 康熙

K'ang Yu-wei 康有為

ke an ch'i fen 各安其分

ke tang ch'i fen 各當其分

ke te ch'i fen 各得其分

ke wu 格物

k'e chi 克己

k'e chi fu li 克己復禮

ken 艮

k'en 肯

ku-tzu 骨子

ku-wen 古文

Ku Yen-wu 顧炎武

kuan 觀

Kuan Chung 管仲

Kuan Feng 關鋒

kuan hsin 觀心

kuan-t'ung 貫通

k'un 坤

kung 公

kung-fu 工夫

kung-hsin 公心

kung-i 公移

kung-li 功利

Kung-yang chuan 公羊傳

kuo 過

Lei Feng 雷鋒

lei-t'ui 類推

[a]*li* 禮

[b]*li* 理

[c]*li* 利

295

Li-chi 禮記
li chih 立志
li-hsing 理性
"Li hsü" 禮序
li-hsüeh 理學
li i fen shu 理一分殊
Li Ta-chao 李大釗
Li Yen-p'ing 李延平
"Li yün" 禮運
Liang Ch'i-ch'ao 梁啟超
liang-chih 良知
Liang Sou[Shu]-ming 梁漱溟
Liu Chi 劉基
liu-hsing 流行
Liu Shao 劉邵
Lo Ch'in-shun 羅欽順
Lu Chiu-yüan 陸九淵
Lu Hsiang-shan 陸象山
Lü 呂
Meng-tzu tzu-i shu-cheng 孟子字義疏證
min chih fu-mu 民之父母
ming 命
ming hsin chien hsing 明心見性
ming li 明理
ming ming-te 明明德
Ming T'ai-tzu 明太子
mo-fan 模範
Mo Tzu 墨子
Nan k'ang chün 南康軍
nei 內
nei-chao 內照
Nei-kuan ching 內觀經
Ou-yang Hsiu 歐陽修
pa 霸
Pa Jen 巴人
Pai-wen 伯溫
p'an 畔
pao en 報恩
pen-hsing 本性
pen-t'i 本體
p'eng tang 朋黨
"P'eng tang lun" 朋黨論
pien-shih 變事
p'ien 偏
piao-hsien 表現

"Po-jo wu-chih lun" 般若無知論
pu ch'i 不齊
pu chün-p'ing 不均平
pu tang 不黨
san kang 三綱
Seng Chao 僧肇
Shen Hsiu 神秀
Shen Hui 神會
Sheng-hsüeh hsin-fa 聖學新法
sheng-i 生意
sheng-jen 聖人
Sheng-tsu 聖祖
"Sheng-yü" 聖諭
Sheng-yü kuang-hsün 聖諭廣訓
[a]shih 是
[b]shih 事
[c]shih 士
shih-fei chih hsin 是非之心
shih li 實理
shih-ta-fu 士大夫
shu 恕
Shu ching 書經
Shun 舜
so 所
ssu 私
Ssu-k'u ch'üan-shu ts'ung-mu t'i-yao 四庫
　　全書總目提要
Ssu-ma Kuang 司馬光
ssu-yü 私欲
Su Shih 蘇軾
ta kung 大公
ta kung, wu ssu 大公無私
Tai Chen 戴震
t'ai chi 太極
tang 黨
tao 道
tao-hsüeh 道學
tao-li 道理
Tao-sheng 道生
Tao-te ching 道德經
Tao-yüan 道原
t'ao 逃
T'ao Ch'ien 陶潛
te 德
ti 帝

296

t'i 體

t'i jen 體仁

t'i pieh 體別

t'ien 天

t'ien-chih yu li 天秩有理

t'ien-chüeh 天爵

t'ien-chün 天君

t'ien-fen 天分

t'ien-hsü 天叙

t'ien-hsü yu tien 天叙有典

t'ien-li 天理

T'ien-t'ai 天台

t'ien-tao 天道

t'ien-t'i 天梯

t'ing-ming yü 聽命於

t'ou 透

tsa 雜

tsai 宰

tsai Mao Tse-tung ssu-hsiang te yang-kuang yü-lu p'u-yü hsia 在毛澤東思想的陽光雨露哺育下

ts'ai 材

ts'ang 藏

Tseng Tzu 曾子

Tso chuan 左傳

tsun te-hsing 尊德性

t'ui 推

t'ui chi chi jen 推己及人

t'ui-lei 推類

Tung Chung-shu 董仲舒

[a]*t'ung* 通

[b]*t'ung* 統

T'ung-chih 同治

t'ung hsin 同心

t'ung tao 同道

Tzu-ching 子靜

Tzu Lu 子路

tzu-ming 自明

Tzu Ssu 子思

tzu-te 自得

tzu tzu 子子

wai 外

Wang An-shih 王安石

Wang Pi 王弼

Wang Yang-ming 王陽明

wei 位

wei ching wei i 惟精惟一

wei fa 未發

wo 我

wu 物

wu chih 無知

wu fen 無分

wu ke yü pi, tse chih chin yü ts'e 物格於彼則知盡於此

wu shih su-yün 無適俗韻

wu ssu 無私

wu tang 無黨

wu yü 無欲

Wu Yü-pi 吳與弼

Yao 堯

yeh 業

Yeh Ts'ai 葉采

Yen Fu 嚴復

Yen Hui 嚴回

Yen Tzu 顏子

Yen Yüan 嚴元

yin 隱

yin jen shih chiao 因人施教

yu fang 有方

yu jen t'i shih 猶仁體事

yu wai chih hsin 有外之心

[a]*yü* 欲

[b]*yü* 踰

Yü 禹

yü-lu 語錄

yüan 元

Yüan Ts'ai 袁采

Yung-cheng 雍正

SELECTED BIBLIOGRAPHY

WESTERN LANGUAGE SOURCES

Abrams, Meyer H. *The Mirror and the Lamp*. New York: Oxford University Press, 1953.

Alitto, Guy. "The Conservative as Sage: Liang Shu-ming." In *The Limits of Change: Essays on Conservative Alternatives in Republican China*, ed. Charlotte Furth. Cambridge, Mass.: Harvard University Press, 1976.

Arendt, Hannah. *The Life of the Mind: Willing*. New York: Harcourt Brace Jovanovich, 1978.

Ayers, William. *Chang Chih-tung and Educational Reform in China*. Cambridge, Mass.: Harvard University Press, 1971.

Bartlett, Thomas C. "Ku Yen-Wu's Response to 'The Demise of Human Society.'" Ph.D. dissertation, Princeton University, 1985.

Berkeley, George. "Three Dialogues." In *Essays, Principles, Dialogues*, ed. Mary W. Calkins. New York: Charles Scribner's Sons, 1929.

Berlin, Isaiah. "Two Concepts of Liberty." In *Four Essays on Liberty*. Oxford: Oxford University Press, 1969.

Black, Max. *Models and Metaphors: Studies in Language and Philosophy*. Ithaca, N.Y.: Cornell University Press, 1962.

Blofeld, John. *The Zen Teaching of Huang Po*. New York: Grove Press, 1980.

Bloom, Irene. "On the Matter of the Mind: The Metaphysical Basis of the Expanded Self." In *Individualism and Holism: Studies in Confucian and Taoist Values*, ed. Donald J. Munro. Ann Arbor: Center for Chinese Studies, University of Michigan, 1985.

————, trans. and ed. *Knowledge Painfully Acquired: The K'un-chih chi by Lo Ch'in-shun*. New York: Columbia University Press, 1987.

Bury, R. G., trans. *Sextus Empiricus*. Loeb Classical Library. Cambridge, Mass.: Harvard University Press, 1955.

Chaffee, John W. "Education and Examinations in Sung Society (960–1279)." Ph.D. dissertation, University of Chicago, 1979.

————. *The Thorny Gates of Learning in Sung China: A Social History of Examinations*. Cambridge: Cambridge University Press, 1985.

Chan, Wing-tsit, trans. *The Platform Scripture*. New York: St. John's University Press, 1963.

————. *Instructions for Practical Living and Other Neo-Confucian Writings by Wang Yang-ming*. New York: Columbia University Press, 1963.

————. "The Evolution of the Neo-Confucian Concept of *Li* as Principle." *Tsing-hua Journal of Chinese Studies* 4 (February 1964), 123–49.

————. *Reflections on Things at Hand*. New York: Columbia University Press, 1967.

————. "Chu Hsi's Completion of Neo-Confucianism." In *Études Song: Sung Studies in Memoriam Étienne Balazs*, ed. Françoise Aubin, 2d ser., no. 1 (1973), 59–90.

————. "Patterns for Neo-Confucianism: Why Chu Hsi Differed from Ch'eng I." *Journal of Chinese Philosophy* 5 (June 1978).

————, ed. *Chu Hsi and Neo-Confucianism*. Honolulu: University of Hawaii Press, 1986.

Chang, Carson. *The Development of Neo-Confucian Thought*. 2 vols. New York: Bookman, 1962.

Chou Yang. *The Fighting Task Confronting Workers in Philosophy and the Social Sciences*. Beijing: Foreign Languages Press, 1963.

Coker, Francis W. *Organismic Theories of the State*. New York: Columbia University Press, 1910.

Conze, Edward, ed. *Buddhist Texts through the Ages*. New York: Philosophical Library, 1954.

Cornford, Francis M. *From Religion to Philosophy*. New York: Harper, 1957.

————. *Plato's Timaeus*. New York: Library of Liberal Arts, 1959.

Danto, Arthur. "Postscript: Philosophical Individualism in Chinese and Western Thought." In *Individualism and Holism: Studies in Confucian and Taoist Values*, ed. Donald J. Munro. Ann Arbor: Center for Chinese Studies, University of Michigan, 1985.

Dardess, John W. *Confucianism and Autocracy: Professional Elites in the Founding of the Ming Dynasty*. Berkeley: University of California Press, 1983.

Davidson, Donald. *Inquiries into Truth and Interpretation*. Oxford: Clarendon Press, 1984.

Davidson, Steven Craig. "Tung Chung-shu and the Origins of Imperial Confucianism." Ph.D. dissertation, University of Wisconsin, 1982.

de Bary, William Theodore. "Individualism and Humanitarianism in Late Ming Thought." In *Self and Society in Ming Thought*, ed. William Theodore de Bary and the Conference on Ming Thought. New York: Columbia University Press, 1970.

————. *Neo-Confucian Orthodoxy and the Learning of the Mind-and-Heart*. New York: Columbia University Press, 1981.

————, ed. *Sources of Chinese Tradition*. New York: Columbia University Press, 1964.

de Coulanges, Fustel. *The Ancient City* (1864), trans. Willard Small. Garden City, N. Y.: 1956.

Demiéville, Paul. "Le miroir spirituel." *Sinologica* (Basel) 1, no. 1 (1948), 112–37.

Derrida, Jacques. "White Mythology: Metaphor in the Text of Philosophy." In *Jacques Derrida: Margins of Philosophy*, trans. Alan Bass. Chicago: University of Chicago Press, 1982.

Descartes, René. *Meditations on First Philosophy*, trans. Laurence J. Lafleur. Indianapolis: Library of Liberal Arts, 1976.

Dubs, Homer H., trans. *The Works of Hsuntze*. London: Probsthain, 1928.

Dyson, Freeman. "Disturbing the Universe." *New Yorker*, 13 August 1979, 69.

Ebrey, Patricia B. *Family and Property in Sung China*. Princeton: Princeton University Press, 1983.

Elman, Benjamin A. "Philosophy (*i-li*) versus Philology (*k'ao-cheng*): The *Jen-hsin tao-hsin* Debate," *T'oung Pao* 69, nos. 4–5 (1983), 175–222.

————. *From Philosophy to Philology: Intellectual and Social Aspects of Change in Late Imperial China*. Cambridge, Mass.: Council on East Asian Studies, Harvard University, 1984.

————. "Criticism as Philosophy: Conceptual Change in Ch'ing Dynasty Evidential Research." *Tsing-hua Journal of Chinese Studies* 17, nos. 1–2 (December 1985; published 1987), 165–98.

Elwes, R. H., trans. *Ethics*. In *The Chief Works of Benedict de Spinoza*. New York: Dover, 1955.

Evans, Gillian R. *Augustine on Evil*. Cambridge: Cambridge University Press, 1982.

Evans-Pritchard, Edward E. *Nuer Religion*. Oxford: Oxford University Press, 1956.

Fairbank, John K., ed. *Chinese Thought and Institutions*. Chicago: University of Chicago Press, 1957.

Fernandez, James. "The Mission of Metaphor in Expressive Culture." *Current Anthropology* 15 (June 1974), 119–45.

Fingarette, Herbert. *Confucius—The Secular as Sacred*. New York: Harper and Row, 1972.

Forke, Alfred. *World Conception of the Chinese*. London: Probsthain, 1952.

Foxley, Barbara, trans. *Émile or Education, by J. J. Rousseau*. Everyman's Library. London: E. P. Dutton, 1933.

Fung Yu-lan. "The Philosophy at the Basis of Traditional Chinese Society." In *Ideological Differences and World Order*, ed. Filmer S. C. Northrop. New Haven: Yale University Press, 1949.

——. *History of Chinese Philosophy*, trans. Derk Bodde. 2 vols. Princeton: Princeton University Press, 1952.

Graf, Olaf. *Tao und Jen* (Tao and *jen*). Wiesbaden: Otto Harrassowitz, 1970.

Graham, Angus C. *Two Chinese Philosophers*. London: Lund Humphries, 1958.

Grieder, Jerome B. *Hu Shih and the Chinese Renaissance*. Cambridge, Mass.: Harvard University Press, 1970.

Haeger, John W. "The Intellectual Context of Neo-Confucian Syncretism." *Journal of Asian Studies* 31 (May 1972), 499–513.

Hale, David G. *The Body Politic*. The Hague: Mouton, 1971.

Hamilton, Edith, and Huntington Cairns, eds. *The Collected Dialogues of Plato*. New York: Bollingen, 1961.

Hardie, W.F.R. *Aristotle's Ethical Theory*. Oxford: Oxford University Press, 1968.

Hatch, George C. "The Thought of Su Hsün (1009–1066): An Essay in the Social Meaning of Intellectual Pluralism in the Northern Sung." Ph.D. dissertation, University of Washington, 1972.

Hsiao Kung-chuan. *Rural China: Imperial Control in the Nineteenth Century*. Seattle: University of Washington Press, 1967.

―――. *A Modern China and a New World: K'ang Yu-wei, Reformer and Utopian, 1858–1927*. Seattle: University of Washington Press, 1975.

Hsieh Yu-wei. "Filial Piety and Chinese Society." In *Philosophy and Culture East and West*, ed. Charles A. Moore. Honolulu: University of Hawaii Press, 1962.

Hsü Dau-lin. "The Myth of the 'Five Human Relations' of Confucius." *Monumenta Serica* 29 (1970–1971), 27–37.

Hymes, Robert P. "Prominence and Power in Sung China: The Local Elite of Fu-chou, Chiang-hsi." Ph.D. dissertation, University of Pennsylvania, 1979.

―――. "On Academies, Community Institutions, and Lu Chiu-yüan." Unpublished paper prepared for the "Conference on Neo-Confucian Education: The Formative Stage." Princeton, New Jersey, 1984. Cited by permission of the author.

Jensen, Lionel M. "Wang Yang-ming and the Quest for Authenticity: An Essay on the Chinese Hermeneutic Tradition and the Individual." M.A. thesis, Washington University, 1980.

Kenny, Anthony, trans. and ed. *Descartes' Philosophical Letters*. Oxford: Oxford University Press, 1970.

Kenyon, Cecelia M. "Conceptions of Human Nature in American Political Thought: 1630–1826." Ph.D. dissertation, Radcliffe College, 1949.

King, Ambrose Y. C. "The Individual and Group in Confucianism: A Relational Perspective." In *Individualism and Holism: Studies in Confucian and Taoist Values*, ed. Donald J. Munro. Ann Arbor: Center for Chinese Studies, University of Michigan, 1985.

Kohn, Livia. *Seven Steps to the Tao: Sima Chengzhen's "Zuowanglun."* *Monumenta Serica* Monographs, no. 20. St. Augustin/Nettetal, 1987.

―――. "Taoist Insight Meditation—The Tang Practice of *Neiquan*." Ann Arbor: Center for Chinese Studies, University of Michigan, forthcoming.

Lakoff, George, and Mark Johnson. "Conceptual Metaphor in Everyday Language." *Journal of Philosophy* 77 (August 1980), 453–86.

Lamotte, Étienne. *La Somme du Grand Véhicule d'Asanga (Mahā-yānasamgraha)*. Louvain: Institut Orientaliste Louvain-la-Neuve, 1973.

Latham, R. E., trans. *Lucretius: On the Nature of the Universe*. Baltimore: Penguin, 1951.

Lau, D. C., trans. *Lao Tzu Tao Te Ching*. Baltimore: Penguin, 1963.

Legge, James, trans. *The Li Ki*. Vol. 27 in F. Max Müller, ed., *Sacred Books of the East*. London: Oxford University Press, 1926.

————, trans. *The Chinese Classics*. Vol. 1, *Confucian Analects*, *The Great Learning*, *The Doctrine of the Mean*. Vol. 2, *The Works of Mencius*. Vol. 3, *The Shoo King, or The Book of Historical Documents*. Hong Kong: Hong Kong University Press, 1960.

Lewis, C. S. *The Allegory of Love*. Oxford: Clarendon Press, 1958.

Long, A. A. *Hellenistic Philosophy*. New York: Charles Scribner's Sons, 1974.

McCracken, D. J. *Thinking and Valuing*. London: Macmillan, 1950.

MacDonald, Margaret. "The Language of Political Theory." In *Logic and Language*, ed. Antony Flew. Oxford: Basil Blackwell, 1955.

McKeon, Richard, ed. *The Basic Works of Aristotle*. New York: Random House, 1941.

Mair, Victor H. "Language and Ideology in the Written Popularizations of the *Sacred Edict*." In *Popular Culture in Late Imperial China*, ed. David Johnson et al. Berkeley: University of California Press, 1985.

Mao Tse-tung. *Talks at the Yenan Forum on Art and Literature*. Beijing: Foreign Languages Press, 1960.

Mather, Richard B. "The Controversy over Conformity and Naturalness During the Six Dynasties." *Journal of the History of Religions* 9, nos. 2–3 (1969–1970), 160–80.

Meisner, Maurice. *Li Ta-chao and the Origins of Chinese Marxism*. Cambridge, Mass.: Harvard University Press, 1967.

Mercer, Philip C. *Sympathy and Ethics*. Oxford: Oxford University Press, 1972.

Metzger, Thomas A. *Escape from Predicament*. New York: Columbia University Press, 1977.

Mote, F. W. "The Growth of Chinese Despotism." *Oriens Extremus* 8 (August 1961), 1–41.

Munro, Donald J. *The Concept of Man in Early China*. Stanford: Stanford University Press, 1969.

———. *The Concept of Man in Contemporary China*. Ann Arbor: University of Michigan Press, 1977.

———. "The Concept of 'Interest' in Chinese Thought." *Journal of the History of Ideas* 41 (April–June 1980), 179–97.

———, ed. *Individualism and Holism: Studies in Confucian and Taoist Values*. Ann Arbor: Center for Chinese Studies, University of Michigan, 1985.

Nash, Ronald H. *The Light of the Mind: St. Augustine's Theory of Knowledge*. Lexington: University Press of Kentucky, 1969.

Needham, Joseph. *Science and Civilisation in China*. 6 vols. to date. Cambridge: Cambridge University Press, 1956–.

Needham, Rodney. *Symbolic Classification*. Santa Monica, Calif.: Goodyear, 1979.

Pepper, Stephen C. *World Hypotheses: A Study in Evidence*. Berkeley: University of California Press, 1948.

Peterson, Willard J. "Fang I-chih: Western Learning and the 'Investigation of Things.' " In William Theodore de Bary, ed. *The Unfolding of Neo-Confucianism*. New York: Columbia University Press, 1970.

———. *Bitter Gourd: Fang I-chih and the Impetus for Intellectual Change*. New Haven: Yale University Press, 1979.

Plamenatz, John. *Man and Society: A Critical Examination of Some Important Social and Political Theories from Machiavelli to Marx*. 2 vols. New York: McGraw-Hill, 1963.

Plato's Phaedo, trans. R. S. Bluck. New York: Library of Liberal Arts, n.d.

Qiu Hansheng. "Chu Hsi's Doctrine of Principle." In *Chu Hsi and Neo-Confucianism*, ed. Wing-tsit Chan. Honolulu: University of Hawaii Press, 1986.

Robinet, Isabel. "The Taoist Immortal: Jesters of Light and Shadow, Heaven and Earth." *Journal of Chinese Religions* 13–14 (1985–1986), 88–96.

———. *Méditation Taoiste*. Paris: Dervy Livres, 1979.

Robinson, Richard H. *Early Mādhyamika in India and China*. Madison: University of Wisconsin Press, 1967.

Robinson, Thomas M. *Plato's Psychology*. Toronto: University of Toronto Press, 1970.

Rorty, Richard. *Philosophy and the Mirror of Nature*. Princeton: Princeton University Press, 1979.

Russell, Bertrand. *A History of Western Philosophy*. New York: Simon and Schuster, 1945.

Scheler, Max. *The Nature of Sympathy*, trans. Peter Heath. New Haven: Yale University Press, 1954.

Schirokauer, Conrad. "Chu Hsi's Political Career: A Study in Ambivalence." In Arthur F. Wright and Denis C. Twitchett, eds. *Confucian Personalities*. Stanford: Stanford University Press, 1962.

———. "Chu Hsi and Hu Hung." In *Chu Hsi and Neo-Confucianism*, ed. Wing-tsit Chan. Honolulu: University of Hawaii Press, 1986.

Schwartz, Benjamin. *In Search of Wealth and Power: Yen Fu and the West*. Cambridge, Mass.: Harvard University Press, 1983.

Shaughnessy, Edward L. "The Composition of the 'Zhouyi.' " Ph.D. dissertation, Stanford University, 1983.

Shryock, J. K. *The Study of Human Abilities: The Jen Wu Chih of Liu Shao*. New Haven: American Oriental Society, 1937.

Smith, Norman Kemp. *New Studies in the Philosophy of Descartes*. New York: Russell and Russell, 1963.

Sparrow, Carroll M., trans. *St. Augustine on Free Will*. Charlottesville: University of Virginia Press, 1947.

Stacey, Judith. *Patriarchy and Socialist Revolution in China*. Berkeley: University of California Press, 1983.

Suzuki, Daisetz T., trans. *The Laṅkāvatārā-sūtra*. London: Routledge and Kegan Paul, Ltd., 1973.

T'an Po-fu and Wen Kung-wen. *The Kuan-tzu*. Carbondale, Ill.: Lewis Maverick, 1954.

T'ang Chün-i. "The Development of the Concept of Moral Mind from Wang Yang-ming to Wang Chi." In *Self and Society in Ming Thought*, ed. William Theodore de Bary and the Conference on Ming Thought. New York: Columbia University Press, 1970.

Thompson, Laurence G. *Ta T'ung Shu: The One-World Philosophy of K'ang Yu-wei*. London: George Allen and Unwin, 1958.

Tillman, Hoyt C. *Utilitarian Confucianism: Ch'en Liang's Challenge to Chu Hsi*. Cambridge, Mass.: Harvard University Press, 1982.

Tomoeda, Ryūtarō. "The System of Chu Hsi's Philosophy." In *Chu Hsi and Neo-Confucianism*, ed. Wing-tsit Chan. Honolulu: University of Hawaii Press, 1986.

Tu Wei-ming. Review of *Hsin-t'i yü hsing-t'i* (Mind and human nature) by Mou Tsung-san. *Journal of Asian Studies* 30 (May 1971), 642–47.

———. *Neo-Confucian Thought in Action: Wang Yang-ming's Youth (1472–1509)*. Berkeley: University of California Press, 1976.

———. "The Continuity of Being: Chinese Visions of Nature." In Tu Wei-ming, *Confucian Thought: Selfhood as Creative Transformation*, Albany: State University of New York Press, 1985.

Ulam, S. M. *Adventures of a Mathematician*. New York: Charles Scribner's Sons, 1976.

Wai Weilin. "Ch'an Metaphors." *Philosophy East and West* 29 (1979).

Wakeman, Frederic. "The Price of Autonomy: Intellectuals in Ming and Ch'ing Politics." *Daedalus* (September 1972).

Waley, Arthur, trans. *The Analects of Confucius*. New York: Modern Library, 1938.

Walton-Vargo, Linda Ann. "Education, Social Change, and Neo-Confucianism in Sung-Yuan China: Academies and the Local Elite in Ming Prefecture (Ningpo)." Ph.D. dissertation, University of Pennsylvania, 1978.

Watson, Burton, trans. *Han Fei-tzu*. New York: Columbia University Press, 1964.

Wayman, Alex. "The Mirror as a Pan-Buddhist Metaphor-Simile." *History of Religions* 13 (May 1974), 251–69.

Wei Cheng-t'ung. "Chu Hsi on the Standard and the Expedient." In *Chu Hsi and Neo-Confucianism*, ed. Wing-tsit Chan. Honolulu: University of Hawaii Press, 1986.

Wilhelm, Richard, trans. (English trans. from the German by Cary F. Baynes.) *The I Ching or Book of Changes*. 2 vols. London: Routledge and Kegan Paul, 1960.

Wright, Mary. *The Last Stand of Chinese Conservatism*. Stanford: Stanford University Press, 1962.

CHINESE AND JAPANESE SOURCES

Chan, Wing-tsit. *Chu hsüeh lun chi* (Collected essays on Chu Hsi). Taipei: Hsüeh-sheng shu-chü, 1982.

Chang Li-wen. *Chu Hsi ssu-hsiang yen-chiu* (Study of Chu Hsi's thought). Beijing: Chung-kuo she-hui k'e-hsüeh ch'u-pan she, 1981.

———. "Lun Chu Hsi che-hsüeh te luo-chi chieh-kou" (A discussion of the logical structure of Chu Hsi's philosophy). *Che-hsüeh yen-chiu* (Philosophical investigations), no. 4 (1981), 49–50.

Ch'en Ching-chih. *Chung-kuo chiao-yü shih* (A history of Chinese education). Taipei: Commercial Press, 1963.

Ch'en P'an. *Ta-hsüeh Chung-yung chin shih* (Modern explanation of the *Great Learning* and the *Doctrine of the Mean*). Taipei: Kuo-li pien-i kuan, 1966.

Ch'eng Hao and Ch'eng I. *Erh Ch'eng ch'üan-shu* (Complete works of the two Ch'engs). *Ssu-pu pei-yao* ed.

———. *I-shu* (Written legacy). In *Erh Ch'eng ch'üan-shu*.

———. *Ts'ui-yen* (Pure words). In *Erh Ch'eng ch'üan-shu*.

———. *Wai-shu* (Additional works). In *Erh Ch'eng ch'üan-shu*.

Ch'eng I. *I chuan* (Commentary on the *Book of Changes*). In *Erh Ch'eng ch'üan-shu*.

———. *Ching shuo* (Explanation of the classics). In *Erh Ch'eng ch'üan-shu*.

Ch'ien Mu. *Chu Tzu hsüeh t'i-kang* (Selected studies on Master Chu). Taipei: San-min shu-chü, 1971.

———. *Chu Tzu hsin hsüeh-an* (A new scholarly report on Chu Hsi). 5 vols. Taipei: San-min shu-tien, 1971.

Ch'ing Sheng-tsu. *Sheng-tsu jen huang-ti sheng-hsün* (Sacred edicts of the emperor K'ang-hsi). Vol. 4 in *Shih Ch'ao sheng-hsün* (Sacred edicts of the Ten Reigns). 100 vols. Shanghai, ca. 1900.

Ch'ing Shih-tsung. "Sheng-yü kuang-hsün hsü" (Preface to the "Sacred Edict" of Emperor K'ang-hsi). In *Sheng-yü kuang-hsün* (Amplified expositions on the "Sacred Edict"). N.p., 1800.

———. *Hsien huang-ti sheng-hsün* (Sacred edicts of Emperor Yung-cheng). Vol. 10 in *Shih Ch'ao sheng-hsün*.

Chu Hsi. *Chu Tzu yü-lei* (Classified conversations of Master Chu

Hsi). 1473. Reprint ed. in 8 vols. Taipei: Cheng-chung shu-chü, 1962.

———. *Chu Tzu yü-lei ta-ch'üan* (Complete edition of the *Classified Conversations of Master Chu Hsi*), ed. Li Ching-te, 1207; ed. Yamagataya Shoshi, Kyoto, 1668. Reprint ed. in 8 vols. Kyoto: Chūbun Shoten, 1973.

———. *Chu Tzu ch'üan-shu* (Complete works of Master Chu). Facsimile reprint of the 1885 reprint of the 1715 ed., 2 vols. Taipei: Kuang-hsüeh she, 1977.

———. *Hsiao hsüeh chi-chu* (Collected commentaries on the *Elementary Learning*). *Ssu-pu pei-yao* ed.

———. *Hui-an hsien-sheng Chu Wen-kung wen-chi* (Collection of literary works of Master Chu). *Ssu-pu ts'ung-k'an* ed.

Chung-kuo che-hsüeh shih (History of Chinese philosophy). 2 vols. Beijing: Chung-hua shu-chü, 1980.

Hou Wai-lu. *Chung-kuo ssu-hsiang t'ung-shih* (General history of Chinese thought). 5 vols. Beijing: Jen-min ch'u-pan she, 1963.

Hsiung Shih-li. *Hsin wei-shih lun* (New idealism). Taipei: Kuang-wen shu-chü, 1962.

Liang Sou [Shu]-ming. *Tung Hsi wen-hua chi ch'i che-hsüeh* (Eastern and Western cultures and their philosophies). Taipei: Tzu-yu hsüeh jen pien-chi pu, 1960.

Liu Shao-ch'i. "Jen te chieh-chi hsing" (Man's class nature). In *Lun ssu-hsiang* (On thought). Beijing: Ch'ün-chung shu-tien, 1949.

Mao Li-jui. *Chung-kuo ku-tai chiao-yü shih* (History of China's premodern education). Beijing: Jen-min chiao-yü ch'u-pan she, 1982.

Mou Tsung-san. *Hsin-t'i yü hsing-t'i* (Mind and human nature). 3 vols. Taipei: Cheng-chung shu-chü, 1968–1969.

Okada Takehiko. "Sō min no Shushigaku" (Chu Hsi studies of the Sung and Ming). In *Shushigaku taikei* (Introduction to Chu Hsi studies). Tokyo: Meitoku shuppansha, 1974.

Ou-yang Hsiu ch'üan-chi (Complete works of Ou-yang Hsiu). 2 vols. Taipei: Shih-chieh shu-chü, 1961.

Shimada Kenji. *Shushigaku to Yōmeigaku* (Chu Hsi studies and Yang-ming studies). Tokyo: Iwanami shoten, 1967.

Sun Wei-pen. *Kung-ch'an tang yüan ying-tang tsen-yang tui-tai kejen li-i he tang te li-i?* (How should a Communist party member treat individual interest and party interest?). Shenyang: Liao-ning jen-min ch'u-pan she, 1956.

Suzuki Chūsei. "Sōdai Bukkyō kessha no kenkyū" (A study of Buddhist societies in the Sung period). *Shigaku zasshi* (Journal of historical studies) 52 (1941), 91–97.

Ta Ch'ing Shih-tsung hsien (Yung-cheng) huang-ti shih-lu (Veritable records of the Yung-cheng emperor). Taipei: Hua-lien ch'u-pan she, 1964.

Tai Chen. *Meng-tzu tzu-i su-cheng* (Evidential explanation of the meaning of terms in the *Mencius*). Beijing: Hsin-hua shu-tien, 1982.

Takakusu Junjirō and Watanabe Kaikyoku, eds. *Taishō shinshū dai-zōkyō* (The Taishō edition of the Chinese Buddhist canon). 85 vols. Tokyo: Taishō shinshū daizōkyō kankōkai, 1927; reprint ed., 1968.

T'ang Chün-i. "Hsien-Ch'in ssu-hsiang chung chih t'ien-ming kuan" (The concept of *t'ien-ming* in pre-Ch'in thought). *Hsin-ya hsüeh-pao* (Journal of New Asia College) 3, no. 2 (1957), 1–33.

————. *Chung-kuo che-hsüeh yüan lun* (On the bases of Chinese phi-losophy). 2 vols. Hong Kong: Hsin-ya yen-chiu so, 1966–1968.

Ting Ta-nien. *Kung-ch'an chu-i jen-sheng kuan* (The Communist view of life). Shanghai: Hua tung jen-min ch'u-pan she, 1953.

Tomoeda Ryūtarō. *Shushi no shisō keisei* (The form of Chu Hsi's thought). Tokyo: Shunjūsha, 1969.

————. "Shushi no gakumon ron" (On some questions concerning Chu Hsi). In *Shushigaku taikei* (Introduction to Chu Hsi stud-ies). Tokyo: Meitoku shuppansha, 1974.

Wang Hsien-ch'ien, ed. *Hsün-tzu chi-chieh* (*Hsün-tzu* with collected annotations). Taipei: Shih-chieh shu-chü, 1957.

Wang P'i-chiang, ed. *T'ang jen ch'üan-ch'i hsiao-shuo* (Tang ro-mances). Reprint ed. Taipei: Shih-chieh shu-chü, 1969.

INDEX

abilities (*ts'ai, yeh*), differences in, 186
ability to discriminate between right
    and wrong (*shih-fei chih hsin*), 9, 31
above form (*hsing erh shang*), 5, 64
Abrams, Meyer H., 108
Absolute Truth (*chen ti*), 83
academies, 18, 21
action, Western concept distinct from
    Confucian, 125
affair (ᵇ*shih*), 117
ālaya, 122
all-in-One, 95
allotment: heavenly (*t'ien-fen*), 50, 55;
    human (*jen-fen*), 50
altruism: and Buddhism, 16–17; and
    clan behavior, 150; and kinship duty,
    8, 10, 13–14, 54, 67, 113–114, 141–
    142; outside the family, 146–148
Amplified Expositions on the Sacred Edict
    (*Sheng-yü kuang-hsün*), 204, 205
Analects, 5, 8, 21, 55, 65, 67, 81, 99, 128,
    133, 134, 136, 145, 159, 164, 172, 184,
    208
approve, to (ᵃ*shih*), 31
Aristotle, 46, 105, 106, 112, 135–138,
    141
aspiration (*chih*), 161
Augustine, 75, 105, 106, 174, 176
authorities, external: Confucian teach-
    ers, 169–170; implications of Chu Hsi
    thought, 189–191; emperors, 165–169

balance scale image, 39, 177–178, 181
become enlightened about his mind
    and his nature (*ming hsin chien hsing*),
    80
Bentham, Jeremy, 175
Bergson, 135, 218
blood, 59
Bloom, Irene, 205

body image, 27, 28, 76, 98
bond (*kang*), 48, 56
Bonds, Three (*san-kang*), 48
Book of Changes, 47, 51, 116, 119, 217
Book of History, 159, 166, 208
Book of Odes, 46
Book of Rites (*Li-chi*), 21
bounded, spatially (*yu fang*), 102
brightening the bright virtue (*ming
    ming-te*), 91
Buddhism: and altruism, 16–17; Confu-
    cian criticism of, 12, 17, 56, 76–80,
    169–170; and dreams, 82; egalitarian-
    ism, 12, 16–17; enlightenment, 217;
    equal worth, 12–13; explanatory fic-
    tions in, 194; false Confucians and,
    15; images (mirror), 82, 84, (moon),
    82, (seed), 122, (water), 63, 197;
    meditation, 129–131; and mind, 9,
    78, 80, 89, 128; monasticism, 12, 77,
    80, 95, 189; one-many relationship,
    60, 62–63; One-Mind principle, 60,
    65–66, 95, 118; self-cultivation, 18,
    130; separation, psychological, 75–80,
    93, 103, 104; in Sung Dynasty, 11; so-
    cieties, 11–12; and true Confucians,
    170; universal love and, 138

Chaffee, John, 156
Ch'an (Meditation) school of Bud-
    dhism, 13, 17, 60, 62, 76, 77, 82, 132,
    194
Chang Chih-tung, 225
Chang Nan-hsien, 130
Chang Tsai, 70, 99, 221
Chan-jan, 60
channels (*ch'ü*), 64
chao (illuminate), 83, 85–86; (reflect),
    85–86

311